Congratulations, Tom
and good luck in the future

Steve

Mark Twain's
MISSISSIPPI

Page 1: An overview of the Mississippi near St. Louis, painted by Paulus Roetter, ca. 1857.

Pages 2–3: River bluff aspens at Perrot State Park, Wisconsin.

Left: The city a river built—a Henry Lewis painting of St. Louis in 1848.

WEATHERVANE BOOKS NEW YORK

Mark Twain's MISSISSIPPI

By T. H. Watkins

Also Selected Excerpts from Mark Twain's
LIFE ON THE MISSISSIPPI

A
PICTORIAL
HISTORY
OF
AMERICA'S
GREATEST
RIVER

Dawn at Lake Itasca—source of the Mississippi.

Contents

Introduction

THE QUOTATION THAT FOLLOWS describes the homeland of a writer's heart. The book from which it is taken is *The Adventures of Huckleberry Finn,* published in 1885. The river is the Mississippi. The writer is Samuel Langhorne Clemens—Mark Twain:

Two or three days and nights went by; I reckon I might say they swum by, they slid along so quiet and smooth and lovely. Here is the way we put in the time. It was a monstrous big river down there—sometimes a mile and a half wide; we run nights, and laid up and hid daytimes; soon as night was most gone we stopped navigating and tied up—nearly always in the dead water under a tow-head; and then cut young cottonwoods and willows, and hid the raft with them. Then we set out the lines. Next we slid into the river and had a swim so as to freshen up and cool off; then we set down on the sandy bottom where the water was about knee deep, and watched the daylight come. Not a sound anywheres—perfectly still—just like the whole world was asleep, only sometimes the bullfrogs a-cluttering maybe. The first thing to see, looking away over the water, was a kind of dull line—that was the woods on t'other side; you couldn't make nothing else out; then a pale place in the sky; then more paleness spreading around; then the river softened up away off, and warn't black any more, but gray; you could see little dark spots drifting along ever so far away—trading scows, and such things; and long black streaks—rafts; sometimes you could hear a sweep screaking; or jumbled-up voices, it was so still, and sounds come so far; and by and by you could see a streak on the water which you know by the look of the streak that there's a snag there in a swift current which breaks on it and makes that streak look that way; and you see the mist curl up off of the water, and the east reddens up, and the river, and you make out a log cabin in the edge of the woods, away on the bank on t'other side of the river, being a woodyard, likely, and piled by them cheats so you can throw a dog through it anywheres; then the nice breeze springs up, and comes fanning you from over there, so cool and fresh and sweet to smell on account of the woods and the flowers; but sometimes not that way, because they've left dead fish laying around, gars and such, and they do get pretty rank; and next you've got the full day, and everything smiling in the sun, and the songbirds just going it!

In the summer of 1973, I stood on a grassy, wooded point of land near Cairo, Illinois, at the confluence of the Mississippi and Ohio rivers and watched just such a dawn arrive and a day begin. It was all quite as Twain described it—although Twain's trading scows were supplanted by snuffling, grumbling, snub-nosed barge tugs, and there was a smell more of diesel oil than of dead fish in the morning breeze. I was impressed at that time not only by the accuracy of the description in its progression of details neatly set down, but by the living experience he had been able to convey in a few spare and simple words; it was not just the physical essence of a river morning that had been given reality, but a man's deep love for it.

It is not given to many men to write so surely about anything, much less to sustain passion to the length of so great a book as *Huckleberry Finn.* The novel is the best of his best work, and it is no accident that it, like *The Adventures of Tom Sawyer, The Tragedy of*

Pudd'nhead Wilson, and *Life on the Mississippi,* derives its strength and surety from a very specific environment: the river, the country of the river, and the people of the river. Like many another American writer (William Faulkner and John Steinbeck come immediately to mind), this greatest of American writers created his enduring work on the foundation of a landscape of heart, mind, and memory; whenever he abandoned that landscape, his work suffered, either just missing the touch of greatness, as in *The Innocents Abroad* and *Roughing It,* or sometimes degenerating into mawkish storytelling, as in *The Prince and the Pauper,* or pallid, self-conscious attempts at "art," as in *The Personal Recollections of Joan of Arc.* It is a dictum older than venial sin that a writer must write about what he knows, and while Twain knew about a great many things (as he was more than willing to admit), he knew nothing so well as he knew this river and its people, and that familiarity gave us a body of literature that will endure for as long as human beings care to pick up books and read them.

THE CAREER OF JOHN STEINBECK, Carey McWilliams once observed, "suggests the existence of a special literary providence. For he was the right man, at the right place, at the right time." Much the same could be said for Mark Twain, for the river of his homeland was not the Kennebec, the Potomac, the Humboldt, the Colorado, or any other of the hundreds of rivers that have been important to the life and history of America; his river was the Mississippi, nothing less than *the* American river, just as Twain was to be *the* American writer. Providence, notoriously fickle, has rarely matched man and place so brilliantly.

First, the river: It is the overwhelming geographic fact in the eastern one-third of the United States, coursing 2,348 miles from its source in northern Minnesota to its end in a muddy, deltaic welter at the Gulf of Mexico; with its tributaries—among them the Missouri, the Wisconsin, the Illinois, and the Ohio—it drains an area of 1,243,700 square miles, nearly two and one-half times that of any other river system in the country, and at its mouth discharges an average of 611,000 cubic feet of water per second. Its watershed encompasses all or part of twenty-two of the contiguous

forty-eight states, and in those hundreds of millions of acres lies some of the richest agricultural land the world has ever known.

If the Mississippi looms hugely in our geography, it is no less huge a fact in our history. From the day in October 1528, when Cabeza de Vaca's desperate expedition first sighted its mouth, to the weeks of May and June 1973, when the river spread ruin in one more of its ancient rampages, much of the history of this country has been shaped by the algebra of the Mississippi. Its possession was the key to the interior of a continent, and four nations struggled to control it until it became an indisputably American river with the Louisiana Purchase of 1803. From that time forward, the river became the chief artery of the new heartland of America.

Even before Jefferson's incredible purchase, Americans had been spilling west across the mountains, still seeking the ultimate earthly Eden of escape and promise that had driven their ancestors to cross the Atlantic nearly two centuries before. What they had found in this first, trans-Appalachian West was not Eden, but it was quite as fruitful as that fertile crescent of biblical times from which they believed all civilization had sprung. By the thousands and then the scores of thousands, they filtered into the valley of the Mississippi, inexorably driving the Indians out, laying waste to whole forests, planting their farms and plantations, bickering over land speculations large and small, creating villages where there had been woods, towns where there had been villages, and cities where there had been towns, and filling the inland network of waterways with a bewildering variety of craft—barges, flatboats, rafts, keelboats, and finally, triumphantly, the puffing, crenelated wonders called steamboats.

The period from about 1830 to the beginning of the Civil War endowed the Mississippi with that agglomeration of fact and legend that endures in the national consciousness as the permanent image of the river-that-was, a landscape of collective memory peopled by roistering keelboatmen and flatboatmen, who wrestled their clumsy vessels up and down the river by day and frolicked profanely in the dives and bordellos of Natchez-under-the-hill and New Orleans by night; by sturdy, pioneering farmers who loosed the repressed passions of their fundamentalism at riverside camp meetings; by patrician gentlemen and beautiful, white-gowned ladies who gathered on the verandas of pillared mansions in the middle of sugar, rice, and cotton fiefdoms; by hot-blooded young blades who indulged in duels with careless enthusiasm and pursued elegant fornication in velvet-walled brothels; by river pirates and grisly bandits who made the Natchez Trace synonymous with organized terror; by steamboat pilots who navigated their massive wedding-cakes-on-water through all the treacheries of the river with a combination of encyclopedic knowledge, natural skill, instinct, and brimstone profanity; by sweat-shined black stevedores and field hands who expressed the stifling agony of slavery in fitful, short-lived rebellions and in a body of music that is one of the richest legacies of America; by occasional fur trappers who wandered into the river towns, smelling of grease and far places, trading, drinking hugely, spreading tales of wild adventure, of seas of elk and buffalo, of mountains as high as the sky; by stray Indians, riverboat gamblers, harlots, flimflam men, merchants, whiskey traders, marginal entrepreneurs of every stripe—a veritable stew of humanity that trembled and boiled in the transitional zone between an older, fast-settling frontier and the raw, mysterious newness of the frontier that lay immediately to the west, beyond the river and the prairie.

Whatever the reality of this national memory, it did not long survive the Civil War, which like a jolt of adrenalin accelerated the creation of a machine civilization in America. Wracked by four years of conflict, the plantation economy of the South never regained the flavor and importance of its antebellum years. The tentacles of railroad tracks crept everywhere through the valley of the Mississippi, gutting the river trade on which fortunes had been built and sounding the death knell for the steamboat era—vestiges of which, nevertheless, managed to survive well into the twentieth century. One after the other, railroad—and later, highway—bridges thrust across the river, obliterating its historic role as a natural barrier. Modest cities swelled to metropolitan stature, as cluttered, crowded, and constrained as metropolises anywhere.

With the twentieth century came the whole-souled enthusiasm of the engineers, who set about to improve the Mississippi. They dredged and kept clear a major shipping channel along much of the river's course, thus destroying adventure even as they revitalized the river's role as an avenue of commerce. They built miles of levees to hold the river back from towns and farmland, and built dams, locks, canals, spillways, and floodways in a mighty effort to control and even reverse the processes of nature—and very nearly succeeded. Today, concretized, channeled, structured, the river lies stripped of almost any romance save that which imagination and memory can supply, left with only seasonal tantrums of flooding to remind us that it will remain long after we are gone. If a man cared to stretch for an allegory, he could see the history of America writ small in the history of this river.

IT WAS FORTUNATE FOR HIM, and fortunate for us, that Mark Twain was privileged to know the Mississippi in its glory, and to know it early enough and long enough for the river to color the spectrum of his soul. He was born Samuel Langhorne Clemens on November 30, 1835—the year of Halley's Comet—in the Missouri hamlet of Florida, some eighty miles west of the river. Four years later his father, chasing the lorelei of opportunity that always evaded him, moved the family to Hannibal, a somnolent farming village on the banks of the Mississippi a little more than a hundred miles north of St. Louis. Here, in this river town of less than five hundred people, Samuel Clemens spun out the days of his boyhood and adolescence, his mind storing up memories like a Silas Marner raking in golden guineas.

It was no grasshopper's life. The family never escaped genteel poverty under the best of circumstances, and when his father died in 1847, young Sam was apprenticed to a printer, a position that supplied his family with much-needed income and himself with an equally desirable education. At eighteen, wanderlust caught at him, as it did most young men of that time and place, and he became a tramp printer for four years, drifting downriver to St. Louis, then to New York and Philadelphia, back to the river again at St. Louis, and finally to Keokuk, Iowa, where he conceived the vague notion of sailing off for adventure in South America.

South America had to get along without him, for on his way downriver to New Orleans, Clemens persuaded the pilot of the steamer *Paul Jones* to take him on as a "cub" and "learn" him the river. In the next three years—perhaps the happiest period in his life—as cub and pilot he did indeed learn the river. That experience remained, forever after, one of the talismans of his soul, something to be clutched at for solace and reassurance, much as he relied upon the remembrance of his boyhood days in Hannibal. "I loved the profession far better than any I have followed since," he wrote twenty years later, "and I took a measureless pride in it. The reason is plain: a pilot, in those days, was the only unfettered and entirely independent human being that lived in the earth."

Whether he would in fact have contentedly spent the rest of his days dodging snags and calculating currents on the Mississippi cannot be answered, for the Civil War put an end to this bright new career by interrupting the riverboat trade for the next four years. He went west to the mines of the Comstock Lode in the Territory of Nevada, and found yet another career as a reporter for the *Territorial Enterprise* of Virginia City. From there he went to San Francisco, earning a fairly comfortable niche in the circle of bohemian *literati* that infested the city. The publication of his short story "Jim Smiley and His Jumping Frog" in 1865 brought him a whisper of fame, and he journeyed to New York to see whether anything good could be made of it. More than forty years later, he had published twenty-one books and countless stories and articles, and had established himself as one of the most effective lecture-entertainers of the nineteenth century. By the time of his death in 1910—again, the year of Halley's Comet—he had achieved a degree of financial, critical, and popular success that few writers have ever enjoyed in their lifetimes.

But it had been a strangely confused and rootless life, made bitter by a combination of temperament and circumstance. For most of his productive life, Mark Twain was haunted by monstrous, unspecified guilts and vexed by rages that shook him to his marrow, rages so intense they seemed almost ancestral. He was plagued by his own inconsistencies: his contempt for greed and his clamoring hunger for money, which drove him to many personal cruelties and to such fabulous money-making schemes as the notoriously unworkable and expensive Paige Typesetting Machine; his instinct for skepticism and his ready vulnerability to cloying sentimentality; his stated disregard for class, respectability, and propriety, and his almost constant pursuit

of it; his innate sensuality and his almost hysterical prudery; his professed love of naked truth and his willingness to lie when the occasion suited; his horror for the excesses and inhumanity of the machine civilization and the fascination that pulled him to it like a filing to a magnet; his love of individual men and his hatred for "the damned human race." Death took his wife and three of his four children before it claimed him. In characteristic fashion, Twain managed to blame both himself and the universe for each death. In the end, he remained uncertain (but rarely in public) of his own genius, never fully trusting the art of *Huckleberry Finn* and frequently naming as his most important book the "refined" and purple-prosed *Personal Recollections of Joan of Arc*.

Small wonder, then, that he looked back to the river days as his one landscape of freedom and joy; the attractive thing about memories is that a man can control them, as he cannot control the world around him. We can reasonably assume that as he lay trembling on the edge of his last sleep, one of his final images would have been that of a vigorous young man at the wheel of a proud steamboat, bellowing orders down a speaking tube and cursing with a flash of joy in his eyes, or that of a boy on a raft heading for Jackson's Island on a river where it was forever summer.

WHILE THE MISSISSIPPI and its people lay at the heart of his best work, Twain wrote only one book that was "about" the river—*Life on the Mississippi*. It is a curiously divided book, one section being almost antithetical to the other, and as such it is revealing of Twain himself.

The bulk of the first half of the book was originally published as a series of articles for the *Atlantic Monthly* in 1875, "Old Times on the Mississippi." Dealing almost exclusively with his days as a cub pilot, this section is, as Bernard DeVoto called it, "a study in pure ecstasy." Like *Tom Sawyer,* it is deliberately nostalgic and pretends to nothing else. Its artistry is sure, and its use of memory an exercise in pure craftsmanship. Taken alone, it is one of the three or four best things Twain ever wrote.

But it was not long enough to make a book, or so Twain thought. In the spring of 1882, he set out to fill out the rest of the book by traveling once more on the river from New Orleans to St. Paul. The chapters that narrate this journey are clearly inferior to the first half of the book—with such notable exceptions as his account of the revisit to Hannibal and his delineation of Uncle Mumford, one of the last of the old-time river pilots. It lacks the core of feeling that dominates the first half. It is loosely organized, occasionally flip, and frequently purely reportorial in a second-rate fashion. Parts are downright banal, some are padded outrageously, and there is a lamentable air of self-consciousness throughout—almost a kind of posturing.

The reasons for his literary dichotomy are illuminating. In 1874, when he began writing "Old Times on the Mississippi" for the *Atlantic*, Twain was still a relatively young man, relatively newly married (since 1870). *The Innocents Abroad, Roughing It,* and *The Gilded Age* had established him solidly in the eastern literary world, and his lecture tours were consistent successes. He was by no means rich, but he had his reasonable expectations. He had tasted bitterness in the death of his infant son and the sporadic invalidism of his wife, Livy, and had experienced the first of the many slumps that would torment his writing life, but gall had not yet overtaken him. When he set down his recollections of the river, his heart was still open to the innocence and joy to be found in his memory of the river-that-was.

By 1882, when he started on his journey to recapture the river, his life and temperament had altered considerably. The publication of *Tom Sawyer* in 1876 had been such a fiasco of mismanagement that he forever after hated his publisher, Elisha Bliss, with a passion that was extreme even for him. His estrangement from his old San Francisco friend and mentor, Bret Harte, had reached a poisonous stage. Problems of plot and structure in *Huckleberry Finn*, the book in him that cried to be written, had been frustrating him for more than six years. The completion of *The Prince and the Pauper* had given his family great satisfaction, and he himself considered it his first work of "art," but somewhere in his writer's heart he must have known that it was nothing less than a sell-out to literary respectability. He was comparatively rich now, but spending money like a fool at a fire and perpetually uncertain of security. He had made his first investment in the Paige Typesetting Machine in 1880, and already that gro-

tesque contraption had begun to sap his energies. Altogether, Twain approached the Mississippi in 1882 as a frustrated, too often angry man whose principal concern was to get a job of work done as quickly as possible—and the second half of the book shows it.

If Twain had changed, so had the river, although he kept his lamentations for that change to a minimum. In fact, he spent a great deal of time celebrating the "progress" and "enterprise" which had transformed the river of his youth. Still, the changes had to rankle him, as they did in St. Louis: "Half a dozen sound-asleep steamboats where I used to see a solid mile of wide-awake ones! This was melancholy, this was woeful. The absence of the pervading and jocund steamboatmen . . . was explained. He was absent because he is no more. His occupation is gone, his power has passed away, he is absorbed into the common herd, he grinds at the mill." The river he had known and worshiped had succumbed to the industrial revolution. Like Twain himself, the river had been stripped of innocence, and in this sense in *Life on the Mississippi,* as in no other of his books, the river and the man became one.

Selected excerpts from *Life on the Mississippi* are at the core of the present volume. This is only as is should be, for any book on the Mississippi that does not rely heavily upon the work of Twain is only half a book. No one has written better on the days of its glory. At the same time, there was more to the Mississippi's story than Twain himself gave his genius to, and so I have attempted here to give a brief history of the river, from its beginnings to the present. Similarly, this book tries to give the river a more comprehensive pictorial treatment than it has received before.

Mark Twain's Mississippi, then, is a collection of images: the reminiscent view, as in the excerpts from the first half of *Life on the Mississippi;* the reportorial view, as in the excerpts from the second half of his book and in portions of my own text; the purely historical view; and the graphic view. The book is a montage of impressions, as broad in scope as it had to be to illuminate the life and history of this most American of all American rivers.

T. H. WATKINS

THE RIVER I

The beginning of a midcontinental journey: water from Lake Itasca spills over rocks and becomes a river.

The Father of Waters

FOUR TIMES THE ICE CAME, beginning about one million years ago, when the topmost half of the North American continent entered an epoch that was periodically so intensely and continuously frigid that in some parts of the land snow refused to melt during the brief summers. Winter after winter, century after century, the snow accumulated in two enormous packs of ice hundreds, then thousands, of feet thick. One, called the Cordilleran Sheet, was centered in the mountains of what is now western Canada; the other, called the Laurentide Sheet, was centered in an area near Hudson Bay. Inching with timeless deliberation, the sheets spread until they joined to cover all of Canada, most of Alaska, and much of the north-central United States. Then the climate warmed and the ice slowly retreated, only to come again and retreat again in four successive sheets, the last retreat beginning as little as twelve thousand years ago.

With each advance and retreat, the ice shaped the land, splitting and polishing the granite of mountains, gouging long trenches, scooping out huge basins, and forming bowllike depressions where sediments collapsed beneath its weight. In the wake of each of its retreats, it left windrows and tailings of gravel, rocks, and house-sized boulders. And lakes, thousands of lakes —finger lakes, heart lakes, lakes hardly bigger than ponds, lakes as big as countries. One of this myriad was a small lake in the northwest quarter of the state of Minnesota, a lake in the shape of an awkward, three-pointed star, an unprepossessing lake utterly dwarfed by the oceanlike sweep of Lake Superior just 150 miles to the east—a lake called Itasca.

But it is here at this living remnant of the Ice Age that the Mississippi River known to history begins its 2,348-mile journey to the sea.

It is not a particularly impressive beginning. No wider than the stone s-throw of a very small boy and not deep enough to wet a wader's thigh, the river nowadays trickles over a man-made dam of rocks and boulders at an outlet on the tip of Lake Itasca's northern arm and flows away from the lake through a narrow avenue of reeds. There is little in this clear, shallow, creeklike stream to inspire epic poetry or suggest the dimensions of its role in the past and present life of middle America. Until comparatively recently, in fact, this beginning was a monumental unknown.

The first "organized" attempt to discover the source of the Mississippi River began as a peculiar offshoot of the exploring expedition of Major Stephen Harriman Long of the U.S. Army Corps of Engineers in 1823. Long's assignment was to explore and document the physical characteristics of a vast triangle of land to the west and north of Fort Snelling in Minnesota; but before he could set out from the fort, an Italian of indeterminate scientific background, Giacomo Beltrami, attached himself to the expedition through the intercession of Major Lawrence Taliaferro, United States agent for the Indian tribes of the Upper Mississippi. Beltrami was a romantic stricken with a vision of the American wilderness that would have done justice to Jean Jacques Rousseau. This wilderness, he wrote, was an arena for "feelings of intense and new delight. The sublime traits of nature; phenomena which fill the soul with astonishment, and inspire it at the same time with

Like a checkerboard of wealth, Mississippi farmland spreads to the horizon near Raddle, Illinois—heartland country.

almost heavenly ecstasy! . . . sentiments of faith and piety, perfect and profound." Embracing the sublime, Beltrami cast himself in the mold of the great explorers, including Columbus, and was obsessed with the notion that he and he alone would discover the source of the Mississippi River.

Beltrami and the dour, unenthralled Long did not get on well. Among other things, Beltrami was given to spread-eagling himself on rocks and weeping over the immense Beauty-of-it-all, a habit regarded with both amusement and annoyance by the pragmatic American and his crew. After a series of disagreements, Beltrami finally abandoned the expedition at Pembina, on the upper reaches of the Minnesota River. With a party of Chippewa guides, he slogged and paddled eastward through prairie bogs and rivulets until a Sioux war party caused his guides to disappear. Undaunted, the stubborn romantic continued on his own, struggling blindly through the moist countryside, driven nearly insane by mosquitoes, deerflies, and gnats, before encountering a friendly Chippewa subchief by the name of Cloudy Weather, who aided him through the remainder of his exploration. The climax came when Beltrami stumbled upon a tiny, heart-shaped lake between the watersheds of the Mississippi and Red rivers.

Without instruments or any particular experience in such matters, he perused the lake and the surrounding countryside and concluded that this little spring-fed lake, which he named Julia after a European acquaintance, was the true and ultimate source of both the Mississippi and the Red. Even in recollection, as set down in his book *A Pilgrimage in Europe and America Leading to the Discovery of the Sources of the Mississippi* (London, 1828), the moment struck him as one of cosmic import: "I feel with pride," he wrote, "that I have been more than human in not trembling then . . . and the phenomenon of that lake, which is only surmounted by the Heavens! . . . Those enchanting situations! That silence! That sombre solitude! My poor savage repast! My bark porringer! What an assemblage of wonders, of thoughts, and of feelings, surrounding the eyes, and the soul!"

HOWEVER UNHINGED HE BECAME in his memory of that stupendous discovery, Beltrami was dead wrong; Lake Julia was just one more lake in a wilderness of lakes. In the years following his curious expedition, several other men, some on official business, some not, attempted to ascertain the true source of the river. But it continued to elude them until 1832, when a young geologist—and later ethnologist—named Henry Rowe Schoolcraft put together a small private party and headed north in an attempt to settle the question once and for all. In his book *Narrative of an Expedition Through the Upper Mississippi to Itasca Lake* (New York, 1834), Schoolcraft outlined the events of a climactic day in prose considerably less hysterical, but no less evocative, than that of Beltrami: "In crossing this highland [a seven-mile stretch between the Schoolcraft River and the east arm of Lake Itasca], our Indian guide, Oza Windib, led the way, carrying one of the canoes and other baggage. The whole party were arranged Indian file, and marched rapidly a distance—then put down their burthens a few moments, and again pressed forward. . . . Every step we made in treading these sandy elevations, seemed to increase the ardor with which we were carried forward. The desire of reaching the actual source of a stream so celebrated as the Mississippi —a stream which LaSalle had reached the mouth of, a century and a half (lacking a year) before, was perhaps predominant; and we followed our guide down the sides of the last elevation, with the expectation of momentarily reaching the goal of our journey. What had been long sought, at last appeared suddenly. On turning out of a thicket, into a small weedy opening, the cheering sight of a transparent body of water burst upon our view. It was Itasca Lake—the source of the Mississippi."

The little lake had been long known to French voyageurs (though not as the source of the Mississippi) as Lac La Biche, but Schoolcraft, in the tradition of American explorers, felt that it should be rechristened, this time with a name that matched its newly discovered significance. Taking the Latin words for "truth" and "head"—*veritas* and *caput*—he contrived a proper noun from the last two syllables of the former and the first syllable of the latter and came up with "Itasca"—a rather primitive abbreviation for "true head." For nearly fifty years Schoolcraft's discovery was accepted as the definitive version of the Mississippi's source, but in 1881 another contention was put forward by Frederick Glazier, who maintained that the source was in fact a tiny body of water—now called Elk Lake—just north of Lake Itasca. In a Beltrami-like gesture, he graced his nominee with the name of Glazier Lake, and it was twenty-five years more before the United States Geological Survey settled the question by declaring that, while the whole basin might logically be considered the source of the Mississippi, the basin's waters were not united into a river until they flowed from the tiny outlet at the northern arm of Lake Itasca.

T HROUGHOUT ALL SUCH EXPLORATIONS and debates, of course, the Mississippi itself knew precisely where it began—and where it was going. It had had experience enough in such matters already, even though the Mississippi cannot be described as an "old" river. Geologically speaking, the age of a river has less to do with the number of years it has been around than with the work it has accomplished in its lifetime. Each river is born, so to speak, with a single task, which is to reduce the terrain through which it flows to a sea-level plain, and the degree to which this job has been completed is the measure of its relative age. Thus, in its youth a river will cut deeply and vigorously, forming sharp, V-shaped canyons, creating many rapids, and gathering unto itself an accretion of tumbling tributaries, each of which joins with the main stream in the task of tearing down the land and carrying it to the sea; in its middle age, a river will have created broad, U-shaped valleys where there once had been canyons, and it will flow through these valleys much more slowly and gently than in its youth; by the time of its old age, the work of its life is nearly done, and a river will meander sluggishly through a valley that has become so broad as to be almost undiscernible.

On this scale a river like the Colorado, even though it is an estimated twelve million years old, must be considered a "young" river, for it is still in the process of slicing canyons into the land along most of its length, hampered in its efforts by the fact that its plateau has risen thousands of feet at one time or another in the past and continues to rise. The Mississippi, on the other hand, because it is blessed with a more stable basin, might be considered middle-aged in spite of its probably being younger in years than the Colorado. In the case of the Mississippi, at least half of its work may be said to be done; and as on many rivers of appreciable length in the world today, the three stages of life may be traced accurately along its course.

Over its first three hundred miles or so, the Missis-

Glimmering like a silver dollar, Lake Pontchartrain and the curving Mississippi bracket the bridge of land that holds New Orleans.

sippi displays many of the characteristics of a young river—although not from the very beginning. Gurgling out of Lake Itasca, it does not curve immediately south, but wanders for a few miles in a northerly direction through a forest of red pine, jack pine, white pine, balsam fir, and tamarack, following a course probably laid down when the last of the ice shrank from the region. Breaking out of the forest into the surrounding prairie, the river nearly loses itself in bogs and marshlands before turning east and entering a chain of lakes, chief among them Cass and Winnibigoshish. It is a wildly moist country through which the river passes in its early stages, a country of ponds and rivulets and lakes, of marsh grass, reeds, wild celery, and wild rice, of spongelike meadows interrupted by stands of pine forest, a country haunted by the mournful laugh of the loon and sometimes at dawn or dusk the inelegant, guttural squawk of the magnificent great blue heron as he whispers through the air on six feet of wings.

Near Grand Rapids, Minnesota, the river finally curves south, turned aside by a gentle rise of land that prevents it from flowing east into Lake Superior. Here, the river takes on muscle and purpose, slashing between steep, rising banks, tumbling in small rapids and occasional falls. By the time it has traveled the 513 miles between its source and the Falls of St. Anthony, at Minneapolis, dropping more than seven hundred feet along the way, it has become a river to be reckoned with, hundreds of yards in width, fast, and sometimes dangerous.

Below Minneapolis, as it is enriched by the Minnesota, the St. Croix, the Chippewa, and the Wisconsin, the river widens even more, entering what might be called its middle-aged section, flowing through a landscape that will be characteristic of it through most of the eight hundred miles to Cairo, Illinois. It is a landscape of forested bluffs, many of them hundreds of feet high, that border its spreading valley, and the river itself is spotted with islands crowded with tall cottonwood trees, land areas that range in size from "towheads" no more than ten yards across to bona fide islands the size of Jackson's Island opposite Hannibal, Missouri, where Mark Twain's boyhood found "the great Mississippi, the majestic, the magnificent Mississippi, rolling its mile-wide tide along, shining in the sun." In many places these islands are gathered in the center of the river in a bewildering maze that obscures the Mississippi proper. In such subworlds are found a wilderness of birds—wood ducks, mallards, ringnecks, teals, widgeons, herons, long-necked egrets with feathers so brightly white they hurt the eyes, redwing blackbirds, kingfishers, woodpeckers, robins and finches.

Beneath the water lies a world that often borders on the outlandish: in addition to such unremarkable creatures as green sunfish and bass, the water moves with long-whiskered catfish that can reach a hundred pounds in weight, alligator gars that are sometimes ten feet long, paddlefish with finger-like snouts half the length of their bodies, shovelnose sturgeons that wriggle along the river bottom in search of food, and alligator snapping turtles with ridgeback shells and punishing jaws.

It is an almost unrelieved green-and-blue world, this world of the central Mississippi, from the iridescent light green of the algal scum of stagnant island pools and inlets to the dark, dark green of forested bluffs, from the steel-blue of the quiet waters to the deep blue void of the sky, enhanced and emphasized by the roseate glow of dawns and sunsets so consistently spectacular as to become monotonous. Here and there is a touch of earth, a rusty clay bank or a shining tan sandbar with a matching piece of driftwood trapped on its edge, or a flash of color in pink hyacinths and yellow marigolds.

The gray-blue of the Mississippi itself remains unaltered until it reaches a point near Alton, Illinois, where the wide Missouri pours in a load of silt and debris from across one-third of the continent. Even though dammed and controlled almost beyond recognition along much of its length, there is still a hint of the power of the Missouri that Francis Parkman found so monumental in *La Salle and the Discovery of the Great West* more than a century ago. At the confluence of the two rivers, Parkman wrote, "a torrent of yellow mud rushed furiously athwart the calm blue current of the Mississippi, boiling and surging and sweeping in its course logs, branches, and uprooted trees." The Missouri, he said, was "that savage river . . . descending from its mad career through a vast unknown of barbarism, pouring its turbid floods into the bosom of its gentler sister." There is less turbulence in the meeting now, but there is no questioning the fact that it is a clash of types; for many miles down the river, the blue current of the Mississippi and the muddy brown current of the Missouri simply refuse to mix, flowing side-by-side in a kind of watery saraband.

By the time the river has reached Cairo, Illinois, however, the mix has been accomplished. The river is thicker and wider here but not so impressive as the mighty Ohio, which pours a broad, slow-moving torrent of clear water into the Mississippi at this point. So dominant in size is the Ohio, that many people give it, and not the upper Mississippi, the distinction of being the main stem of the river system. Be that as it may, the combination of the upper Mississippi with its many tributaries and the Ohio with its own tributaries creates a lusty giant of a river, and the water that flows the remaining one thousand miles to the Gulf of Mexico is the Mississippi of legend.

THIS REMAINING THOUSAND-MILE STRETCH represents the river's old age, for it flows along on a bed of its own deltaic deposits so deep that at times the surface of the river is higher than the surrounding countryside. Meandering in loops and bends, turning back on itself time and time again, the river wanders with antic inconsistency through a marvelously rich floodplain so immense that in places it stretches unbroken to the horizon. In times past, the river had a way of changing its bed unpredictably, confounding steamboat pilots and converting prosperous riverport towns into moribund country villages with no ready access to the water. Yet perhaps the most dramatic manifestation of the river's perversity in such matters was its habit of snipping off bits and pieces of itself like a worm shedding sections of its body. This occurred when the force of its current wore away the neck of a river loop completely, providing the river with a new and more convenient channel. For a time the loop would remain an appendage of the river until silt closed up its two ends, transforming it into what is called an oxbow or horseshoe lake. Scores of such lakes are scattered through the country of the lower river, testaments to the Mississippi's whim of steel.

Today the floodways and reinforced levees of the U.S. Army Corps of Engineers have combined to restrain the river in its ancient wanderings, holding it to a predictable bed and arresting its lake-manufacturing activities. But the river is by no means tamed, as it proceeds to demonstrate from time to time with the frequently devastating floods of the "June rise." The river is older than the memory of man, and it has been about its business for a long time; it will still be about its business, it seems to remind us, long after the last of mankind's dams and levees have been stripped away.

Swollen with the added waters of the St. Francis, Arkansas, and Yazoo rivers, together with dozens of smaller streams, creeks, and trickles, the Mississippi enters its very own country when it enters the state of Louisiana. Eons ago, the Gulf of Mexico extended deep into Louisiana, as well as its neighboring state of Mississippi, but with the inexorability of a modern land-fill engineer, the river gradually inched into the gulf on a foundation of midcontinental debris, ultimately smothering several thousand square miles of open sea and building the present "bird-foot" delta that distinguishes the toe of Louisiana. The river's load of mud is still prodigious, even though not quite so much as the 406 million tons a year that Mark Twain reported in *Life on the Mississippi* ninety years ago ("This mud," he wrote, "solidified, would make a mass a mile square and two hundred and forty-one feet high"). Yet progress has slowed the river's land-making, simply because its mouth is now so close to the edge of the continental shelf that much of the sediment is spewed into water hundreds of feet deep.

This river country is a land of marshes, bogs, and swamps (not unlike the land of the river's beginning), of rice farms and fields of sugar cane, of long bayous that creep sluggishly toward the sea, of dark cypress forests festooned with the peculiar gauze of Spanish moss, of glades of saw grass, of hundreds of thousands of wintering migratory birds from the northern reaches of the Mississippi Flyway, of such common creatures as possums, muskrats, nutrias, and deer, and such uncommon creatures as alligators and water moccasins, each in its own fashion quite as deadly as the other. It is a moist and tropical land, hot, humid, and bitterly vulnerable to the sweeping destruction of hurricanes that boil up in the Gulf of Mexico. Darkly mysterious, this land is an appropriate setting for the journey's end of a river that has so captivated the passion and imagination of men.

Snipped off from the river like so much string, Oxbow Lake near Aitkin, Minnesota, documents the Mississippi's fickle nature.

In the land where the river rises, dark, medieval forests of fir crowd the banks of Lake Itasca, Minnesota—a body of water whose peaceful aspect in no way hints at the turbulence of the river to which it gives birth.

Constantly rising and falling, eating into the earth of its banks, the Mississippi keeps at its task of carrying the land all the way to the Gulf of Mexico—and leaving behind such victims as this toppled cottonwood at Crow Wing State Park, Minnesota.

For much of the first two hundred miles of its journey, the Mississippi runs along in
no particularly impressive fashion, but by the time it reaches La Crosse, Wisconsin, as shown
above, it has become a river of muscle and dimension.

One of the riches of the Mississippi
environment is the existence of
pockets of sudden beauty and delicacy,
such as this bed of daisies in Perrot
State Park, Wisconsin.

Land that has enriched a nation and fed the world: below, a "picture-postcard" farm near Garnaville, Iowa, where the corn may or may not be as high as an elephant's eye, and at the left a view of the delta land twenty miles south of Venice, Louisiana.

The river in its middle age, with gentle, wooded bluffs, tree-crowded islands, and a sky that has no end—a scene above Hannibal, Missouri.

In the nineteenth century, it was foggy mornings like this that made steamboat pilots call up every encyclopedic bit of knowledge and experience they had to avoid disaster.

The Mississippi harbors an abundance of life: on its lower reaches, the common (or American) egret ornaments its world.

A sundown view of Jackson's Island near Hannibal, where Tom Sawyer,
Huckleberry Finn, and the young Sam Clemens searched out a world
of mystery and adventure.

As unearthly as a surrealistic painting, the outlandish
trunks of cypress trees thrust up from the dark waters
of a delta swamp.

At Bayou Teche, Louisiana, Spanish moss festoons
trees with a brooding grace.

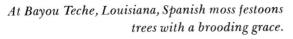

The Children of the Valley

MAN KNOWS A GREAT DEAL about this river, or likes to think he does. He knows where it starts and where it ends, and quite a bit of what it does along the way. He has calculated its currents, navigated it, charted its depths, studied its flora and fauna, spanned it with bridges, set up walls of concrete levees, dredged it, dammed it, and called it his own.

But there are ghosts on the river, ghosts infinitely more vague than the explorers, voyageurs, keelboatmen, and steamboat pilots who flick across the pages of our books in pale imitation of life. We cannot invest these other ghosts with even that limited measure of reality, for they derive from a time far back beyond the dimmest edge of man's racial memory, the ghosts of the river valley's first human residents.

What we do not know, we can guess. We do not know when they came, but we can guess that like the other native peoples of North and South America, they descended from those who had crossed over the land mass that bridged the eastern and western hemispheres during the last Ice Age, somewhere between 12,000 and 35,000 years ago. We can guess that while others of this great exodus spread directly south along the western edge of the continent, following the game that lived in the ice-free valleys, some wandered eastward along the edge of the great ice mass all the way to its southernmost tip, not far from what is now the confluence of the Mississippi and Ohio rivers. Many of these spread south down the valley of the embryonic river, and some may actually have continued south into Mexico, Central America, and even South America. Others remained in the valley and some returned north, following in the wake of the receding ice.

We do not know what this early man looked like or much about how he lived, but we can guess that his body was squat and powerful, mostly bone and muscle, that his brain was capable of little ruminative thought, and that he was not much given to verbal communication. We do know that he traveled in small, probably familial bands, and that he was primarily a hunter, stalking the mighty beasts of the Pleistocene Era—principally the mastodon and the prehistoric bison—with spears and arrows, the most advanced toolmaking achievements of the Stone Age. He was built and programmed for survival, survival alone in a world in which it was not easily managed.

How many there were we cannot even guess with any accuracy, but we do know that these people were present, at one time or another, in most of the valley of the Mississippi. Excavations on the shores of Lake Itasca, the very source of the river, have unearthed the splintery bones of *Bison occidentalis* mixed together with discarded Stone Age tools and weapons that are estimated to be at least eight thousand years old; and similarly ancient artifacts have been discovered in various regions of the valley, all the way down to the mouth of the river. The country of the Mississippi was then, as it is today, capable of supporting a rich abundance of life—including human life.

Over the course of more than a hundred centuries, the people of the valley gradually evolved from a brutally primitive condition to one that in some aspects

An overview of the Mississippi at Effigy Mounds National Monument, Iowa,
where the children of the valley built a civilization lost in the dark of history.

In a rare early attempt to depict the Indians of the valley realistically, a French artist by the name of DeBatz rendered the above group of "Atakapa" Indians in 1835.

at least could be called sophisticated. They developed language, social structure, and religious forms; instead of heaping rocks over the bodies of their dead, or just leaving them for carrion, they learned to bury them, often with the trappings of ceremony that suggested a powerful belief in the ghosts and mysteries of a spirit world. They became, many of them, sedentary or semi-sedentary rather than nomadic; besides hunting their meat, they foraged for natural vegetable foods and also started an agriculture in the cultivation of a prim-itive maize, or corn.

Perhaps as long ago as 1000 B.C., they began to display a turn for art, expressed in the painting and incising of pottery, much of it quite intricate. Their technology developed to the point where they were making not only better weapons than the crude spears of their ancestors, but a whole array of woodworking tools that enabled

them to fashion such things as dug-out canoes. The most dramatic manifestation of advancing technology took place three or four thousand years ago in the country between the Mississippi and Lake Superior, whose people may have been the first metal-working people in history; during the time of what has been named the Old Copper Culture, these river-and-woodland people dug raw copper out of the ground and worked it into spear and arrow points, knives, awls, axes, gouges, brace-lets and necklaces.

Mini-civilizations like the Old Copper Culture came and went over the years, leaving little to mark their passing, but about a thousand years before the birth of Christ, a new civilization began to develop, evidences of which can be seen today in many places along the river. It was the civilization of a people infatuated with the rituals of death, who buried their dead in mounds

The mound-builders exposed: "Huge Mound and the Manner of Opening Them,"
a section of a panoramic painting by Dr. Montroville W. Dickeson and I. J. Egan, ca. 1850.

Assinboin
Chippewa
LAKE SUPERIOR
Sauk
Fox
Santee Dakota
Winnebago
Kickapoo
Iowa
Miami
LAKE MICHIGAN
Oto
ILLINOIS R.
MISSISSIPPI R.
Illini
MISSOURI R.
Missouri
Ohio R.
Osage
Shawnee
Arkansas R.
Quapaw
Chickasaw
Tunica
Yazoo
Caddo
Koroa
Choctaw
Waco
Taensa
Alabama
Natchez
Biloxi
Atakapa
Chitimacha
GULF OF MEXICO

INDIAN TRIBES IN THE MISSISSIPPI RIVER VALLEY

ranging from a few feet in height and diameter to hillocks the size of small buildings. Hundreds of these mounds have been discovered and preserved, from a small site within walking distance of the source of the Mississippi in Itasca State Park, Minnesota, to a 1,374-acre site high on the bluffs overlooking the river at Effigy Mounds National Monument, Iowa, and a 224-acre site some six miles east of the river at Cahokia Mounds State Park, Illinois. This mound-building civilization possessed three distinct periods: The first, the Adena Culture, began about two thousand years ago and lasted until about A.D. 200. It was succeeded by the richest and most complex, the Hopewellian, centered in the region of the upper Mississippi and Ohio valleys; the Hopewellian Culture featured an advanced agriculture, extensive trade with people as far away as the Rocky Mountains on the west and New England on the east, and huge temple mounds (as well as burial mounds) surrounded by immense earthen walls. The Hopewellian period was succeeded, in turn, by the Mississippian Culture, beginning about A.D. 700 and centering in the valley of the lower Mississippi between St. Louis and Memphis. Rich and vigorous, like the Hopewellian, the Mississippian Culture soon spread throughout much of the southeastern corner of the United States.

THE CIVILIZATION OF THE MOUND-BUILDERS of the Mississippi was remarkably long-lived, and vestiges of it remained among scattered and isolated tribes of the Southeast until well after the first European contact. By then, however, most of the rest of the people of the valley had undergone a few more centuries of development, shifting about from region to region, enjoying dominance here, suffering conquest there, becoming diluted with further migrations from all directions of the compass, separating into the many-leveled language stocks and tribes known to history.

In the lower valley, most of the people based their lives on agriculture and were generally sedentary, with few territorial ambitions. If most of them retained few other forms from the Mississippian Culture, they did adhere relatively closely to its patterns of settlement. Their warfare was largely defensive in nature and limited in ferocity; their inability to withstand for long

By the time this drawing of a Sioux camp appeared in Harpers Magazine *in 1857,*
the Sioux were already being pushed across the river to the Great Plains.

the intrusion of Europeans is suggested by the number of names among them that simply disappeared from the rolls of human population: the Caddoes, Kichais, Wacos, Taensas, Tawaconis, Tunicas, Chitimachas, and Atakapas of Louisiana; the Choctaws, Chickasaws, Natchez, and Houmas of Mississippi; the Arkansas and Quapaws of Arkansas . . .

North of these, in the land where the Ohio, the Missouri, and the Illinois rivers meet the Mississippi, the people were somewhat less settled than their southern neighbors, but in many instances hardly less dependent upon agriculture for their basic foods. To the west of the Mississippi lay the Missouris, the Osages, and the Iowas, and farther to the west a veritable congeries of tribal identities—the Illinois, the Sauks, the Foxes, the Miamis, the Potawatomies, the Mascoutens, and the Kickapoos—made a rich and semi-indolent pool of life

in the fertile bottomlands. They would fight, and sometimes fight well, when pushed to it, but for the most part they preferred a peaceful existence of hunting, fishing, and tending small individual plots of corn, squash, beans, and pumpkins.

It was a different tale altogether in the country comprising the present states of Wisconsin and Minnesota. Here, the vaguely westering Chippewas skirmished almost constantly with the Sioux for domination of the upper reaches of the river, particularly the wild rice marshes, which provided a reliable staple. The issue was not thoroughly settled even by the seventeenth century, but the Chippewas had at least driven the Sioux from most of eastern Minnesota, forcing them south and west across the river. (It was the Chippewas, it should be noted, who named the river *Mechesebe* —"Great River"—which through the normal processes

An Ojibway woman and child, painted by George Catlin in 1834.

*The family unit: a Louisiana Indian, his wives, and his children, troop along
a bayou swamp in an evocative painting by Alfred Baisseau.*

of linguistic corruption has come down to us as "Mississippi.") North of the battleground of the Sioux and Chippewas lay the country of the Assiniboins, the Winnebagos, and the Crees, and to the east the country of the Menominees, the Ottawas, and the Hurons. While not residents of the valley, each of these tribes made its presence felt there to some degree, but none possessed the influence of the malevolent and ambitious Iroquois, who lay even farther east, in the region of upstate New York. In time, the power of the Iroquois became such that it struck terror into the hearts of Indians as far west as the prairies of Iowa.

For these people of the Mississippi Valley, strong and weak alike, were to become enmeshed in a game of global politics and nation-building, a game in which they were little more than pawns to be used, used against one another and used up, a game outside their experience or comprehension. Not many would survive. Today, only the Chippewas of Minnesota remain in significant numbers in the land of their ancestry; copper-skinned and stoic, protected by government fiat, they still pole their flat-bottomed boats through weedy marshes to harvest wild rice—a thin, living remnant of those dimly remembered children of the valley who once hunted the great mastodon beneath the shadow of a mountain of ice.

This So Renowned River

THE EUROPEAN DISCOVERERS of the Mississippi had other things on their minds. This was not unusual. The discovery of the heartland river of America, like so much else in the sweeping geography of this country, was an accident, the fortuitous by-product of the myth-chasing that drove men with over-heated imaginations into adventures that were at once fascinating and monumentally ill-conceived.

The New World was a vast unknown, and it was a psychological imperative of the sixteenth-century mind that it therefore be filled with many rich and wonderful things: one-breasted Amazons who rode trained griffins and harvested pearls like so many beans in a beanpatch; El Dorado, the Gilded Man, whose subjects paid him annual tribute with his own weight in gold; Gran Quivira, a land whose people ate from golden plates and slept beneath trees festooned with golden bells; the country of Antillia, whose seven cities were paved with gold. Whatever the particular myth, its dominant theme was the dream of gold or comparable wealth.

It was this dream that in 1519 impelled Hernán Cortés, the first and definitive conquistador, into the slaughter that destroyed the rule of the Aztecs in central Mexico. In the same year that dream caused a navigator by the name of Piñeda to head for the east coast of Florida to see what he might see (and even if he found no gold, he might at least discover the fabled passage through the continent to the great South Sea, another imperative that would shape the exploration of America). A storm interrupted his plans by blowing him west into the Gulf of Mexico, whose previously unknown coast he navigated from western Florida to the eastern edge of Mexico. On the way, it is possible that he discovered the Mississippi River, for on a crude chart of his travels there appears the mouth of a large river which he named *Rio del Spiritu Sancto* ("River of the Holy Ghost"). In 1524 a copy of this chart was appended to a superbly stylized rendering of the Aztec City of Mexico, identified only as "Cortes's Map"; it may be the first cartographic depiction of the Mississippi.

Piñeda's discovery remains speculative, but the next European encounter with the Mississippi has more solid documentation. In 1527, Pánfilo de Narváez was appointed governor of the great blank of Florida, "which meant," as Bernard DeVoto has written, "that he was licensed to conquer and exploit it." To satisfy this worthy goal, Narváez put together an expedition of four hundred men and eighty horses, and in the spring of 1528 set out from Cuba. With the expedition was its treasurer, Cabeza de Vaca, whose responsibility was to see that the crown received its 20 percent share of any loot that Narváez might appropriate. Their destination was the southwestern boundary of Florida, as almost the entire coast of the Gulf of Mexico was then known, not far north of the present city of Tampico in Mexico.

Disaster struck almost immediately, as storms drove Narváez and his party east across the gulf, killing nearly half their horses and placing them somewhere near Tampa Bay. Putting ashore, they began the grand adventure of conquest by supposing they could march overland to their original destination in a matter of days.

The "Black Robe" personified: a more than slightly imaginative painting of Father Jacques Marquette by William Lambrecht, 1869.

Nearly two months later, after inching through swamps, sawgrass glades, jungles, and cypress bogs, slowly starving, driven wild by the region's mosquitoes (the ferocity of which may have no equal on earth), sickened with dysentery, malaria, and most likely yellow fever, and constantly harassed by Indians whose belligerence increased the farther west they traveled—they had gone no farther than the Apalachicola River in the present panhandle of Florida. They had found no gold, and nearly half the expedition had died; Narváez abandoned the dream here. They killed and ate their remaining horses and somehow built five boats in which they planned to sail along the gulf coast until they reached Mexico. Only two of the makeshift craft got even as far west as Galveston Bay, where they were wrecked. One of these was captained by Cabeza de Vaca, who had encountered a most wonderful thing on the way—a large river mouth whose rushing current pushed his boat more than two miles out into the gulf, where he still "tooke fresh water within the Sea, because the river ranne into the Sea continually and with great violence."

This could only have been the Mississippi, cutting through one of the three passes of its delta on the way to the sea, but it would be nearly seven years before de Vaca could tell anyone of his discovery. Eighty men crawled out of those two wrecks on the beach of Galveston Bay, only to be captured and enslaved by Indians. Just four were ever heard from again—out of the expedition's original contingent of four hundred. Led by the indomitable de Vaca, the four Spaniards finally stumbled into the frontier outpost of Culiacán on the northwest coast of Mexico in April 1536, after one of the most incredible journeys in the history of mankind—European man's first blind thrust into the country of what would become the American Southwest.

Narváez was not one of these four. He had fancied himself a conquistador in the tradition of Cortés, but while he possessed the instinct for brutality such a role required, he had displayed none of the necessary qualities of leadership. One who did was Hernando De Soto, a veteran of Pizzaro's conquest of Peru in 1533 and the brother-in-law of Vasco Nuñez de Balboa, discoverer of the Pacific Ocean. De Soto had become governor of Cuba and *adelantado* of Florida by 1536, when Cabeza de Vaca stepped out of the desert of northwestern Mexico with seven years' worth of stories to tell. One of these,

Hernando De Soto, who traveled to the banks of the Mississippi in 1542.

enriched by imagination, hope, and remembered terror, concerned seven rich cities. He had not seen the cities, but he had heard wondrous tales of them throughout his immense journey. Exactly where they lay he could not say, except that he knew they were somewhere west of the old expedition's landing in Tampa Bay.

THE STORY VIBRATED throughout New Spain and soon came to the ears of De Soto, who was then planning a second expedition to conquer Florida. Responding to the new myth with enthusiasm, De Soto determined to find de Vaca's lost Seven Cities. After more than two years of preparation, he landed at Tampa Bay in May 1539 with more than seven hundred men and nearly two hundred and fifty horses—the largest European expedition the country north of Mexico had yet seen. It came in handy. With cold-blooded enthusiasm, De Soto pillaged, enslaved, and murdered his way through the Indians of the Southeast, constantly pressing them for information concerning the myth that obsessed him. Those Indians who lived were cooperative enough. Yes, they said, there were such cities—but not here. They lay over this-or-that mountain, near this-or-that river, in someone else's country, always.

With iron determination, De Soto followed the rumors out of Florida, across Georgia, and into parts of North and South Carolina. Here in this rich piedmont land his men wished to establish a colony. There was no gold, but the coast some distance away did hold pearls, they had heard, and the land was so black and moist that a man could mold it in his fist. De Soto would have none of it, as the expedition's chronicler noted: "Since the governor's purpose was to seek another treasure like that of Peru, he had no wish to content himself with good

land or with pearls even though many of them were worth their weight in gold. . . . Thereupon, the governor determined to go in search of that land, and as he was a man, hard and dry of word, and although he was glad to listen and learn the opinion of all, after he had voiced his own opinion he did not like to be contradicted and always did what seemed best to him. Accordingly all conformed to his will . . . although it seemed a mistake to leave the land." It was a mistake, even on De Soto's terms, for if he had lingered and explored just a bit more, he might have encountered the rich placer and quartz gold deposits near Dahlonega, Georgia; as it was, it would be more than three hundred years before their discovery would inspire the first gold rush in America.

De Soto pushed on, west across the Great Smoky Mountains into Tennessee, south into Alabama almost to the gulf, northwest through Mississippi, still killing, still capturing, still chasing the thin specter of the Seven

*De Soto's ambitious expedition landing on the shores of Tampa Bay, Florida,
each man seduced by dreams of gold.*

*The discovery of the Mississippi—although neither De Soto nor his men were quite
as stricken with the moment as this painting by Oscar Berninghaus would suggest.*

Cities. And in May 1541, he reached the Mississippi at a point probably near the present city of Memphis—the first recorded sighting of the Mississippi beyond its mouth. Not only that, the expedition fashioned boats and made the first river crossing. It was a momentous occasion, but De Soto had no more patience for the river than he had had for the land of Georgia; the dream must be followed. The army slogged down the west bank of the river until it reached the valley of the Arkansas, then turned west and marched up that tributary well beyond the eastern boundary of the present state of Oklahoma. Here the quest ended. Half his horses and one-third of his men had died, and De Soto decided to give it up, to return to the Mississippi and from thence to Cuba, perhaps to try again another year.

After wintering in brush huts on the Ouachita River, the expedition murdered its way back to the Mississippi, encamping in March 1542 on the west bank of the river opposite what is now Natchez. This was as far as De Soto went. Ulcerated by nearly three years of frustration and failure, he took to his cot on the banks of the river he had found, and died. His presence had stricken so much awe into the Indians, however, that his men were afraid to let them suspect that this avenging sun-god had died just like other men. They took his body in the dead of night and slipped it into the middle of the river—an act that was as useful symbolically as it was pragmatic. They then made boats once again and set out for the Gulf of Mexico, and from there to Cuba. A little over three hundred of the original seven hundred survived. None of them ever returned.

No Spaniard, in fact, would see the Mississippi again for more than one hundred and fifty years.

IT HAD ALL BEEN A DISAPPOINTMENT to Spain. Almost simultaneously with De Soto, Francisco de Coronado had commandeered his own expedition in search of the

The sun god was dead, but the Indians must not know, and De Soto's wasted body was slipped into the silent waters of the Mississippi.

Seven Cities, this one north and east from the west coast of Mexico; like De Soto's, Coronado's expedition failed, coming up against empty reality on the Kansas plains—possibly no more than three hundred miles from De Soto's westernmost point. These two were the greatest disappointments but not the only ones, and after such failures there was little heart in New Spain or Old Spain for the chasing of dreams.

So the Mississippi, discovered as the result of myth, lay unknown for another century as a result of the failure of myth. But even as the Spanish dream of gold bloomed and faded for the last time, another myth began pushing open another door to the river, this one thousands of miles to the northeast of the Mississippi's mouth. The myth was called, among other things, the Northwest Passage, a water route that was supposed to lead to all

the riches of Cathay through the inconvenience of the North American continent. And just as the Spanish believed—had to believe—in golden cities that were not there, those who sought the Northwest Passage for glory, wealth, God, or king believed in its existence with a lunatic passion.

The first crack in the second door to the Mississippi was opened in August 1535, when Jacques Cartier, a navigator in the employ of Francis I of France, discovered the mouth of the St. Lawrence River in Canada, which he at first imagined was the magical strait itself. But it was only a river, and he sailed up it to a height of land he named Mount Royal. Indians took him up the mountain and showed him the stream-laced country that stretched to the western horizon. Beyond that horizon, they said, were great freshwater seas—the Great Lakes—

and the farthest of these stood at the very edge of the world. Merging fact and wishful speculation, Cartier reckoned that this last sea was either a bay that opened on the Pacific or a lake with a river outlet that also led to the sea. Thus was born the concept of the great western sea whose bordering rivers connected the east and west coasts of the continent; it would be a long time dying, for each time it was disproved, the imaginary western sea simply moved farther inland, beyond the reach of fact but not beyond dream.

With Cartier's journey, France staked its claim on Canada—called New France—but did little about it until the end of the sixteenth century. By then France, nearly poverty-stricken by decades of war and internal division, had learned the value of beaver pelts, the gold of the northern New World that really existed. A haphazard kind of trade with the Indians near the mouth of the St. Lawrence had been developed by French fishermen as early as the 1570s, as they exchanged knives, strap iron, iron kettles, mirrors, and gewgaws for the thick, rich furs that would adorn the backs of princes and others well born. In 1603, Henry of Navarre, the French king, having decided to tap into this new wealth, authorized a group of adventurers to establish a trading colony at a suitable point in New France. The adventurers would be accorded a monopoly on the fur trade, and the crown, of course, would get the "King's Fifth." Among the colonists was Samuel de Champlain, who would ultimately become the first governor of New France.

The first colony was Port Royal, established in 1604 on the mainland of Nova Scotia; but in 1608 Champlain founded the log hut outpost of Quebec just south of the mouth of the St. Lawrence River, and it was here that the fur trade had its center. Each year French trading ships anchored in the river and traders set up displays of Old World goods in the town. Indians, avid for the trappings of civilization, would stream in from as far north as the watershed rivers of Hudson Bay and as far west as the country of the Great Lakes, dressed in savage splendor, their great canoes heaped above the rim with mounds of beaver pelts.

Inexorably, inevitably, from their wilderness outpost of Quebec the exploiters of New France began to probe toward the upper valley of the Mississippi. Champlain's dream, like that of Cartier nearly seventy-five years earlier, was to find the great western sea, and

from that the Pacific Ocean, and much of the exploration he both participated in and fostered before his death in 1635 was inspired by that goal. Yet there were more important considerations, chief among them the necessity to expand the markets of the fur trade, keep the trade routes open, and maintain a constant communication with the Indians who supplied the furs on which the young colony was based—particularly the Hurons, who acted as middlemen, sending their own traders west to barter for furs, then carrying the pelts to Quebec via Lake Huron, Lake Nipissing, and the Ottawa and St. Lawrence rivers.

NONE OF THIS WAS EASILY DONE, for the French expansion of the fur trade had a profound effect on Indian alliances and antagonisms, some of them ancient, some newly inspired by the trade itself. Most important were the attitudes and actions of the Iroquois, who were located in the region of what is now upstate New York but whose influence extended much farther. For years they had enjoyed a virtual monopoly of the fur trade by acting as the principal middlemen in trade with the Dutch outpost at Albany, on the upper Hudson River. Now the Hurons, with the aid and comfort of the French, were cutting into their territory, and the Iroquois expressed their rage at this by nearly a century of vicious warfare against the Hurons, any Indian allies of the Hurons, and the French themselves; at their most effective, the Iroquois several times over this period managed to halt the trade completely, and at their least effective were an almost constant source of harassment and irritation to the French.

To maintain the trade, then, it was necessary to maintain a powerful influence among the Indians of the Great Lakes region and the valleys of the Wisconsin, Illinois, and Mississippi rivers. This end was accomplished by three means, two of them deliberate, one coincidental (and quite illegal). The first were the efforts of licensed traders, who were encouraged to probe for new sources of furs in whatever direction the search led them; the second were the efforts of Jesuit missionaries, the tough soldiers of God who entered the wilderness in search of souls, not furs, but whose presence was of vast importance to the trade; finally, there were the efforts of the *coureurs de bois*, unlicensed and highly

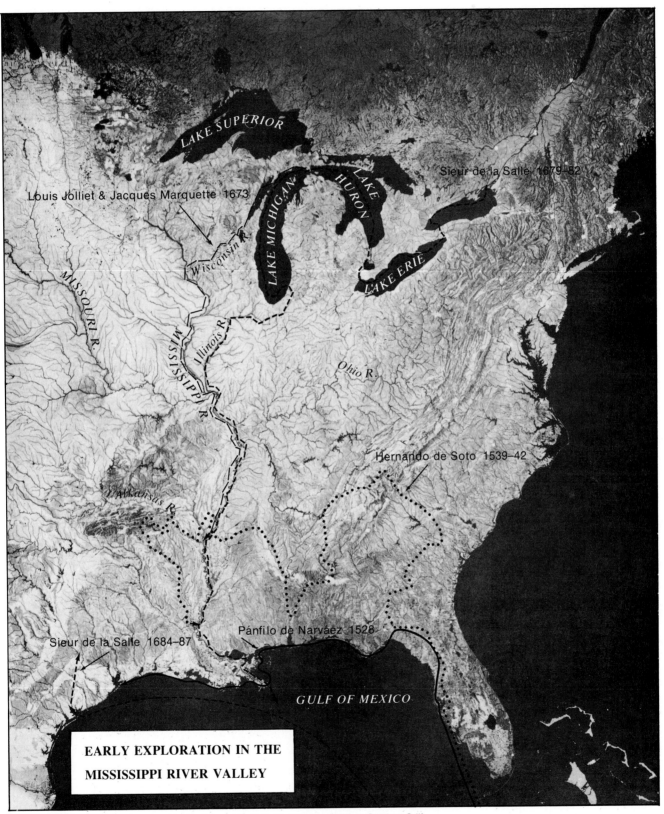

Sieur de la Salle 1679–82

Louis Jolliet & Jacques Marquette 1673

LAKE SUPERIOR

LAKE MICHIGAN

LAKE HURON

LAKE ERIE

MISSOURI R.

Wisconsin R.

MISSISSIPPI R.

Illinois R.

Ohio R.

Hernando de Soto 1539–42

Arkansas R.

Sieur de la Salle 1684–87

Pánfilo de Narváez 1528

GULF OF MEXICO

**EARLY EXPLORATION IN THE
MISSISSIPPI RIVER VALLEY**

illegal traders who nevertheless helped establish the dominance of French influence among the Indians of the Old Northwest.

As French influence expanded west and south, so did knowledge of the country grow, and the second door to the Mississippi opened wider. In 1634, Jean Nicolet, at the instigation of Champlain, headed west for purposes of trade and exploration. Traveling over the ancient water routes of the Indians, Nicolet got as far west as Green Lake, Wisconsin, where the Indians told him of a "great water" just three days' journey to the south. This was the Mississippi, but Nicolet took "great water" to mean a sea, and he returned to Quebec with the certainty that he had been close to reaching the great western sea of myth.

Twenty years later, a *coureur de bois* by the name of Médart Chouart, Sieur des Groseilliers, mounted an independent expedition into the interior, traveling deep into the valley of the Mississippi and—if we are to believe the chronicle of this expedition written several years later by his brother-in-law Pierre Radisson—perhaps discovering the river itself: "By the persuasion of some of them [Indians] we went into ye great river that divides itself in 2, where the hurrons with some Ottanake [Ottowas] & the Indians that had warrs with them had retired. . . . This nation have warrs against those of the forked river. It is so called because it has 2 branches, the one towards the west, the other towards the South, which we believe runns towards Mexico, by the tokens they gave us." The "fork" Radisson described may well have been the point at which the Missouri empties its brown flood into the Mississippi.

Father Jacques Marquette, a seeker of souls who helped rediscover the Mississippi River.

I N 1663, Jean Baptiste Colbert, chief minister to Louis XIV, persuaded the king to declare New France a royal colony, rather than the semi-independent entrepreneurial outpost it had been since the beginning of the century. As *intendent*—the personal representative of the king—Colbert appointed Jean Talon, and under his administration both the fur trade and the colony flourished mightily. He not only forced a temporary (but remarkably long-lived) peace on the Iroquois, officially claimed the whole vast territory surrounding the Great Lakes as the domain of the king, licensed a body of new fur traders, and established a line of trading posts and missions as far west as the Fox River below Lake Michigan, but he also engineered an expedition that led to the second documented discovery of the Mississippi River.

This was the 1673 venture of Louis Jolliet, whose mission was to open new trade sources and discover whether Radisson's "forked river" did indeed lead into the Gulf of Mexico (or, hopefully, the Pacific Ocean, for that great hope had not yet died), and Father Jacques Marquette, a Jesuit whose mission and ambition were to find and convert new souls from among the savages. Jolliet's mission was paramount, for there was yet much speculation on the geography of the river. Some of it was expressed by Father Claude Dablon, a Jesuit missionary familiar with the country of the Wisconsin River. He was writing in 1669: "It [the Mississippi] seems to form an inclosure, as it were, for all our lakes,

Marquette and Jolliet on the banks of the Mississippi in 1673, doing the work of God and king—and empire.

rising in the regions of the North and flowing toward the south, until it empties into the sea—supposed by us to be either the vermilion [Gulf of California] or the Florida sea [Gulf of Mexico], as there is no knowledge of any large rivers in that direction except those which empty into these two Seas." (The river emptying into the Gulf of California, of course, was the Colorado.) The question of the river's direction had to be resolved, so that New France's future exploitation of it could be determined.

In May 1673, Jolliet and Marquette left the Straits of Mackinac between lakes Huron and Michigan, paddled down Lake Michigan to Green Bay, entered the Fox River, then portaged from its headwaters to those of the Wisconsin River, the first Europeans to enter this principal tributary of the Mississippi. Here, the narrative of the expedition says, "We left the waters flowing to Quebec, four or five hundred leagues from here, to float on those that would thenceforward take us through strange lands." Strange, and lit with destiny.

On June 17, 1673, Jolliet and Marquette spun out of the mouth of the Wisconsin River and entered the Mississippi, "this so renowned river." By the end of June, they had passed the mouth of the Missouri. "I have seen nothing more dreadful," Marquette said. "An accumulation of large and entire trees, branches, and floating islands was issuing from the mouth . . . with such impetuosity that we could not without great danger risk passing through it. So great was the agitation that the water was very muddy and could not become clear." Past the "Big Muddy" they journeyed, each mile a new entry in the book of discovery. They reached the mouth of the Ohio and still continued south in their fragile birchbark canoes, little slips of wood lost on the

"In the name of the most high, mighty, invincible, and victorious Prince, Louis the Great," La Salle claimed the valley of the Mississippi in April 1682.

shining expanse of the river. At a point not far from the mouth of the Arkansas River, they learned from Indians that the Mississippi continued south into the Gulf of Mexico; they learned, too—or thought they did —that the region south of them was a domain of the Spanish (although no Spaniard had set foot on the land since De Soto's death in 1542). Taking no chances, they turned back, entered the mouth of the Illinois River, and by doing so opened up a new water route from Lake Michigan, not the least of their accomplishments.

So THE FRENCH NOW KNEW the lay of the river—and some thought they knew what to do with it. Among these were Louis, Comte de Frontenac, who had re-

placed Talon as *intendent* of New France in 1672, and Robert Cavalier, Sieur de la Salle, a fur trader with much experience in the valley of the Ohio. What these two had in mind was the establishment of a string of trading posts from the mouth of the Wisconsin to the mouth of the Mississippi (providing the Spanish had not done so first), which would create an almost invincible monopoly on the interior fur trade, sealing off any possibility of British intrusions from her colonies on the eastern seaboard, and giving New France two export outlets to the sea. After nearly six years of preparation (including a campaign by La Salle in the Court of Versailles to obtain a kingly grant of a fur monopoly), the grand scheme was launched in April 1679 when La Salle headed a party of thirty-two

of God King of France and of Navarre, Fourteenth of that name, I, this ninth day of April, one thousand six hundred and eighty-two . . . do now take, in the name of his Majesty and of his successors to the crown, possession of this country of Louisiana, the seas, harbors, ports, bays, adjacent straits, and all the nations, people, provinces, cities, towns, villages, mines, minerals, fisheries, streams, and rivers, within the extent of the said Louisiana, from the mouth of the great river St. Louis, otherwise called the Ohio . . . as also along the . . . Mississippi, and the rivers which discharge themselves thereinto, from its source beyond the country of the [Sioux] . . . as far as its mouth at the sea, or Gulf of Mexico."

It had been a journey of 158 years from the unknown to the known on the Mississippi River, a journey charted by the destiny and dreams of nations. And now it was known, from the region of its source (if not the source itself) to its mouth, where the accumulated debris from the heartland of a continent was spewed into the unimaginable depths beyond the continental shelf. Known, and claimed for the first time, claimed for the Sun King of France, Louis XIV, the high, mighty, invincible, and victorious Prince. How well he could hold this inland empire remained to be seen, for the energies that would shape the future of America were gathering like the gray billows of a hurricane over the azure sweep of the Gulf of Mexico.

voyageurs down the Illinois River, where they established the first "settlement" in the Mississippi Valley, Fort Crevecoeur.

Yet another Iroquois rampage interrupted the plans of La Salle and Frontenac, and it was not until the autumn of 1681 that they were able to continue. With a party of twenty-three men, La Salle again descended the Illinois to the Mississippi, and after a remarkably dull journey reached the mouth of the great river for the first time. He found no Spanish, to his great relief, and proceeded to claim an empire in a formal ceremony of possession: "In the name of the most high, mighty, invincible and victorious Prince, Louis the Great," he announced (while his men fired volleys of musketry and shouted "Vive le Roi!") "by the grace

THE
RIVER II

Carl Bodmer's lithographic view of Tower Rock on the Mississippi, drawn in 1835.

The River of Many Nations

IT WAS ONLY FOR EIGHTY YEARS that France governed the long sweep of the Mississippi River, from the bogs of the north to the deep-cutting currents of the river's mouth in Louisiana, but in that length of time the French personality was stamped on the river with such indelibility that much of it has survived for two centuries. Even so, the French adventure of settlement and development was a curiously sporadic and finally abortive affair.

While the voyageurs and Jesuits who formed the cutting edge of France's frontier experience continued their efforts to solidify domination of the upper reaches of the Mississippi, Robert Cavalier, Sieur de la Salle—who had planted the French flag on the sands of the river's mouth in 1681—pressed on to realize his dream of an empire. In 1683 he journeyed to Paris to confront the French court with his plans for colonization, beginning with the establishment of a major fort not far from the river's mouth—and, he hinted untruthfully, not too much farther from Spain's rich silver mines in New Mexico. Like most zealots, La Salle was a persuasive man, and Louis XIV not only approved the project but made La Salle commander of all the territory between the Illinois River and the mouth of the Mississippi. In 1684, with four ships, a company of soldiers, and some two hundred men, women, and children as colonists, La Salle's long hoped-for colonizing expedition set out across the Atlantic.

The mission was a disaster almost from the beginning. Ill with periodic attacks of malaria and given to almost paranoid outbursts of irrationality, La Salle pro-vided progressively deteriorating leadership. Trapped by his own lying insistence that the mouth of the Mississippi lay much farther west than it actually did, his colony was finally "established" on the shores of Matagorda Bay in Texas, where, as historian Francis Parkman described the scene, "among tents and hovels, bales, boxes, casks, spars, dismounted cannon, and pens for fowls and swine, were gathered the dejected men and homesick women who were to . . . hold for France a region large as half Europe." In the end, they held nothing. Scourged by heat, fevers, and hunger, the colonists died off, one by one, until by 1687 there were only about forty left. La Salle finally attempted to lead them overland to the Mississippi River and from there to the safety of Canada. Along the way, a pair of mutinous survivors assassinated him.

La Salle's dream of colonization lingered in the minds of a few men, among them the French minister of marine and colonies, Louis Phelypeaux, Comte de Pontchartrain. He was moved to put the dream into reality in 1698, when he learned that an Englishman by the name of Dr. Daniel Coxe was planning to establish colonies along the lower Mississippi. Pontchartrain promptly organized another four-ship expedition to sail to Louisiana with several hundred colonists under the leadership of Pierre Le Moyne, Sieur d'Iberville. This expedition was more successful; when Coxe's functionary, Captain Lewis Bond, entered the Mississippi River, he found the region occupied by Iberville's men. Bond retreated, never to return.

Iberville established a preliminary settlement called

Reclaiming an empire, Pierre Le Moyne, Sieur d'Iberville, lands at Biloxi, Mississippi, in 1699.

Jean Baptiste Le Moyne, Sieur de Bienville, founder of New Orleans in 1718.

Fort Maurepas east of the Mississippi on the shores of Biloxi Bay, Mississippi, in 1699, and the following year built a small outpost on a bluff overlooking the Mississippi River some forty miles above its mouth. Called Fort de la Boulaye, it was the first European settlement in Louisiana—the first, and perhaps least permanent, for the little fort was abandoned eighteen years later when Iberville's brother, Jean Baptiste Le Moyne, Sieur de Bienville, founded New Orleans on a curve of the river a few miles downstream.

The founding of that magnificent city coincided with the first (and last) flowering of French civilization in the Mississippi Valley. The flowering began in 1717, when the Duke of Orleans, who reigned over France during the years of Louis XV's childhood, turned the administration of the French colony over to the hugely industrious Company of the Indies, or Mississippi Company, under the directorship of John Law, an émigré Scotsman. This company, as historian John Anthony Caruso has written, "undertook to deliver France from bankruptcy by using the anticipated wealth of Louisiana as security" and in the process acquired nearly absolute power in the Mississippi Valley, with monopolies in the fur trade of the lower valley, the slave trade, tobacco and sugar cultivation, mining (most of it for lead, rather than the gold that France hoped to find), exports, imports, and all other forms of mercantile activities. Under the banner of this energetic company, French settlement on the river rapidly evolved from a fairly primitive society to one of prosperity and vigor. Spurred on by a widespread propaganda campaign in France, investors there struggled with one another to buy shares in the Mississippi Company (and thus in Louisiana itself); immigration increased dramatically; bustling little towns popped up along the river, among them Ste. Genevieve, Cahokia, Kaskaskia, and Fort de Chartres. In two generations, one more civilization had been implanted in the valley of the Mississippi.

The people who made up this new civilization were French in their heart and souls, in their attitudes, loyalties, and experience; they were called Creoles, a shrewd, courteous, passionate, and eminently sophisticated society, whose soft tones have colored the fabric of the river's life for more than two hundred years. However French the Creoles were by instinct, though, they did not remain so in fact beyond the second generation, when war and global politics conspired to put an end to the framework of their lives.

For most of the first half of the eighteenth century, France and England had avoided open conflict on the question of dominance of the eastern one-third of the North American continent, like dogs circling each other around a bone. In 1754 the wary circling ended when the French attacked and captured the uncompleted British post of Fort Duquesne (now the site of Pittsburgh), and the French and Indian War began.

For close to ten years, this battle for the control of an empire dragged on, most of it waged in southern Canada and the Ohio Valley. While her coffers steadily emptied, France saw one possession after another fall to the military machine of the British—Louisburg, Fort

Frontenac (both in Canada), Fort Duquesne, Niagara, Ticonderoga, Crown Point, and finally Quebec itself. By 1762 when it became obvious that France was going to lose most, if not all, of Canada, she ceded to Spain (in the secret Treaty of Fontainebleau) the Isle of Orleans and the part of Louisiana that lay west of the Mississippi River, gaining millions of francs in the transaction but losing half an empire. The remaining half was lost in 1763 when, in the Treaty of Paris, France relinquished all of Canada to Great Britain and temporarily left the stage of the North American drama.

Spain, whose fantasizing conquistadors had discovered it more than two hundred years before, now became proprietor of the Mississippi by virtue of effectively controlling navigation from the mouth to well above the confluence of the Missouri River. Yet the Spanish were not alone in this valley. Besides a burgeoning Creole population, which had chosen to remain in spite of Spanish rule, colonial Americans from the eastern seaboard increasingly began to make their presence felt. Even before the war had ended, individual speculators (among them George Washington) and large land-jobbing companies were casting acquisitive glances toward the rich bottomland country of the Ohio and Mississippi valleys, petitioning king and court to grant them the right to purchase millions of acres, and a handful of genuine settlers had begun to trickle across the Appalachian barrier. When the war ended in 1763, the trickles became small rivers of people; ignoring, circumventing, or forcing the revision of British restrictions of their movement west, they filtered into the wandering river valleys, purchasing and selling enormous blocs of land, laying bare forests, burning off meadows, planting corn, tobacco, and wheat, negotiating with, killing, and being

The official 1723 plan for the city of New Orleans; the "Place d'Armes" later became Jackson Square, but the old quarter has changed remarkably little in 250 years.

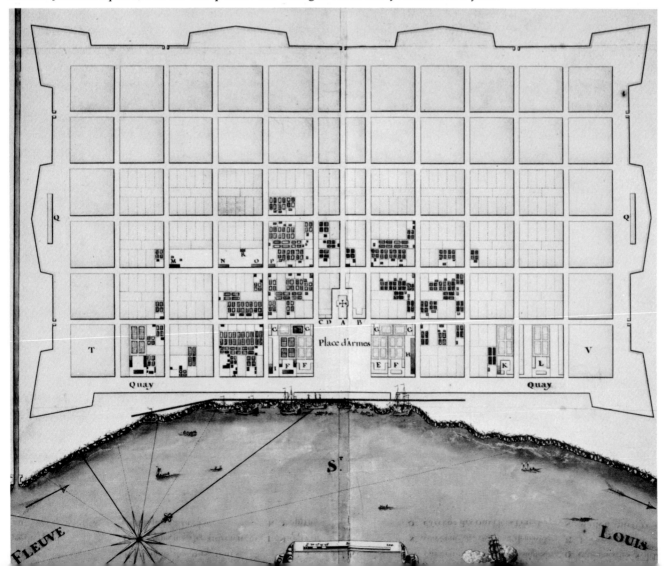

Muscle, sweat, and hope: the beginnings of St. Louis are carved from the Mississippi wilderness in 1764.

killed by Indians, surviving. By the time of the American Revolution, thousands of men, women, and children had created a new frontier stretching from the Monongahela Valley across western Virginia to Kentucky and eastern Tennessee and even filling in pockets of the upper Ohio Valley.

THE REVOLUTION PUT A TEMPORARY HALT to this backwoods inundation, as the British and their various Indian allies initiated some of the most vicious fighting of the entire war in the western country. When the war ended, the tide continued, spearheaded by the kind of horizon-eyed frontiersmen that the Frenchman, F. A. Michaux, described in 1805: "More than half of those who inhabit the borders of the Ohio, are again the first inhabitants, or as they are called in the United States, the *first settlers,* a kind of men who cannot settle upon the soil that they have cleared, and who under pretence

of finding a better land, a more wholesome country, a greater abundance of game, push forward, incline perpetually towards the most distant points of the American population."

Behind these "first settlers" came the real settlers, so many of them that the Spanish, holding for dear life to their possessions of Louisiana and Florida, became nervous. Who knew how far or how hard the people of this vigorous young beast of a nation would push? Spain's first move was to assert its control of the Mississippi by closing the river to American navigation, ignoring the clause in the 1783 Treaty of Paris (ending the Revolutionary War) which had stipulated that "the navigation of the river Mississippi, from its source to the ocean, shall remain forever free and open to . . . the citizens of the United States."

To secure official recognition of this act of closure, Spain then sent a diplomat to Philadelphia to negotiate with the American government, offering as bait the

An Oscar E. Berninghaus painting of colonial Ste. Genevieve, Missouri
—one of the earliest settlements of the Mississippi Valley.

proposal that American trading ships would be allowed to enter Spanish ports around the world (heretofore closed to American shipping). The resulting treaty (Jay-Gardoqui), which provided that the United States would give up the right to navigate the Mississippi for twenty-five years, was sent to Congress for ratification in 1786. The seven northern states, seduced by the prospect of open trade, ratified the agreement; Delaware passed; but the five southern states, with closer ties to the western country, rejected it.

Seven votes were not enough for ratification, and the treaty failed—but by then the harm had been done. The western country raged at what it interpreted as brutal insensitivity to western needs; navigation of the Mississippi was necessary to its very survival, yet a group of eastern mountebanks had been willing to give it up out of a purely selfish interest in trade. Talk of rebellion against the embryonic United States became common, though not generally popular, and various sordid con-

spiracies developed. The most ambitious of these was the enterprise of James Wilkinson, a resident of Kentucky so pleased by his physical similarity to George Washington that he had been known to smile enigmatically whenever someone mistook him for the old general. His scheme, laid before the Spanish governor of Louisiana, Esteban Miró, was simple: in exchange for a trade monopoly in New Orleans, Wilkinson would act as a secret agent for Spain in Kentucky and contrive to foment a revolution that would place the region under the control of the Spanish government. The plan also indicated that the logical man to head up the new non-republic would be Wilkinson himself, the father, as it were, of his own country.

Miró, it turned out, was delighted at the prospect, but circumstances beyond the control of the two conspirators killed the project before it could develop. Kentuckians rejected Wilkinson's talk of revolution, and the king of Spain decided upon conciliation to

From Spain, to France, to America—the Three Flags ceremony of March 9, 1804, as seen in a diorama from the Jefferson National Expansion Memorial, St. Louis.

strengthen his American colonies: after 1789, Americans would be allowed to ship goods through New Orleans for the payment of a 15 percent duty, and immigration to Louisiana would be encouraged by the offer of easy conditions of entry, no religious restrictions, free land, commercial equality, and—perhaps most important—the privilege of selling tobacco at high prices in the crown's New Orleans warehouses. Westerners continued to chafe at the 15 percent duty they had to pay, and few of them chose to immigrate to the papacy of Spanish rule, however tolerant the government of Spain promised to be, but they were no longer completely strangled in their use of the river. Even the duty disappeared in 1795, when the Treaty of San Lorenzo gave Americans the perpetual right to navigate the Mississippi. European wars were bleeding Spain, and its days of glory in the Mississippi Valley were beginning to fade.

They disappeared completely in 1800, when the Treaty of San Ildefonso returned the Louisiana Territory to France—whose people were still the dominant population of the valley, except for a few Americans now scattered here and there on the banks of the river. In 1803, President Thomas Jefferson sent emissaries to Napoleon Bonaparte to negotiate for the purchase of New Orleans, but to the immense surprise of everyone but himself, the dictator of France offered to sell not only New Orleans but all of the Louisiana Territory, a domain that embraced most of the land between the Mississippi River and the Rocky Mountains; his price was $15 million, and the stunned Americans hastened to put their signatures to the agreement. "This accession of territory," Napoleon wrote after the sale, "consolidates the power of the United States forever, and I have given England a maritime rival who sooner or later will humble her pride." On December 30, 1803, the French flag was lowered and the flag of the United States raised in New Orleans. The Mississippi had finally become an American river.

Half of a continent signed away: the final transfer of the Louisiana Territory in 1803.

From Muscle to Steam

IN THE NEARLY SIXTY YEARS between the Louisiana Purchase in 1803 and the beginning of the Civil War in 1861, frontier became civilization in the Mississippi Valley, a transformation that contributed to the emerging concept of Manifest Destiny. As one congressional orator put it, "There is such a thing as a destiny for this American race ... because we, the people of the United States, have spread, are spreading, and intend to spread, and should spread, and go on to spread ... and this our destiny has now become so manifest that it cannot fail but by our own folly."

In 1803 the non-Indian population of the valley was a little over 400,000, most of it confined to portions of eastern Ohio, Kentucky, Tennessee, and Louisiana (whose inhabitants were mostly Creoles, citizens by acquisition); by 1810 it had swelled to 1,178,251 and spread through an area now covered by Indiana, Illinois, Michigan, Missouri, Arkansas, and Mississippi; and by 1860 the population had bloated to 13,263,280 and was scattered over territory that now included Wisconsin, Minnesota, Iowa, and Kansas. This was more than a wave, it was a veritable *tsunami* of human population, inexorable in its growth, promising devastation to any force that attempted to stand in its way.

Which should be enough to explain what happened to the luckless Indians of the valley. In fire and blood, the Stone Age met the Iron Age head on, and it was not the Stone Age that survived. After 1803, as the westering horde spread toward the river, its vanguard included not only frontiersmen and land speculators but Indian commissioners whose task it was to persuade the Indians through cajolery, threats, or any other means at hand to relinquish their ancestral lands to make room for freeholders and plantation lords. (In the Old Northwest, one such commissioner was William Henry Harrison, who was also, not incidentally, a land jobber of respectable dimensions; the acreage he siphoned off for himself and his associates from these acquired Indian lands made him a rich man and ultimately president of the United States.) By 1810 nearly 110 million acres of land had been wrung from the Indians by threats of force, bribery, and numerous treaties made with tribal fragments. The pressures on the natives were enormous. Not only were they being pushed constantly westward, but as they moved, they inevitably encroached on the lands of other tribes and, consequently, had to fight for the privilege of living anywhere.

Out of this welter of desperation, there rose a leader whose name was Tecumseh, a fiery Shawnee chieftain with a native brilliance and a gift for oratory. With his brother, The Prophet, a one-eyed, epileptic *shaman* (who the Indians believed was possessed of spiritual powers), Tecumseh began touring the western tribes in 1805, preaching unity and defiance. "Burn their dwellings!" he shouted before hundreds, then thousands, of Indians who gathered to hear his message. "Destroy their stock. The red people own the country. . . . Burn now. War forever. War upon the living. War upon the dead; dig their very corpses from the grave; our country must give no rest to a white man's bones!"

For all of Tecumseh's firebrand speechmaking, it was not until General William Henry Harrison gathered a

The bustle and muscle of steam—a view of the Mississippi at Memphis, Tennessee, in 1848.

*At New Orleans in 1815, the raw frontier army of Andrew Jackson met the highly
trained army of British General Packenham; the toll: two thousand British dead, six Americans.*

troop of one thousand "Long Knives" in August 1811 that open war broke out. In the Battle of Tippecanoe on November 7, Harrison's men routed some seven hundred Shawnees and destroyed their village of Prophetown, near the banks of the Wabash River in Indiana Territory. The immediate result was a concentrated series of Indian reprisals that set the frontier's edge to burning and terrified settlers even in the well-populated regions of Ohio and Kentucky.

The Indians were encouraged and in some measure supplied by the British at Fort Malden, the British Canadian post on the Detroit River above Lake Erie—although not to the extent claimed by Harrison: "The whole of the Indians on this frontier have been completely armed and equipped from the British King's stores at Malden." Still, the belief in the perfidy of the British was widespread on the frontier, and the West added its voice to the demands for war with England

that were already being raised in the new capital of Washington, D.C., as eastern merchants and shippers chafed under British impressment practices and restraints on American trade. On June 18, 1812, Congress declared that a state of war existed.

IN THE EAST, the War of 1812 was a conflict between maritime powers, one huge and established, the other small and emerging; in the West, it was very largely a struggle between the Stone Age and the Iron Age for domination in the Mississippi Valley. For scarcely a single battle in that country took place without British regulars fighting side by side with Indian allies against the Americans, the last time the Indians of the valley would be employed by a European power to further its own ends.

The tactic was not particularly successful for either

The great treaty gathering at Prairie du Chien in 1825, which set the scene for the Indian cession of most of the upper Mississippi Valley.

the British or the Indians. In the North, the Battle of the Thames on October 5, 1813, in which Tecumseh himself and nearly six hundred other warriors died, scattered the aggressive chieftain's desperate confederation. In the South, the Battle of Horseshoe Bend on March 27, 1814, in which 3,000 troops under Andrew Jackson killed 800 Indians, all but destroyed the Creek Nation. Of all the bitter skirmishes, massacres, and formal battles of the war, these two were the most important to the Americans of the West, so much so that the Battle of New Orleans on January 8, 1815, in which Andrew Jackson's army killed 2,000 British regulars with the loss of only six Americans, was almost anticlimatic (in more ways than one, for the battle was fought two weeks after the war had formally ended with the signing of the Treaty of Ghent). By then the crucial point had been settled: Indian resistance in the Mississippi Valley had been broken.

Broken, but not yet obliterated. Feebly and pathetically, it was expressed once again at the climax of the Black Hawk "War" of 1832, in which more than six hundred Keokuk men, women, and children under the leadership of Chief Black Hawk (who had been forced into war in the first place and who had twice attempted to surrender) were shot down like so many vermin on the banks of the Mississippi in the Bad Axe Massacre.

More aggressively and effectively, it was revived for a final time thirty years later. In August 1862 more than two thousand Sioux warriors launched a forty-day assault on settlements of western Minnesota scattered through the 250 miles between Fort Abercrombie on the Red River and New Ulm on the Minnesota. The death toll was more than five hundred people. General John Pope was dispatched from Washington to direct the campaign of reprisal. Burning with the need to cleanse the wounds of his many Civil War blunders with Indian blood (but not willing to leave his comfortable quarters in St. Paul to do so), he outlined his plans to his commander in the field, Henry Hastings Sibley: "The horrible massacres of women and children and, the outrageous abuse of female prisoners still alive, call for punishment beyond human power to inflict. . . . It is my purpose utterly to exterminate the Sioux. . . . Destroy everything belonging to them and force them out into the plains." Sibley, a reasonable man who knew that simpleminded revenge would serve no useful purpose, did not set out "utterly to exterminate the Sioux," but by the end of the summer of 1863 he *had* pushed them southwest across the Missouri River into the Great Plains, from which they never returned.

The road to progress had finally been cleared.

THE CIVILIZATION that replaced the Indian in the Mississippi Valley was a dichotomous one, with differences in style, attitude, experience, and opportunity. And in those differences lay the seeds of conflict.

The upper valley—comprising Ohio, Indiana, Illinois, Wisconsin, Michigan, Minnesota, and Iowa—was in many respects an extension of early New England, a land of the yeoman farmer, as he was described by Thomas Jefferson: "Cultivators of the earth are the most valuable citizens. They are the most vigorous, the most independent, the most virtuous, and they are tied to their country, and wedded to its liberty and interests, by the most lasting bonds." Henry Clay, writing more than thirty years later, was hardly less flattering in his description of this paragon: "Pioneers," he said, "penetrate into the uninhabited regions of the West. They apply the axe to the forest, which falls before them, or the plough to the prairie, deeply sinking its share in the unbroken wild grasses in which it abounds. They build houses, plant orchards, enclose fields, cultivate the earth, and rear up families around them."

Whether pioneer or son of a pioneer, the typical farmer of the upper valley was a sober, self-consciously industrious sort whose fundamentalist Protestantism was bedded on rock—and if he fell victim to the fevered excitement of the Methodism that swept across the Old Northwest in the 1830s, it merely suggests the degree to which his religious emotions had been repressed through the years. On his 40-, 80-, or 160-acre plot—purchased,

most likely, on credit at exorbitant interest rates from a land-jobbing speculator—he sank his plowshare deeply and planted his rows of corn and stands of wheat and barley, his fields of squash and pumpkins. He raised hogs and chickens and a few beef cattle, and kept a milch cow or two for family use. If he rarely became rich, he usually prospered, as hard work on good land can make men prosper. With a simple, unshakable faith, he believed in Progress and Enterprise and sometimes even in the perfectibility of man.

The society in which he functioned was in most respects an extension of himself—sober and industrious. Whatever color and excitement it possessed was provided by the dips and spurts of commercial enterprise. The cities it erected on the banks of the Mississippi reflected the values of the yeoman farmer; the St. Pauls, Keokuks, Madisons, Dubuques, and Davenports were neat, sturdy, *purposeful* towns with more churches than taverns, more banks than brothels. There was little romance in this society, but its steady uprightness was the heartland strength of America.

The lower valley was another world. It had its share of yeoman farmers with all the virtues and dullnesses of their northern counterparts, but here they barely influenced the quality of life. At the heart of the difference was the institution of slavery, outlawed in the North by the provisions of the Northwest Ordinance of 1787 but carried across the mountains intact from the piedmont lands of the eastern seaboard to the country of the lower river—into western Kentucky and Tennessee, Missouri, Arkansas, Louisiana, and Mississippi. The men who brought it there did not call themselves farmers. They were *planters,* begod, fiercely, proudly individualistic, often bombastic, always colorful. On hundreds, even thousands, of acres of silt-rich bottomland, they planted their money crops: tobacco in Kentucky and Tennessee, as well as grains for the distillation of some of the finest whiskey in the world; cotton, extending in a wide belt on both sides of the river, from western Tennessee through Mississippi and into eastern Louisiana, and from southern Missouri through Arkansas and into eastern Texas; rice in Arkansas, Louisiana, and Mississippi; cane sugar among the bayous of the thick deltaic deposits of Louisiana's southern boot.

A typical plantation was that of Martin W. Philips of Hinds County, Mississippi, who described his operation

The so-called "battle" of Bad Axe in 1832, an encounter that hastened the
end of the Indian presence on the Mississippi.

The tools of the Iron Age: troops of the United States Army
encamped on Wabasha Prairie, Illinois, in 1848.

Natchez, Mississippi, in 1848—where commerce flourished by day and several versions of hell could be found at night.

in 1854: "We now have in this estate 1,168 acres of land; on the place 66 negroes, twenty work horses or mules, five yoke of choice oxen. We plant 270 or 280 acres in cotton, and 125 in corn. We send to the field thirty-four negroes, old and young, rating them at thirty hands; have one carpenter; a woman who cooks for the above, with all the children in charge." They built earthen levees to hold back the river's flood and great, colonnaded mansions on whose verandahs they probably did gather in the summer to hear the darkies singing. They believed in a kind of patrician progress and in the perfectibility of their own culture.

Above all, they had come to believe in slavery, for it was on the ridged and sweating backs of African Coromantees, Fantyns, Mandingoes, Foulahs, Congoes, Angolas, Eboes, Whydahs, Nagoes, and Pawpaws that the foundation of their chosen way of life rested. Quite enough has been written about the institution of slavery—more dismal than peculiar—and it is enough here to note that, while life in thralldom was neither the tortured world the Abolitionists maintained nor the innocent paradise the slavemasters propagandized, there was something in it that dehumanized both master and slave.

Consider the words of planter Charles Tait in 1826: "Our loss of little negroes has been great the past year, but I hope it will not happen again. Let us feed, clothe and house them well, and I do not fear but they will increase rapidly. With the stock we have there is a good prospect for the next generation." When a man can equate human beings with cattle, when he can refer to them as "stock," he has stripped away some of his own humanity, diminished his life. What such attitudes can do to the "stock" itself, we now know altogether too well.

As there was a conflict between humanity and inhumanity in the men who dominated the life of the lower valley, so it was with the river towns their energies erected and informed. They were fearfully exciting and excited places, those towns, where measured respectability seemed always to be warring with venality, bawdry, and violence. Natchez, Mississippi, was typical. "Up on the hill," it was the very picture of small town virtue, even of a kind of elegance, with columned mansions, sturdy business establishments, and wide, bustling streets well shaded by trees. But there was another Natchez—

Natchez-Under-the-Hill, situated at the foot of a two-hundred-foot bluff that rose from the Mississippi. Natchez-Under-the-Hill was the Mississippi crossroads of the Natchez Trace, the ancient Indian and pioneering trail to the interior of the trans-Appalachian West; it was a boisterous, rowdy collection of bordellos, gambling hells, and saloons where on any given night a man could lose his virtue, his money and his life—in that order.

Without perhaps the dramatic intensity of Natchez, most of the other river towns of the lower valley displayed the same schizophrenic characteristics. St. Louis, however, was a special case. Founded in 1764 as a French fur company's trading center, St. Louis was more than a river town; it was the stepping-off point for the vast unknown of the Far West. Smelling of bear grease and far places, dressed in outlandish buckskin and beaver fur, and carrying their monstrous Hawken rifles with them wherever they went, mountain men wandered the city's waterfront streets bent on purposes of drink and gambling. Speaking of Indian troubles, of passes and mountains and deserts, explorers—and later overland settlers and goldseekers—outfitted themselves for adventure beyond imagination from the merchants, wagon-makers, saddlers, and horse-, mule-, and oxen-traders of the city. St. Louis lay on the border between the frontier already subdued and the frontier unconquered that stretched to the western horizon.

Of all the towns of the lower Mississippi, the queen

Dubuque, Iowa, in 1848—as sober, purposeful, and businesslike as any town in the upper Mississippi Valley.

was New Orleans, an original so utterly unique that one Colonel James R. Creecy was driven to verse to describe it in 1829:

> Have you ever been in New Orleans?
>   If not, you'd better go;
> It's a nation of a queer place;
>   day and night a show!
> Frenchmen, Spaniards, West Indians,
>   Creoles, Mustees,
> Yankees, Kentuckians, Tennesseeans,
>   lawyers and trustees,
> Clergymen, priests, friars, nuns,
>   women of all stains;
> Negroes in purple and fine linen,
>   and slaves in rags and chains.
> Ships, arks, steamboats, robbers,
>   pirates, alligators,
> Assassins, gamblers, drunkards
>   and cotton speculators;
> Sailors, soldiers, pretty girls
>   and ugly fortune-tellers;
> Pimps, imps, shrimps, and all
>   sorts of dirty fellows;
> White men with black wives,
>   et vice-versa too.
> A progeny of all colors—
>   an infernal motley crew!
> Yellow fever in February—
>   muddy streets all the year;
> Many things to hope for,
>   and a dev'lish sight to fear!
> Gold and silver bullion—
>   United States' bank-notes,
> Horse-racers, cock-fighters,
>   and beggars without coats.
> Snapping turtles, sugar,
>   sugar-houses, water-snakes,
> Molasses, flour, whiskey,
>   tobacco, corn and johnny-cakes,
> Beef, cattle, hogs, pork,
>   turkeys, Kentucky rifles,
> Lumber, boards, apples, cotton,
>   and many other trifles.
> Butter, cheese, onions, wild
>   beasts in wooden cages,
> Barbers, waiters, draymen,
>   with the highest sort of wages.
> Now and then there are Duels,
>   for very little cause;
> The natives soon forget 'em—
>   they care not much for laws.

Filled with plantations more often than farms and governed by a society that was loose, expansive, ambitious, and somewhat libertine in its morality (at least for men), the civilization of the lower valley was the very antithesis of the middle-American world of the North, the land of early bed and early rising. Yet one thing bound the two regions together, gave Keokuk and Natchez a kind of brotherhood: an absolute dependence upon the Mississippi waterways for commerce and transportation. It was the Mississippi, together with the Ohio and their navigable tributaries, that carried the pork, beef, hams, lard, butter, beans, tanned hides, corn, hay, cheese, ducks and chickens, and barrel staves of the North, and the tobacco, whiskey, cotton, rice, and sugar of the South to New Orleans for sale and shipment to the markets of America and the world. It was the river that gave each region its life.

DURING THE FIRST TWENTY YEARS or so of the nineteenth century, the river trade was dominated by annual fleets of muscle- and current-powered flatboats. Each spring in upriver towns, the boats were constructed, taking as many shapes as innovation could give them but generally falling into three types: the "scow-shed," consisting of a boxlike little shelter placed on an oblong deck; the Alleghany skiff, featuring a long steering oar; and the Kentucky flat, the commonest of the flatboats, which had a cabin at one end and a raised deck at the other, as well as a pair of masts to carry a crude schooner rig when the wind was up and from the right direction. Once built, the boats remained at dockside for most of the summer, taking on loads of produce and livestock from hundreds of square miles around. When the first autumn rains swelled the river, they pushed off for New Orleans. At its height, this flatboat fleet carried an astonishing amount of commerce, as described by historian Walter Havighurst: "Between October and May, 1810–11, nearly a thousand flatboats

Southern plantation life in 1861—as the South would have liked it to be known. How it was is a matter still open to debate.

passed Louisville packed with the produce of the Ohio Valley. Along with the barreled goods went livestock— fifteen hundred hogs grunting at their feed troughs; two million chickens, ducks, and geese cackling and quacking down the river, five hundred horses watching the passing shores. The lesser cargo included two tons of shoe thread, seven tons of country linen, 8,500 boxes of cheese, twenty tons of butter and 380 tons of lard." Once in New Orleans, the cargo was sold, the boats were sold and broken up for firewood, and the crews walked home up the Natchez Trace—and if lucky survived the legendary assaults of that murderer's path.

Flatboating was a one-way trade. It was for the longer, narrower, and less numerous keelboats to attempt the laborious upstream traffic. With their colorful, durable crews, the keelboats were literally hauled up the river along the shore. While men at set-poles in the stern held the boat against the current, rope cordelles were attached to trees, and the boat was pulled upstream until the rope ran out; the cordelles were then untied, run a few hundred feet farther up the river while the set-poles held the boat's position, and retied, and the whole process was repeated. From New Orleans to Louisville, it was a three-month trip of drudgery and danger, and the great keelboats and their roistering, sweating, shouting crews did not long survive the onslaught of technology.

It was steam that killed their trade, steam that soon became the principal motive force on the river, although fleets of one-way flatboats would continue to ply its waters until the 1880s, when steam locomotives sent the flatboats the way of the keelboats. It was a revolution,

New Orleans in 1852—"A nation of a queer place," the poet said, "day and night a show!" It was also the spout of heartland America's cornucopia.

this business of steam, as described by Zadok Cramer in the 1811 edition of his famed pilot's manual, *The Navigator:* "There is now on foot a new method of navigating our western waters, particularly the Ohio and Mississippi rivers. This is with boats propelled by the power of steam. . . . It will be a novel sight, and as pleasing as novel, to see a huge boat working her way up the windings of the Ohio, without the appearance of sail, oar, pole, or any manual labor about her—moving within the secrets of her own wonderful mechanism and propelled by power undiscoverable!—This Plan, if it succeeds, must open to view flattering prospects to an immense country, an interior of not less than two thousand miles of as fine a soil and climate as

the world can produce, and to a people worthy of all the advantages that nature and art can give them. . . . The immensity of the country we have yet to settle, the vast reaches of the bowels of the earth, the unexampled advantage of our water courses, which wind without interruption for a thousand miles, the numerous sources of trade and wealth opening to the enterprising and industrious citizens, are reflections that must rouse the most dull and stupid."

A novel sight, a novel and rousing sight, indeed. It came to the river in the year of *The Navigator's* publication, when Nicholas Roosevelt, applying the principles demonstrated in Robert Fulton's *Clermont*—which had chugged and hissed up the Hudson River in

either side of which spouted the two chimneys of the boat's engines. Someone remarked that it resembled a "floating wedding cake," and no one has ever ventured a better description of the vessels that soon became part of the life and legend of the Mississippi.

By 1820 there were more than sixty steamers on the river between New Orleans and the upriver towns of the Ohio Valley. These early boats were dirty and dangerous, much given to fire, wrecks, and boiler explosions, but while they survived (an average of five years), they were fast, efficient, and immensely profitable for their owners. By the middle of the 1820s, there were 200 steamers in operation; by 1840, more than 400; and by 1860, nearly 1,000. The wharves of Cincinnati, St. Louis, Memphis, Natchez, and New Orleans were crowded all the days of the year with a feast of wedding cakes loading or unloading all the rich produce of the Ohio and Mississippi valleys, and the steamers probed into every navigable tributary where profit might be made—into the upper stem of the Mississippi as far as St. Paul, up the Missouri (eventually, almost to the Rocky Mountains), the Wabash, the Illinois, and the Red.

The men who manned these great machines of the pre-railroad West were a raffish, adventurous, irreverent lot, from the lowliest stevedore to the pilot himself, the aristocrat of the trade. And the passengers who crowded into their staterooms or cabins (or, for the cheapest fare, simply curled up on the open deck) were a melange of frontier river life: southern belles, some of them quite as beautiful as southern men believed them to be, complete with retinues of personal slaves, going to visit families and friends in Memphis or St. Louis; flatboatmen returning to their Ohio Valley homes after a "hoo-raw" in Natchez; northern merchants on their way to New Orleans to see what good they could do themselves; land jobbers (next to home-taught lawyers and stump-speaking politicians perhaps the most ubiquitous form of frontier life) with an eye on the western shore; drummers and peddlers, their carpetbags packed with samples and gadgetry; planters and planters' sons heading toward the manly rites and pleasures of New Orleans; Englishmen and Frenchmen traveling for their health or to see how America worked,

New York just three years before—caused to be built in Pittsburgh a hundred-foot sidewheel steamboat. He called it the *New Orleans,* and in the autumn of 1811 this narrow-hulled pioneer of considerable draft got up steam and headed downriver for the city of her name. In January 1812 she arrived safe and sound to the noise of cheering; the people of the river knew history when they saw it.

In 1816, Henry M. Shreve of Wheeling, West Virginia, set the pattern for all future river steamers when he built and launched the 400-ton *Washington.* Built on a shallow-draft hull to ride the river's snags and sandbars, the *Washington*'s two decks rose high above the water, topped off by a little boxlike pilothouse on

73

A stubby paddlewheeler of 1832.

A "Kentucky flat," a working keelboat of the 1830s.

or did not work, a compulsion that occupied so many foreigners in the nineteenth century; gamblers, many of whom looked the way the movies have decided they must have looked; immigrants, overlanders, housewives, and harlots—anyone who would be carried, could be carried, and no questions asked.

The boats grew larger and larger, filagreed with the intricacies of carpenter's Gothic, looking like even bigger and fancier wedding cakes. Many acquired ballrooms with mirror-covered walls and parquet floors, elegant saloons that might have been lifted intact from New Orleans hotels, bridal suites with Belgian carpets; they carried barbers, cooks, bartenders, and musicians in addition to the regular crew. They grew faster as hull and engine design improved; in 1817 the trip from New Orleans to Louisville consumed twenty-five days and two hours, but in 1858 only four days and nine and one-half hours.

Big, fast, and luxurious, they remained bloody dangerous craft, and riding them was a kind of watery roulette. One estimate has it that four thousand people were killed or injured in steamboat accidents between 1810 and 1850, many of which casualties were the result of what we call today "pilot error." Between 1831 and

The Age of Ripoff comes to the Mississippi Valley in the form of the nonexistent city of Nininger, 1857.

The Mississippi as the highway of commerce is documented in
one of Currier & Ives' most famous prints, 1865.

1833, for example, one out of every eight boats on the river was destroyed through human miscalculation— quite frequently connected with the sport of racing, one of the trade's more lethal pastimes, but as often the result of accidental fires, collisions, and inferior boiler construction or maintenance. It was an exploitive, full-speed-ahead age free of almost any regulatory restrictions; a man was privileged to get away with anything he could, and however much the nineteenth-century riverboat trade may have needed a Ralph Nader, such a critic was quite unthinkable.

Deadly though the boats could be, their contribution to the growth of river trade was incalculable. Every ten years after 1820, the total value of goods hauled down the river to New Orleans doubled, and the city blossomed. In 1834 the actor Tyrone Power described the levees of New Orleans as "bordered by tiers of merchant shipping from every portion of the trading world," and by "numberless steamboats of all sizes" and hundreds of "rude rafts and arks constructed by the dwellers on the hundred waters of the far West." Wealth, he said, was "on all hands accumulating with a rapidity almost partaking of the marvelous." By 1840, New Orleans was the fourth largest city in the United States. Between 1840 and 1850, it handled more export trade than New York City and more than fifty percent of the exports of the entire nation; its commerce, fed in a steady stream from the western rivers, in that decade exceeded the tonnage of the British merchant marine.

And then, in a little over three generations after the *New Orleans* had made her maiden trip down the river from Pittsburgh, the Age of Steam on the Mississippi dribbled away to nothing, reduced and then eliminated by the Age of Gasoline. There was little left of this great era but the ghosts of memory—and the man who gave voice to that national memory with more eloquence than any other was Samuel Clemens, Mark Twain, a child of the Mississippi.

A Man, a Town, and a River

MARK TWAIN always attached profound significance to the fact that he was born in 1835, the year of Halley's Comet. There was something to be said for this, perhaps, for he died in 1910—again the year of Halley's Comet—and he himself had risen to brilliance like a comet, becoming the brightest and most permanent fixture in America's literary firmament. Yet the night sky shining with that cosmic visitor of 1835 was less important to the life of Mark Twain than the ground on which he was born and reared: Florida, Missouri, where he came into the world, and Hannibal, Missouri, where he learned the lessons he had to know in the journey from boy to man.

"The Missouri in which the infant's eyes opened," Bernard DeVoto wrote in *Mark Twain's America,* "was frontier, and that it was frontier is the whole truth about the books of Mark Twain. . . . Necessarily Samuel Clemens was a leaf that took its color from the sun: the sun of Florida and Hannibal shone on Western rural slaveholding communities near the fringe of settlement during years when a boundless vigor was making America something it had not been, something not reducible to a formula." That sun illuminated not only the man, but the books that became part of America's patrimony.

Samuel Clemens came to Hannibal at the age of four and left at eighteen—long enough for the little town to sear its images into his psyche forever, where they became what Winfield Townley Scott called "the bones of art." The town had few pretensions to greatness on its own; founded as a service center for the farms around it (northern Missouri was a region dominated by small farmers, not plantation-owners, for all the fact that it was slave territory), it slept almost without ambition, its streets hot and dusty in the summer, muddy and treacherous in the winter. There were few truly rich people and few truly poor people in the town (the Clemens family was among the latter); most were at that level of society whose women would have fit the description Twain penned as one of the sayings of Pudd'nhead Wilson: "She was not quite what you would call refined. She was not quite what you would call unrefined. She was the kind of person that keeps a parrot." Behind the town rose forested hills, and beyond those stretched the sweep of western prairie; before the town rolled the glimmering Mississippi, in the middle of which lay Jackson's Island, a place of constant temptation to the adventurous instincts of the small boy.

The cutting edge of the frontier had passed the town by but had left its marks in passage; men still sat on benches on Main Street, or on the levee where the town's modest shipments of hemp, hides, pork, lard, and tobacco waited for the next steamboat, and talked of things that could stir the soul of a boy: of Indian raids and seas of buffalo, of frontiersmen with Kentucky rifles and mountain men with Green River knives, of explorers, furs, mountains, deserts, and rivers with names like Yellowstone, Platte, and Sacramento. Yes, the frontier had left the town, but one knew it had been there.

Such tales would have fired a boy's footling urge to wander, and it was the river (which had its own tales to be told) that provided the highway. Twain admitted that at least once in his childhood he had stowed away

"Huck Finn and Jim," one of the sinewy lithographs of the Missouri artist, Thomas Hart Benton.

•

on a southbound steamer; soon caught out, he made it only as far as the next town down the river, where he was put ashore in the hands of a relative and returned to Hannibal. One would like to have been there when he confronted his mother and father; perhaps his explanations would have possessed some of the style and flair that Huckleberry Finn used to such advantage whenever he wished to deceive and/or befuddle the adults who were forever trying to "sivilize" him.

EXCEPT FOR PERIODIC VISITS to relatives and friends in later years, Sam left the town permanently at eighteen. After two years in the East as a tramp printer and writer of occasional newspaper squibs, and a few weeks in Keokuk, Iowa, working in his brother's print-shop, he found himself once again on the river, heading south in the *Paul Jones,* ultimately bound for Brazil, of all places.

Before he got even as far as New Orleans, he became entranced with the notion of learning to become a riverboat pilot, and the *Paul Jones'* pilot, Horace Bixby, agreed to take him on as an apprentice for a fee of $500, on credit (it was later knocked down to $400). For seventeen months following that momentous decision in October 1855, the sandy-haired youth spent his days and nights on the river, learning its snags and bars, its eddies and currents, its islands and towheads, its whims and fancies and dangers. From the *Paul Jones* he went to the *John J. Roe,* and from there to the *Aleck Scott* and then the *A. T. Lacey.* Finally, he began piloting boats that carried cargo exclusively (which unlicensed pilots could do under the free and easy restrictions of those days). On April 9, 1859, in the St. Louis office of the district steamboat inspector, his dream was given full-fledged, official reality: "The inspectors for the district of St. Louis certify that Samuel Clemens, having been duly examined, touching his qualifications as a PILOT of a Steam Boat, is a suitable and safe person to be entrusted with the powers and duties of a Pilot of Steam Boats, and do

The stature of a river pilot warranted the painting of a portrait; this one shows Clemens in 1859.

license him to act as such for one year from this date on the following rivers, to wit on the Mississippi River to and from St. Louis and New Orleans."

Ah, here was glory! Sam Clemens, the river town boy, could strut now, a man taller than all other men on the river, save those who followed his own profession (a profession, mind you, not a trade). He could sip his brandies in Jackson Square in New Orleans, puff at his perpetual cigars while strolling up Market Street in St. Louis, and be fully in touch with himself, the last time he would have that certainty; he could go home to Hannibal and the pubescent, dreaming boys would watch his every move, just as he had watched the pilots in his own youth. Those boys would know what he knew, that he had reached a pinnacle of the river's life, his own life.

The glory ended after a period only a little longer than the months of his apprenticeship. In January 1861 his last command was at the dock in New Orleans when Louisiana seceded from the Union. The boat was seized, and Sam went back to St. Louis as a passenger on the

Uncle Sam. It was the last regularly-scheduled trip on the river for the next four years, for the Civil War had unofficially begun (it would begin historically on April 11, when Fort Sumter in Charleston Harbor was fired on by Confederates). Sam Clemens never piloted a steamboat again.

For the rest of his life, Twain hated war — for humanitarian reasons, certainly, but we are allowed to wonder whether his hatred was not colored by the bitterness he must have felt when he found that men who wished to practice the art of killing one another had put an end to his innocence.

Mark Twain's passport to glory: his pilot's certificate of April 9, 1859.

*Twain in a rakish pose of about 1890—when his
piloting days were a lonesome memory.*

From LIFE ON THE MISSISSIPPI
by MARK TWAIN

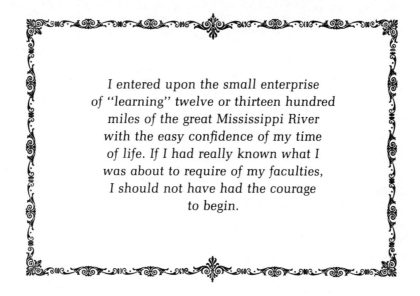

I entered upon the small enterprise of "learning" twelve or thirteen hundred miles of the great Mississippi River with the easy confidence of my time of life. If I had really known what I was about to require of my faculties, I should not have had the courage to begin.

PART ONE

WHEN I was a boy, there was but one permanent ambition among my comrades in our village* on the west bank of the Mississippi River. That was, to be a steamboatman. We had transient ambitions of other sorts, but they were only transient. When a circus came and went, it left us all burning to become clowns; the first negro minstrel show that ever came to our section left us all suffering to try that kind of life; now and then we had a hope that, if we lived and were good, God would permit us to be pirates. These ambitions faded out, each in its turn; but the ambition to be a steamboatman always remained.

Once a day a cheap, gaudy packet arrived upward from St. Louis, and another downward from Keokuk. Before these events, the day was glorious with expectancy; after them, the day was a dead and empty thing. Not only the boys, but the whole village, felt this. After all these years I can picture that old time to myself now, just as it was then: the white town drowsing in the sunshine of a summer's morning;

*Hannibal, Missouri.

the streets empty, or pretty nearly so; one or two clerks sitting in front of the Water Street stores, with their splint-bottomed chairs tilted back against the walls, chins on breasts, hats slouched over their faces, asleep—with shingle-shavings enough around to show what broke them down; a sow and a litter of pigs loafing along the sidewalk, doing a good business in watermelon rinds and seeds; two or three lonely little freight piles scattered about the "levee"; a pile of "skids" on the slope of the stone-paved wharf, and the fragrant town drunkard asleep in the shadow of them; two or three wood flats at the head of the wharf, but nobody to listen to the peaceful lapping of the wavelets against them; the great Mississippi, the majestic, the magnificent Mississippi, rolling its mile-wide tide along, shining in the sun; the dense forest away on the other side; the "point" above the town, and the "point" below, bounding the river-glimpse and turning it into a sort of sea, and withal a very still and brilliant and lonely one. Presently a film of dark smoke appears above one of those remote "points"; instantly a negro drayman, famous for his quick eye and

prodigious voice, lifts up the cry, "S-t-e-a-m-boat a-comin'!" and the scene changes! The town drunkard stirs, the clerks wake up, a furious clatter of drays follows, every house and store pours out a human contribution, and all in a twinkling the dead town is alive and moving. Drays, carts, men, boys, all go hurrying from many quarters to a common center, the wharf. Assembled there, the people fasten their eyes upon the coming boat as upon a wonder they are seeing for the first time. And the boat *is* rather a handsome sight, too. She is long and sharp and trim and pretty; she has two tall, fancy-topped chimneys, with a gilded device of some kind swung between them; a fanciful pilot-house, all glass and "gingerbread," perched on top of the "texas" deck behind them; the paddle-boxes are gorgeous with a picture or with gilded rays above the boat's name; the boiler-deck, the hurricane-deck, and the texas deck are fenced and ornamented with clean white railings; there is a flag gallantly flying from the jack-staff; the furnace doors are open and the fires glaring bravely; the upper decks are black with passengers; the captain stands by the big bell, calm, imposing, the envy of all; great volumes of the blackest smoke are rolling and tumbling out of the chimneys—a husbanded grandeur created with a bit of pitch-pine just before arriving at a town; the crew are grouped on the forecastle; the broad stage is run far out over the port bow, and an envied deck-hand stands picturesquely on the end of it with a coil of rope in his hand; the pent steam is screaming through the gauge-cocks; the captain lifts his hand, a bell rings, the wheels stop; then they turn back, churning the water to foam, and the steamer is at rest. Then such a scramble as there is to get aboard, and to get ashore, and to take in freight and to discharge freight, all at one and the same time; and such a yelling and cursing as the mates facilitate it all with! Ten minutes later the steamer is under way again, with no flag on the jack-staff and no black smoke issuing from the chimneys. After ten more minutes the town is dead again, and the town drunkard asleep by the skids once more.

My father was a justice of the peace, and I supposed he possessed the power of life and death over all men, and could hang anybody that offended him. This was distinction enough for me as a general thing; but the desire to be a steamboatman kept intruding, nevertheless. I first wanted to be a cabin-boy, so that I could come out with a white apron on and shake a table-cloth over the side, where all my old comrades could see me; later I thought I would rather be the deck-hand who stood on the end of the stage-plank with the coil of rope in his hand, because he was particularly conspicuous. But these were only day-dreams—they were too heavenly to be contemplated as real possibilities. By and by one of our boys went away. He was not heard of for a long time. At last he turned up as apprentice engineer or "striker" on a steamboat. This thing shook the bottom out of all my Sunday-school teachings. That boy had been notoriously worldly, and I just the reverse; yet he was exalted to this eminence, and I left in obscurity and misery. There was nothing generous about this fellow in his greatness. He would always manage to have a rusty bolt to scrub while his boat tarried at our town, and he would sit on the inside guard and scrub it, where we all could see him and envy him and loathe him. And whenever his boat was laid up he would come home and swell around the town in his blackest and greasiest clothes, so that nobody could help remembering that he was a steamboatman; and he used all sorts of steamboat technicalities in his talk, as if he were so used to them that he forgot common people could not understand them. He would speak of the "labboard" side of a horse in an easy, natural way that would make one wish he was dead. And he was always talking about "St. Looy" like an old citizen; he would refer casually to occasions when he was "coming down Fourth Street," or when he was "passing by the Planter's House," or when there was a fire and he took a turn on the brakes of "the old Big Missouri"; and then he would go on and lie about how many towns the size of ours were burned down there that day. Two or three of the boys

had long been persons of consideration among us because they had been to St. Louis once and had a vague general knowledge of its wonders, but the day of their glory was over now. They lapsed into a humble silence, and learned to disappear when the ruthless "cub"-engineer approached. This fellow had money, too, and hair-oil. Also an ignorant silver watch and a showy brass watch-chain. He wore a leather belt and used no suspenders. If ever a youth was cordially admired and hated by his comrades, this one was. No girl could withstand his charms. He "cut out" every boy in the village. When his boat blew up at last, it diffused a tranquil contentment among us such as we had not known for months. But when he came home the next week, alive, renowned, and appeared in church all battered up and bandaged, a shining hero, stared at and wondered over by everybody, it seemed to us that the partiality of Providence for an undeserving reptile had reached a point where it was open to criticism.

This creature's career could produce but one result, and it speedily followed. Boy after boy managed to get on the river. The minister's son became an engineer. The doctor's and the postmaster's sons became "mud clerks"; the wholesale liquor dealer's son became a barkeeper on a boat; four sons of the chief merchant, and two sons of the county judge, became pilots. Pilot was the grandest position of all. The pilot, even in those days of trivial wages, had a princely salary—from a hundred and fifty to two hundred and fifty dollars a month, and no board to pay. Two months of his wages would pay a preacher's salary for a year. Now some of us were left disconsolate. We could not get on the river—at least our parents would not let us.

So, by and by, I ran away. I said I would never come home again till I was a pilot and could come in glory. But somehow I could not manage it. I went meekly aboard a few of the boats that lay packed together like sardines at the long St. Louis wharf, and humbly inquired for the pilots, but got only a cold shoulder and short words from mates and clerks. I had to make the best of this sort of treatment for the time being, but I had comforting day-dreams of

a future when I should be a great and honored pilot, with plenty of money, and could kill some of these mates and clerks and pay for them.

MONTHS afterward the hope within me struggled to a reluctant death, and I found myself without an ambition. But I was ashamed to go home. I was in Cincinnati, and I set to work to map out a new career. I had been reading about the recent exploration of the river Amazon by an expedition sent out by our government. It was said that the expedition, owing to difficulties, had not thoroughly explored a part of the country lying about the headwaters, some four thousand miles from the mouth of the river. It was only about fifteen hundred miles from Cincinnati to New Orleans, where I could doubtless get a ship. I had thirty dollars left; I would go and complete the exploration of the Amazon. This was all the thought I gave to the subject. I never was great in matters of detail. I packed my valise, and took passage on an ancient tub called the *Paul Jones*, for New Orleans. For the sum of sixteen dollars I had the scarred and tarnished splendors of "her" main saloon principally to myself, for she was not a creature to attract the eye of wiser travelers.

When we presently got under way and went poking down the broad Ohio, I became a new being, and the subject of my own admiration. I was a traveler! A word never had tasted so good in my mouth before. I had an exultant sense of being bound for mysterious lands and distant climes which I never have felt in so uplifting a degree since. I was in such a glorified condition that all ignoble feelings departed out of me, and I was able to look down and pity the untraveled with a compassion that had hardly a trace of contempt in it. Still, when we stopped at villages and wood-yards, I could not help lolling carelessly upon the railings of the boiler-deck to enjoy the envy of the country boys on the bank. If they did not seem to discover me, I presently sneezed to attract their attention, or moved to a position where they could not help seeing me. And as soon as I knew they saw me I gaped and stretched, and gave other signs of being mightily bored with traveling.

I kept my hat off all the time, and stayed where the wind and the sun could strike me, because I wanted to get the bronzed and weather-beaten look of an old traveler. Before the second day was half gone I experienced a joy which filled me with the purest gratitude; for I saw that the skin had begun to blister and peel off my face and neck. I wished that the boys and girls at home could see me now.

We reached Louisville in time—at least the neighborhood of it. We stuck hard and fast on the rocks in the middle of the river, and lay there four days. I was now beginning to feel a strong sense of being a part of the boat's family, a sort of infant son to the captain and younger brother to the officers. There is no estimating the pride I took in this grandeur, or the affection that began to swell and grow in me for those people. I could not know how the lordly steamboatman scorns that sort of presumption in a mere landsman. I particularly longed to acquire the least trifle of notice from the big stormy mate, and I was on the alert for an opportunity to do him a service to that end. It came at last. The riotous pow-wow of setting a spar was going on down on the forecastle, and I went down there and stood around in the way —or mostly skipping out of it—till the mate suddenly roared a general order for somebody to bring him a capstan bar. I sprang to his side and said: "Tell me where it is—I'll fetch it!"

If a rag-picker had offered to do a diplomatic service for the Emperor of Russia, the monarch could not have been more astounded than the mate was. He even stopped swearing. He stood and stared down at me. It took him ten seconds to scrape his disjointed remains together again. Then he said impressively: "Well, if this don't beat h—l!" and turned to his work with the air of a man who had been confronted with a problem too abstruse for solution.

I crept away, and courted solitude for the rest of the day. I did not go to dinner; I stayed away from supper until everybody else had fin-

ished. I did not feel so much like a member of the boat's family now as before. However, my spirits returned, in instalments, as we pursued our way down the river. I was sorry I hated the mate so, because it was not in (young) human nature not to admire him. He was huge and muscular, his face bearded and whiskered all over; he had a red woman and a blue woman tattooed on his right arm—one on each side of a blue anchor with a red rope to it; and in the matter of profanity he was sublime. When he was getting out cargo at a landing, I was always where I could see and hear. He felt all the majesty of his great position, and made the world feel it, too. When he gave even the simplest order, he discharged it like a blast of lightning, and sent a long, reverberating peal of profanity thundering after it. I could not help contrasting the way in which the average landsman would give an order with the mate's way of doing it. If the landsman should wish the gangplank moved a foot farther forward, he would probably say: "James, or William, one of you push that plank forward, please"; but put the mate in his place, and he would roar out: "Here, now, start that gang-plank for'ard! Lively, now! *What*'re you about! Snatch it! *snatch* it! There! there! Aft again! aft again! Don't you hear me? Dash it to dash! are you going to *sleep* over it! '*Vast* heaving. 'Vast heaving, I tell you! Going to heave it clear astern? WHERE're you going with that barrel! *for'ard* with it 'fore I make you swallow it, you dash-dash-dash-*dashed* split between a tired mud-turtle and a crippled hearse-horse!"

I wished I could talk like that. . . .

WHAT with lying on the rocks four days at Louisville, and some other delays, the poor old *Paul Jones* fooled away about two weeks in making the voyage from Cincinnati to New Orleans. This gave me a chance to get acquainted with one of the pilots, and he taught me how to steer the boat, and thus made the fascination of river life more potent than ever for me.

It also gave me a chance to get acquainted

with a youth who had taken deck passage—more's the pity; for he easily borrowed six dollars of me on a promise to return to the boat and pay it back to me the day after we should arrive. But he probably died or forgot, for he never came. It was doubtless the former, since he had said his parents were wealthy, and he only traveled deck passage because it was cooler.*

I soon discovered two things. One was that a vessel would not be likely to sail for the mouth of the Amazon under ten or twelve years; and the other was that the nine or ten dollars still left in my pocket would not suffice for so impossible an exploration as I had planned, even if I could afford to wait for a ship. Therefore it followed that I must contrive a new career. The *Paul Jones* was now bound for St. Louis. I planned a siege against my pilot, and at the end of three hard days he surrendered. He agreed to teach me the Mississippi River from New Orleans to St. Louis for five hundred dollars, payable out of the first wages I should receive after graduating. I entered upon the small enterprise of "learning" twelve or thirteen hundred miles of the great Mississippi River with the easy confidence of my time of life. If I

*"Deck" passage—*i. e.,* steerage passage.

had really known what I was about to require of my faculties, I should not have had the courage to begin. I supposed that all a pilot had to do was to keep his boat in the river, and I did not consider that that could be much of a trick, since it was so wide.

The boat backed out from New Orleans at four in the afternoon, and it was "our watch" until eight. Mr. Bixby, my chief, "straightened her up," plowed her along past the sterns of the other boats that lay at the Levee, and then said, "Here, take her; shave those steamships as close as you'd peel an apple." I took the wheel, and my heartbeat fluttered up into the hundreds; for it seemed to me that we were about to scrape the side off every ship in the line, we were so close. I held my breath and began to claw the boat away from the danger; and I had my own opinion of the pilot who had known no better than to get us into such peril, but I was too wise to express it. In half a minute I had a wide margin of safety intervening between the *Paul Jones* and the ships; and within ten seconds more I was set aside in disgrace, and Mr. Bixby was going into danger again and flaying me alive with abuse of my cowardice. I was stung, but I was obliged to admire the easy confidence with which my chief loafed

A MISSISSIPPI SIDE-WHEEL STEAMBOAT

from side to side of his wheel, and trimmed the ships so closely that disaster seemed ceaselessly imminent. When he had cooled a little he told me that the easy water was close ashore and the current outside, and therefore we must hug the bank, up-stream, to get the benefit of the former, and stay well out, down-stream, to take advantage of the latter. In my own mind I resolved to be a down-stream pilot and leave the up-streaming to people dead to prudence.

Now and then Mr. Bixby called my attention to certain things. Said he, "This is Six-Mile Point." I assented. It was pleasant enough information, but I could not see the bearing of it. I was not conscious that it was a matter of any interest to me. Another time he said, "This is Nine-Mile Point." Later he said, "This is Twelve-Mile Point." They were all about level with the water's edge; they all looked about alike to me; they were monotonously unpicturesque. I hoped Mr. Bixby would change the subject. But no; he would crowd up around a point, hugging the shore with affection, and then say: "The slack water ends here, abreast this bunch of China trees; now we cross over." So he crossed over. He gave me the wheel once or twice, but I had no luck. I either came near chipping off the edge of a sugar-plantation, or I yawed too far from shore, and so dropped back into disgrace again and got abused.

The watch was ended at last, and we took supper and went to bed. At midnight the glare of a lantern shone in my eyes, and the night watchman said:

"Come, turn out!"

And then he left. I could not understand this extraordinary procedure; so I presently gave up trying to, and dozed off to sleep. Pretty soon the watchman was back again, and this time he was gruff. I was annoyed. I said:

"What do you want to come bothering around here in the middle of the night for? Now, as like as not, I'll not get to sleep again to-night."

The watchman said:

"Well, if this ain't good, I'm blessed."

The "off-watch" was just turning in, and I heard some brutal laughter from them, and such remarks as "Hello, watchman! ain't the new cub turned out yet? He's delicate, likely. Give him some sugar in a rag, and send for the chambermaid to sing 'Rock-a-by Baby,' to him."

About this time Mr. Bixby appeared on the scene. Something like a minute later I was climbing the pilot-house steps with some of my clothes on and the rest in my arms. Mr. Bixby was close behind, commenting. Here was something fresh — this thing of getting up in the middle of the night to go to work. It was a detail in piloting that had never occurred to me at all. I knew that boats ran all night, but somehow I had never happened to reflect that somebody had to get up out of a warm bed to run them. I began to fear that piloting was not quite so romantic as I had imagined it was; there was something very real and worklike about this new phase of it.

It was a rather dingy night, although a fair number of stars were out. The big mate was at the wheel, and he had the old tub pointed at a star and was holding her straight up the middle of the river. The shores on either hand were not much more than half a mile apart, but they seemed wonderfully far away and ever so vague and indistinct. The mate said:

"We've got to land at Jones's plantation, sir."

The vengeful spirit in me exulted. I said to myself, "I wish you joy of your job, Mr. Bixby; you'll have a good time finding Mr. Jones's plantation such a night as this; and I hope you never *will* find it as long as you live."

Mr. Bixby said to the mate:

"Upper end of the plantation, or the lower?"

"Upper."

"I can't do it. The stumps there are out of water at this stage. It's no great distance to the lower, and you'll have to get along with that."

"All right, sir. If Jones don't like it, he'll have to lump it, I reckon."

And then the mate left. My exultation began to cool and my wonder to come up. Here was a man who not only proposed to find this plantation on such a night, but to find either end of it you preferred. I dreadfully wanted to ask a question, but I was carrying about as many short answers as my cargo-room would admit of, so I held my peace. All I desired to ask Mr.

Bixby was the simple question whether he was ass enough to really imagine he was going to find that plantation on a night when all plantations were exactly alike and all of the same color. But I held in. I used to have fine inspirations of prudence in those days.

Mr. Bixby made for the shore and soon was scraping it, just the same as if it had been daylight. And not only that, but singing:

"Father in heaven, the day is declining," etc.

It seemed to me that I had put my life in the keeping of a peculiarly reckless outcast. Presently he turned on me and said:

"What's the name of the first point above New Orleans?"

I was gratified to be able to answer promptly, and I did. I said I didn't know.

"Don't *know?*"

This manner jolted me. I was down at the foot again, in a moment. But I had to say just what I had said before.

"Well, you're a smart one!" said Mr. Bixby. "What's the name of the *next* point?"

Once more I didn't know.

"Well, this beats anything. Tell me the name of *any* point or place I told you."

I studied awhile and decided that I couldn't.

"Look here! What do you start out from, above Twelve-Mile Point, to cross over?"

"I—I—don't know."

"You—you—don't know?" mimicking my drawling manner of speech. "What *do* you know?"

"I—I—nothing, for certain."

"By the great Caesar's ghost, I believe you! You're the stupidest dunderhead I ever saw or ever heard of, so help me Moses! The idea of *you* being a pilot—*you!* Why, you don't know enough to pilot a cow down a lane."

Oh, but his wrath was up! He was a nervous man, and he shuffled from one side of his wheel to the other as if the floor was hot. He would boil awhile to himself, and then overflow and scald me again.

"Look here! What do you suppose I told you the names of those points for?"

I tremblingly considered a moment, and then

the devil of temptation provoked me to say: "Well to—to—be entertaining, I thought."

This was a red rag to the bull. He raged and stormed so (he was crossing the river at the time) that I judged it made him blind, because he ran over the steering-oar of a trading-scow. Of course the traders sent up a volley of red-hot profanity. Never was a man so grateful as Mr. Bixby was; because he was brimful, and here were subjects who could *talk back.* He threw open a window, thrust his head out, and such an irruption followed as I never had heard before. The fainter and farther away the scowmen's curses drifted, the higher Mr. Bixby lifted his voice and the weightier his adjectives grew. When he closed the window he was empty. You could have drawn a seine through his system and not caught curses enough to disturb your mother with. Presently he said to me in the gentlest way:

"My boy, you must get a little memorandum-book; and every time I tell you a thing, put it down right away. There's only one way to be a pilot, and that is to get this entire river by heart. You have to know it just like A B C."

That was a dismal revelation to me; for my memory was never loaded with anything but blank cartridges. However, I did not feel discouraged long. I judged that it was best to make some allowances, for doubtless Mr. Bixby was "stretching." Presently he pulled a rope and struck a few strokes on the big bell. The stars were all gone now, and the night was as black as ink. I could hear the wheels churn along the bank, but I was not entirely certain that I could see the shore. The voice of the invisible watchman called up from the hurricane-deck:

"What's this, sir?"

"Jones's plantation."

I said to myself, "I wish I might venture to offer a small bet that it isn't." But I did not chirp. I only waited to see. Mr. Bixby handled the engine-bells, and in due time the boat's nose came to the land, a torch glowed from the forecastle, a man skipped ashore, a darky's voice on the bank said: "Gimme de k'yarpet-bag, Mass' Jones," and the next moment we were standing up the river again, all serene. I

reflected deeply awhile, and then said—but not aloud—"Well, the finding of that plantation was the luckiest accident that ever happened; but it couldn't happen again in a hundred years." And I fully believed it *was* an accident, too.

By the time we had gone seven or eight hundred miles up the river, I had learned to be a tolerably plucky up-stream steersman, in daylight; and before we reached St. Louis I had made a trifle of progress in night work, but only a trifle. I had a note-book that fairly bristled with the names of towns, "points," bars, islands, bends, reaches, etc.; but the information was to be found only in the note-book—none of it was in my head. It made my heart ache to think I had only got half of the river set down; for as our watch was four hours off and four hours on, day and night, there was a long four-hour gap in my book for every time I had slept since the voyage began.

IN THE PILOT-HOUSE

My chief was presently hired to go on a big New Orleans boat, and I packed my satchel and went with him. She was a grand affair. When I stood in her pilot-house I was so far above the water that I seemed perched on a mountain; and her decks stretched so far away, fore and aft, below me, that I wondered how I could ever have considered the little *Paul Jones* a large craft. There were other differences, too. The *Paul Jones's* pilot-house was a cheap, dingy, battered rattletrap, cramped for room; but here was a sumptuous glass temple; room enough to have a dance in; showy red and gold window-curtains; an imposing sofa; leather cushions and a back to the high bench where visiting pilots sit, to spin yarns and "look at the river"; bright, fanciful "cuspidores," instead of a broad wooden box filled with sawdust; nice new oilcloth on the floor; a hospitable big stove for winter; a wheel as high as my head, costly with inlaid work; a wire tiller-rope; bright brass knobs for the bells; and a tidy, white-aproned, black "texas-tender," to bring up tarts and ices and coffee during midwatch, day and night. Now this was "something like"; and so I began to take heart once more to believe that piloting was a romantic sort of occupation after all. The moment we were under way I began to prowl about the great steamer and fill myself with joy. She was as clean and as dainty as a drawing-room; when I looked down her long, gilded saloon, it was like gazing through a splendid tunnel; she had an oil-picture, by some gifted sign-painter, on every stateroom door; she glittered with no end of prism-fringed chandeliers; the clerk's office was elegant, the bar was marvelous, and the barkeeper had been barbered and upholstered at incredible cost. The boiler-deck (*i.e.*, the second story of the boat, so to speak) was as spacious as a church, it seemed to me; so with the forecastle; and there was no pitiful handful of deck-hands, firemen, and roustabouts down there, but a whole battalion of men. The fires were fiercely glaring from a long row of furnaces, and over them were eight huge boilers! This was unutterable pomp. The mighty engines—but enough of this. I had never felt so fine before. And when I found that the regiment of natty servants respectfully "sir'd" me, my satisfaction was complete. . . .

AT the end of what seemed a tedious while, I had managed to pack my head full of islands, towns, bars, "points," and bends; and a curiously inanimate mass of lumber it was, too. However, inasmuch as I could shut my eyes and reel off a good long string of these

names without leaving out more than ten miles of river in every fifty, I began to feel that I could take a boat down to New Orleans if I could make her skip those little gaps. But of course my complacency could hardly get start enough to lift my nose a trifle into the air, before Mr. Bixby would think of something to fetch it down again. One day he turned on me suddenly with this settler:

"What is the shape of Walnut Bend?"

He might as well have asked me my grandmother's opinion of protoplasm. I reflected respectfully, and then said I didn't know it had any particular shape. My gun-powdery chief went off with a bang, of course, and then went on loading and firing until he was out of adjectives.

I had learned long ago that he only carried just so many rounds of ammunition, and was sure to subside into a very placable and even remorseful old smoothbore as soon as they were all gone. That word "old" is merely affectionate; he was not more than thirty-four. I waited. By and by he said:

"My boy, you've got to know the *shape* of the river perfectly. It is all there is left to steer by on a very dark night. Everything else is blotted out and gone. But mind you, it hasn't the same shape in the night that it has in the daytime."

"How on earth am I ever going to learn it, then?"

"How do you follow a hall at home in the dark? Because you know the shape of it. You can't see it."

"Do you mean to say that I've got to know all the million trifling variations of shape in the banks of this interminable river as well as I know the shape of the front hall at home?"

"On my honor, you've got to know them *better* than any man ever did know the shapes of the halls in his own house.

"I wish I was dead!"

"Now I don't want to discourage you, but—"

"Well, pile it on me; I might as well have it now as another time."

"You see, this has got to be learned; there isn't any getting around it. A clear starlight night throws such heavy shadows that, if you didn't know the shape of a shore perfectly, you would claw away from every bunch of timber, because you would take the black shadow of it for a solid cape; and you see you would be getting scared to death every fifteen minutes by the watch. You would be fifty yards from shore all the time when you ought to be within fifty feet of it. You can't see a snag in one of those shadows, but you know exactly where it is, and the shape of the river tells you when you are coming to it. Then there's your pitch-dark night; the river is a very different shape on a pitch-dark night from what it is on a star-light night. All shores seem to be straight lines, then, and mighty dim ones, too; and you'd run them

A DANGEROUS SNAG

for straight lines, only you know better. You boldly drive your boat right into what seems to be a solid, straight wall (you knowing very well that in reality there is a curve there), and that wall falls back and makes way for you. Then there's your gray mist. You take a night when there's one of these grisly, drizzly, gray mists, and then there isn't *any* particular shape to a shore. A gray mist would tangle the head of the oldest man that ever lived. Well, then, different kinds of *moonlight* change the shape of the river in different ways. You see—"

"Oh, don't say any more, please! Have I got to learn the shape of the river according to all these five hundred thousand different ways? If I tried to carry all that cargo in my head it would make me stoop-shouldered."

"*No!* you only learn *the* shape of the river; and you learn it with such absolute certainty that you can always steer by the shape that's *in your head*, and never mind the one that's before your eyes."

"Very well, I'll try it; but, after I have learned it, can I depend on it? Will it keep the same form and not go fooling around?

Before Mr. Bixby could answer, Mr. W. came in to take the watch, and he said:

"Bixby, you'll have to look out for President's Island, and all that country clear away up above the Old Hen and Chickens. The banks are caving and the shape of the shores changing like everything. Why, you wouldn't know the point above 40. You can go up inside the old sycamore snag, now."*

So that question was answered. Here were leagues of shore changing shape. My spirits were down in the mud again. Two things seemed pretty apparent to me. One was, that in order to be a pilot a man had got to learn more than any one man ought to be allowed to know; and the other was, that he must learn it all over again in a different way every twenty-four hours.

That night we had the watch until twelve.

Now it was an ancient river custom for the two pilots to chat a bit when the watch changed. While the relieving pilot put on his gloves and lit his cigar, his partner, the retiring pilot, would say something like this:

"I judge the upper bar is making down a little at Hale's Point; had quarter twain with the lower lead and mark twain* with the other."

"Yes, I thought it was making down a little, last trip. Meet any boats?"

"Met one abreast the head of 21, but she was away over hugging the bar, and I couldn't make her out entirely. I took her for the *Sunny South*— hadn't any skylights forward of the chimneys."

And so on. And as the relieving pilot took the wheel his partner** would mention that we were in such-and-such a bend, and say we were abreast of such-and-such a man's woodyard or plantation. This was courtesy; I supposed it was *necessity*. But Mr. W. came on watch full twelve minutes late on this particular night—a tremendous breach of etiquette; in fact, it is the unpardonable sin among pilots. So Mr. Bixby gave him no greeting whatever, but simply surrendered the wheel and marched out of the pilot-house without a word. I was appalled; it was a villainous night for blackness, we were in a particularly wide and blind part of the river, where there was no shape or substance to anything, and it seemed incredible that Mr. Bixby should have left that poor fellow to kill the boat, trying to find out where he was. But I resolved that I would stand by him anyway. He should find that he was not wholly friendless. So I stood around, and waited to be asked where we were. But Mr. W. plunged on serenely through the solid firmament of black cats that stood for an atmosphere, and never opened his mouth. "Here is a proud devil!" thought I; "here is a limb of Satan that would rather send us all to destruction than put himself under obligations to me, because I am not yet one of the salt of the earth and privileged to

*It may not be necessary, but still it can do no harm to explain that "inside" means between the snag and the shore.—M. T.

*Two fathoms. Quarter twain is 2¼ fathoms, 13½ feet. Mark three is three fathoms.

**"Partner" is technical for "the other pilot."

snub captains and lord it over everything dead and alive in a steamboat." I presently climbed up on the bench; I did not think it was safe to go to sleep while this lunatic was on watch.

However, I must have gone to sleep in the course of time, because the next thing I was aware of was the fact that day was breaking, Mr. W. gone, and Mr. Bixby at the wheel again. So it was four o'clock and all well—but me; I felt like a skinful of dry bones, and all of them trying to ache at once.

Mr. Bixby asked me what I had stayed up there for. I confessed that it was to do Mr. W. a benevolence—tell him where he was. It took five minutes for the entire preposterousness of the thing to filter into Mr. Bixby's system, and then I judge it filled him nearly up to the chin; because he paid me a compliment—and not much of a one either. He said:

"Well, taking you by and large, you do seem to be more different kinds of an ass than any creature I ever saw before. What did you suppose he wanted to know for?"

I said I thought it might be a convenience to him.

"Convenience! D—nation! Didn't I tell you that a man's got to know the river in the night the same as he'd know his own front hall?"

"Well, I can follow the front hall in the dark if I know it *is* the front hall; but suppose you set me down in the middle of it in the dark and not tell me which hall it is; how am *I* to know?"

"Well, you've *got* to, on the river!"

"All right. Then I'm glad I never said anything to Mr. W."

"I should say so! Why, he'd have slammed you through the window and utterly ruined a hundred dollars' worth of window-sash and stuff."

I was glad this damage had been saved, for it would have made me unpopular with the owners. They always hated anybody who had the name of being careless and injuring things.

I went to work now to learn the shape of the river; and of all the eluding and ungraspable objects that ever I tried to get mind or hands on, that was the chief. I would fasten my eyes upon a sharp, wooded point that projected far into the river some miles ahead of me, and go to laboriously photographing its shape upon my brain; and just as I was beginning to succeed to my satisfaction, we would draw up toward it and the exasperating thing would begin to melt away and fold back into the bank! If there had been a conspicuous dead tree standing upon the very point of the cape, I would find that tree inconspicuously merged into the general forest, and occupying the middle of a straight shore, when I got abreast of it! No prominent hill would stick to its shape long enough for me to make up my mind what its form really was, but it was as dissolving and changeful as if it had been a mountain of butter in the hottest corner of the tropics. Nothing ever had the same shape when I was coming down-stream that it had borne when I went up. I mentioned these little difficulties to Mr. Bixby. He said:

"That's the very main virtue of the thing. If the shapes didn't change every three seconds they wouldn't be of any use. Take this place where we are now, for instance. As long as that hill over yonder is only one hill, I can boom right along the way I'm going; but the moment it splits at the top and forms a V, I know I've got to scratch to starboard in a hurry, or I'll bang this boat's brains out against a rock; and then the moment one of the prongs of the V swings behind the other, I've got to waltz to larboard again, or I'll have a misunderstanding with a snag that would snatch the keelson out of this steamboat as neatly as if it were a sliver in your hand. If that hill didn't change its shape on bad nights there would be an awful steamboat graveyard around here inside of a year."

It was plain that I had got to learn the shape of the river in all the different ways that could be thought of—upside down, wrong end first, inside out, fore-and-aft, and "thort-ships"— and then know what to do on gray nights when it hadn't any shape at all. So I set about it. In the course of time I began to get the best of this knotty lesson, and my self-complacency moved to the front once more. Mr. Bixby was all fixed, and ready to start it to the rear again. He opened on me after this fashion:

"How much water did we have in the middle

crossing at Hole-in-the-Wall, trip before last?"

I considered this an outrage. I said:

"Every trip, down and up, the leadsmen are singing through that tangled place for three-quarters of an hour on a stretch. How do you reckon I can remember such a mess as that?"

"My boy, you've got to remember it. You've got to remember the exact spot and the exact marks the boat lay in when we had the shoalest water, in every one of the five hundred shoal places between St. Louis and New Orleans; and you mustn't get the shoal soundings and marks of one trip mixed up with the shoal soundings and marks of another, either, for they're not often twice alike. You must keep them separate."

When I came to myself again, I said:

"When I get so that I can do that, I'll be able to raise the dead, and then I won't have to pilot a steamboat to make a living. I want to retire from this business. I want a slush-bucket and a brush; I'm only fit for a roustabout. I haven't got brains enough to be a pilot; and if I had I wouldn't have strength enough to carry them around, unless I went on crutches."

"Now drop that! When I say I'll learn* a man the river, I mean it. And you can depend on it, I'll learn him or kill him."

THERE was no use in arguing with a person like this. I promptly put such a strain on my memory that by and by even the shoal water and the countless crossing-marks began to stay with me. But the result was just the same. I never could more than get one knotty thing learned before another presented itself. Now I had often seen pilots gazing at the water and pretending to read it as if it were a book; but it was a book that told me nothing. A time came at last, however, when Mr. Bixby seemed to think me far enough advanced to bear a lesson on water-reading. So he began:

"Do you see that long, slanting line on the face of the water? Now, that's a reef. Moreover,

*"Teach" is not in the river vocabulary.

it's a bluff reef. There is a solid sand-bar under it that is nearly as straight up and down as the side of a house. There is plenty of water close up to it, but mighty little on top of it. If you were to hit it you would knock the boat's brains out. Do you see where the line fringes out at the upper end and begins to fade away?"

"Yes, sir."

"Well, that is a low place; that is the head of the reef. You can climb over there, and not hurt anything. Cross over, now, and follow along close under the reef—easy water there—not much current."

I followed the reef along till I approached the fringed end. Then Mr. Bixby said:

"Now get ready. Wait till I give the word. She won't want to mount the reef; a boat hates shoal water. Stand by—wait—*wait*—keep her well in hand. *Now* cramp her down! Snatch her! snatch her!"

He seized the other side of the wheel and helped to spin it around until it was hard down, and then we held it so. The boat resisted, and refused to answer for a while, and next she came surging to starboard, mounted the reef, and sent a long, angry ridge of water foaming away from her bows.

"Now watch her; watch her like a cat, or she'll get away from you. When she fights strong and the tiller slips a little, in a jerky, greasy sort of way, let up on her a trifle; it is the way she tells you at night that the water is too shoal; but keep edging her up, little by little, toward the point. You are well up on the bar now; there is a bar under every point, because the water that comes down around it forms an eddy and allows the sediment to sink. Do you see those fine lines on the face of the water that branch out like the ribs of a fan? Well, those are little reefs; you want to just miss the ends of them, but run them pretty close. Now look out—look out! Don't you crowd that slick, greasy-looking place; there ain't nine feet there; she won't stand it. She begins to smell it; look sharp, I tell you! Oh, blazes, there you go! Stop the starboard wheel! Quick! Ship up to back! Set her back!"

The engine bells jingled and the engines answered promptly, shooting white columns of steam far aloft out of the 'scape-pipes, but it was too late. The boat had "smelt" the bar in good earnest; the foamy ridges that radiated from her bows suddenly disappeared, a great dead swell came rolling forward, and swept ahead of her, she careened far over to larboard, and went tearing away toward the shore as if she were about scared to death. We were a good mile from where we ought to have been when we finally got the upper hand of her again.

During the afternoon watch the next day, Mr. Bixby asked me if I knew how to run the next few miles. I said:

"Go inside the first snag above the point, outside the next one, start out from the lower end of Higgins's woodyard, make a square crossing, and—"

"That's all right. I'll be back before you close up on the next point."

But he wasn't. He was still below when I rounded it and entered upon a piece of the river which I had some misgivings about. I did not know that he was hiding behind a chimney to see how I would perform. I went gaily along, getting prouder and prouder, for he had never left the boat in my sole charge such a length of time before. I even got to "setting" her and letting the wheel go entirely, while I vaingloriously turned my back and inspected the stern marks and hummed a tune, a sort of easy indifference which I had prodigiously admired in Bixby and other great pilots. Once I inspected rather long, and when I faced to the front again my heart flew into my mouth so suddenly that if I hadn't clapped my teeth together I should have lost it. One of those frightful bluff reefs was stretching its deadly length right across our bows! My head was gone in a moment; I did not know which end I stood on; I gasped and could not get my breath; I spun the wheel down with such rapidity that it wove itself together like a spider's web; the boat answered and turned square away from the reef, but the reef followed her! I fled, but still it followed, still it kept—right across my bows! I never looked to see where I was going, I only fled. The awful crash was imminent. Why didn't that villain

come? If I committed the crime of ringing a bell I might get thrown overboard. But better that than kill the boat. So in blind desperation, I started such a rattling "shivaree" down below as never had astounded an engineer in this world before, I fancy. Amidst the frenzy of the bells the engines began to back and fill in a curious way, and my reason forsook its throne —we were about to crash into the woods on the other side of the river. Just then Mr. Bixby stepped calmly into view on the hurricane-deck. My soul went out to him in gratitude. My distress vanished; I would have felt safe on the brink of Niagara with Mr. Bixby on the hurricane-deck. He blandly and sweetly took his toothpick out of his mouth between his fingers, as if it were a cigar—we were just in the act of climbing an overhanging big tree, and the passengers were scudding astern like rats—and lifted up these commands to me ever so gently:

"Stop the starboard! Stop the larboard! Set her back on both!"

The boat hesitated, halted, pressed her nose among the boughs a critical instant, then reluctantly began to back away.

"Stop the larboard! Come ahead on it! Stop the starboard! Come ahead on it! Point her for the bar!"

I sailed away as serenely as a summer's morning. Mr. Bixby came in and said, with mock simplicity:

"When you have a hail, my boy, you ought to tap the big bell three times before you land, so that the engineers can get ready."

I blushed under the sarcasm, and said I hadn't had any hail.

"Ah! Then it was for wood, I suppose. The officer of the watch will tell you when he wants to wood up."

I went on consuming, and said I wasn't after wood.

"Indeed? Why, what could you want over here in the bend, then? Did you ever know of a boat following a bend up-stream at this stage of the river?"

"No, sir—and I wasn't trying to follow it. I was getting away from a bluff reef."

"No, it wasn't a bluff reef; there isn't one within three miles of where you were."

"But I saw it. It was as bluff as that one yonder."

"Just about. Run over it!"

"Do you give it as an order?"

"Yes. Run over it!"

"If I don't, I wish I may die."

"All right; I am taking the responsibility."

I was just as anxious to kill the boat, now, as I had been to save it before. I impressed my orders upon my memory, to be used at the inquest, and made a straight break for the reef. As it disappeared under our bows I held my breath; but we slid over it like oil.

"Now, don't you see the difference? It wasn't anything but a *wind* reef. The wind does that."

"So I see. But it is exactly like a bluff reef. How am I ever going to tell them apart?"

"I can't tell you. It is an instinct. By and by you will just naturally *know* one from the other, but you never will be able to explain why or how you know them apart."

It turned out to be true. The face of the water, in time, became a wonderful book — a book that was a dead language to the uneducated passenger, but which told its mind to me without reserve, delivering its most cherished secrets as clearly as if it uttered them with a voice. And it was not a book to be read once and thrown aside, for it had a new story to tell every day. Throughout the long twelve hundred miles there was never a page that was void of interest, never one that you could leave unread without loss, never one that you would want to skip, thinking you could find higher enjoyment in some other thing. There never was so wonderful a book written by man; never one whose interest was so absorbing, so unflagging, so sparklingly renewed with every reperusal. The passenger who could not read it was charmed with a peculiar sort of faint dimple on its surface (on the rare occasions when he did not overlook it altogether); but to the pilot that was an *italicized* passage; indeed, it was more than that, it was a legend of the largest capitals, with a string of shouting exclamation-points at the end of it, for it meant that a wreck or a rock was buried there that could tear the life out of the strongest vessel that ever floated. It is the faintest and simplest expression the water ever makes, and the most hideous to a pilot's eye. In truth, the passenger who could not read this book saw nothing but all manner of pretty pictures in it, painted by the sun and shaded by the clouds, whereas to the trained eye these were not pictures at all, but the grimmest and most dead-earnest of reading-matter.

Now when I had mastered the language of this water, and had come to know every trifling feature that bordered the great river as familiarly as I knew the letters of the alphabet, I had made a valuable acquisition. But I had lost something, too. I had lost something which could never be restored to me while I lived. All the grace, the beauty, the poetry, had gone out of the majestic river! I still kept in mind a certain wonderful sunset which I witnessed when steamboating was new to me. A broad expanse of the river was turned to blood; in the middle distance the red hue brightened into gold, through which a solitary log came floating, black and conspicuous; in one place a long, slanting mark lay sparkling upon the water; in another the surface was broken by boiling, tumbling rings, that were as many-tinted as an opal; where the ruddy flush was faintest, was a smooth spot that was covered with graceful circles and radiating lines, ever so delicately traced; the shore on our left was densely wooded, and the somber shadow that fell from this forest was broken in one place by a long, ruffled trail that shone like silver; and high above the forest wall a clean-stemmed dead tree waved a single leafy bough that glowed like a flame in the unobstructed splendor that was flowing from the sun. There were graceful curves, reflected images, woody heights, soft distances; and over the whole scene, far and near, the dissolving lights drifted steadily, enriching it every passing moment with new marvels of coloring.

I stood like one bewitched. I drank it in, in a speechless rapture. The world was new to me, and I had never seen anything like this at home. But as I have said, a day came when I began to

cease from noting the glories and the charms which the moon and the sun and the twilight wrought upon the river's face; another day came when I ceased altogether to note them. Then, if that sunset scene had been repeated, I should have looked upon it without rapture, and should have commented upon it, inwardly, after this fashion: "This sun means that we are going to have wind to-morrow; that floating log means that the river is rising, small thanks to it; that slanting mark on the water refers to a bluff reef which is going to kill somebody's steamboat one of these nights, if it keeps on stretching out like that; those tumbling 'boils' show a dissolving bar and a changing channel there; the lines and circles in the slick water over yonder are a warning that that troublesome place is shoaling up dangerously; that silver streak in the shadow of the forest is the 'break' from a new snag, and he has located himself in the very best place he could have found to fish for steamboats; that tall dead tree, with a single living branch, is not going to last long, and then how is a body ever going to get through this blind place at night without the friendly old landmark?"

No, the romance and beauty were all gone from the river. All the value any feature of it had for me now was the amount of usefulness it could furnish toward compassing the safe piloting of a steamboat. Since those days, I have pitied doctors from my heart. What does the lovely flush in a beauty's cheek mean to a doctor but a "break" that ripples above some deadly disease? Are not all her visible charms sown thick with what are to him the signs and symbols of hidden decay? Does he ever see her beauty at all, or doesn't he simply view her professionally, and comment upon her unwholesome condition all to himself? And doesn't he sometimes wonder whether he has gained most or lost most by learning his trade?

ON THE MISSISSIPPI DELTA

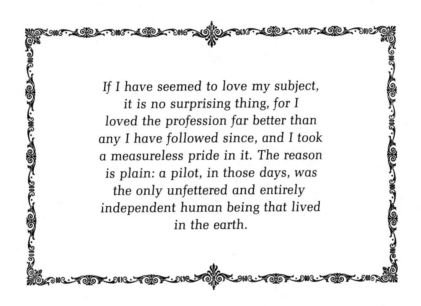

If I have seemed to love my subject,
it is no surprising thing, for I
loved the profession far better than
any I have followed since, and I took
a measureless pride in it. The reason
is plain: a pilot, in those days, was
the only unfettered and entirely
independent human being that lived
in the earth.

PART TWO

WHOSOEVER has done me the courtesy to read my chapters which have preceded this may possibly wonder that I deal so minutely with piloting as a science. It was the prime purpose of those chapters; and I am not quite done yet. I wish to show, in the most patient and painstaking way, what a wonderful science it is. Ship-channels are buoyed and lighted, and therefore it is a comparatively easy undertaking to learn to run them; clear-water rivers with gravel bottoms, change their channels very gradually, and therefore one needs to learn them but once; but piloting becomes another matter when you apply it to vast streams like the Mississippi and the Missouri, whose alluvial banks cave and change constantly, whose snags are always hunting up new quarters, whose sand-bars are never at rest, whose channels are forever dodging and shirking, and whose obstructions must be confronted in all nights and all weathers without the aid of a single lighthouse or a single buoy; for there is neither light nor buoy to be found anywhere in all this three or four thousand miles of villainous river.* I feel justified in enlarging upon this great science for the reason that I feel sure no one has ever yet written a paragraph about it who had piloted a steamboat himself, and so had a practical knowledge of the subject. If the theme was hackneyed, I should be obliged to deal gently with the reader; but since it is wholly new, I have felt at liberty to take up a considerable degree of room with it.

When I had learned the name and position of every visible feature of the river; when I had so mastered its shape that I could shut my eyes and trace it from St. Louis to New Orleans; when I had learned to read the face of the water as one would cull the news from the morning paper; and finally, when I had trained my dull memory to treasure up an endless array of soundings and crossing-marks, and keep fast hold of them, I judged that my education was complete; so I got to tilting my cap to the side of my head, and wearing a toothpick in my mouth at the wheel. Mr. Bixby had his eye on these airs. One day he said:

"What is the height of that bank yonder, at Burgess's?"

"How can I tell, sir? It is three-quarters of a mile away."

"Very poor eye — very poor. Take the glass."

*True at the time referred to; not true now (1882).

I took the glass and presently said:

"I can't tell. I suppose that that bank is about a foot and a half high."

"Foot and a half! That's a six-foot bank. How high was the bank along here last trip?"

"I don't know; I never noticed."

"You didn't? Well, you must always do it hereafter."

"Why?"

"Because you'll have to know a good many things that it tells you. For one thing, it tells you the stage of the river—tells you whether there's more water or less in the river along here than there was last trip."

"The leads tell me that." I rather thought I had the advantage of him there.

"Yes, but suppose the leads lie? The bank would tell you so, and then you would stir those leadsmen up a bit. There was a ten-foot bank here last trip, and there is only a six-foot bank now. What does that signify?"

"That the river is four feet higher than it was last trip."

"Very good. Is the river rising or falling?"

"Rising."

"No, it ain't."

"I guess I am right, sir. Yonder is some driftwood floating down the stream."

"A rise *starts* the driftwood, but then it keeps on floating awhile after the river is done rising. Now the bank will tell you about this. Wait till you come to a place where it shelves a little. Now here: do you see this narrow belt of fine sediment? That was deposited while the water was higher. You see the driftwood begins to strand, too. The bank helps in other ways. Do you see that stump on the false point?"

"Ay, ay, sir."

"Well, the water is just up to the roots of it. You must make a note of that."

"Why?"

"Because that means that there's seven feet in the chute of 103."

"But 103 is a long way up the river yet."

"That's where the benefit of the bank comes in. There is water enough in 103 *now*, yet there may not be by the time we get there, but the bank will keep us posted all along. You don't run close chutes on a falling river, up-stream, and there are precious few of them that you are allowed to run at all down-stream. There's a law of the United States against it. The river may be rising by the time we get to 103, and in that case we'll run it. We are drawing—how much?"

"Six feet aft—six and a half forward."

"Well, you do seem to know something."

"But what I particularly want to know is, if I have got to keep up an everlasting measuring of the banks of this river, twelve hundred miles, month in and month out?"

"Of course!"

My emotions were too deep for words for a while. Presently I said:

"And how about these chutes? Are there many of them?"

"I should say so! I fancy we sha'n't run any of the river this trip as you've ever seen it run before—so to speak. If the river begins to rise again, we'll go up behind bars that you've always seen standing out of the river, high and dry, like a roof of a house; we'll cut across low places that you've never noticed at all, right through the middle of bars that cover three hundred acres of river; we'll creep through cracks where you've always thought was solid land; we'll dart through the woods and leave twenty-five miles of river off to one side; we'll see the hind side of every island between New Orleans and Cairo."

"Then I've got to go to work and learn just as much more river as I already know."

"Just about twice as much more, as near as you can come at it."

"Well, one lives to find out. I think I was a fool when I went into this business."

"Yes, that is true. And you are yet. But you'll not be when you've learned it."

"Ah, I never can learn it!"

"I will see that you *do*."

By and by I ventured again:

"Have I got to learn all this thing just as I know the rest of the river—shapes and all— and so I can run it at night?"

"Yes. And you've got to have good fair marks from one end of the river to the other, that will

help the bank tell you when there is water enough in each of these countless places — like that stump, you know. When the river first begins to rise, you can run half a dozen of the deepest of them; when it rises a foot more you can run another dozen; the next foot will add a couple of dozen, and so on: so you see you have to know your banks and marks to a dead moral certainty, and never get them mixed; for when you start through one of those cracks, there's no backing out again, as there is in the big river; you've got to go through, or stay there six months if you get caught on a falling river. There are about fifty of these cracks which you can't run at all except when the river is brimful and over the banks.''

"This new lesson is a cheerful prospect."

"Cheerful enough. And mind what I've just told you; when you start into one of those places you've got to go through. They are too narrow to turn around in, too crooked to back out of, and the shoal water is always *up at the head*; never elsewhere. And the head of them is always likely to be filling up, little by little, so that the marks you reckon their depth by, this season, may not answer for next."

"Learn a new set, then, every year?"

"Exactly. Cramp her up to the bar! What are you standing up through the middle of the river for?"

The next few months showed me strange things. On the same day that we held the conversation above narrated we met a great rise coming down the river. The whole vast face of the stream was black with drifting dead logs, broken boughs, and great trees that had caved in and been washed away. It required the nicest steering to pick one's way through this rushing raft, even in the daytime, when crossing from point to point; and at night the difficulty was mightily increased; every now and then a huge log, lying deep in the water, would suddenly appear right under our bows, coming head-on; no use to try to avoid it then; we could only stop the engines, and one wheel would walk over that log from one end to the other, keeping up a thundering racket and careening the boat in a way that was very uncomfortable to pas-

sengers. Now and then we would hit one of these sunken logs a rattling bang, dead in the center, with a full head of steam, and it would stun the boat as if she had hit a continent. Sometimes this log would lodge and stay right across our nose, and back the Mississippi up before it; we would have to do a little crawfishing, then, to get away from the obstruction. We often hit *white* logs in the dark, for we could not see them until we were right on them, but a black log is a pretty distinct object at night. A white snag is an ugly customer when the daylight is gone.

Of course, on the great rise, down came a swarm of prodigious timber-rafts from the headwaters of the Mississippi, coal-barges from Pittsburg, little trading-scows from everywhere, and broadhorns from "Posey County," Indiana, freighted with "fruit and furniture" — the usual term for describing it, though in plain English the freight thus aggrandized was hoop-poles and pumpkins. Pilots bore a mortal hatred to these craft, and it was returned with usury. The law required all such helpless traders to keep a light burning, but it was a law that was often broken. All of a sudden, on a murky night, a light would hop up, right under our bows, almost, and an agonized voice, with the backwoods "whang" to it, would wail out:

"Whar'n the — you goin' to! Cain't you see nothin', you dash-dashed aig-suckin', sheep-stealin', one-eyed son of a stuffed monkey!"

Then for an instant, as we whistled by, the red glare from our furnaces would reveal the scow and the form of the gesticulating orator, as if under a lightning flash, and in that instant our firemen and deck-hands would send and receive a tempest of missiles and profanity, one of our wheels would walk off with the crashing fragments of a steering-oar, and down the dead blackness would shut again. And that flatboatman would be sure to go into New Orleans and sue our boat, swearing stoutly that he had a light burning all the time, when in truth his gang had the lantern down below to sing and lie and drink and gamble by, and no watch on deck. Once at night, in one of those forest-bordered crevices (behind an island)

which steamboatmen intensely describe with the phrase "as dark as the inside of a cow," we should have eaten up a Posey County family, fruit, furniture, and all, but that they happened to be fiddling down below and we just caught the sound of the music in time to sheer off, doing no serious damage, unfortunately, but coming so near it that we had good hopes for a moment. These people brought up their lantern, then, of course; and as we backed and filled to get away, the precious family stood in the light of it—both sexes and various ages—and cursed us till everything turned blue. Once a coal-boatman sent a bullet through our pilot-house when we borrowed a steering-oar of him in a very narrow place. . . .

BUT I am wandering from what I was intending to do; that is, make plainer than perhaps appears in the previous chapters some of the peculiar requirements of the science of piloting. First of all, there is one faculty which a pilot must incessantly cultivate until he has brought it to absolute perfection. Nothing short of perfection will do. That faculty is memory. He cannot stop with merely thinking a thing is so and so; he must *know* it; for this is eminently one of the "exact" sciences. With what scorn a pilot was looked upon, in the old times, if he ever ventured to deal in that feeble phrase "I think," instead of the vigorous one, "I know!" One cannot easily realize what a tremendous thing it is to know every trivial detail of twelve hundred miles of river and know it with absolute exactness. If you will take the longest street in New York, and travel up and down it, conning its features patiently until you know every house and window and lamp-post and big and little sign by heart, and know them so accurately that you can instantly name the one you are abreast of when you are set down at random in that street in the middle of an inky black night, you will then have a tolerable notion of the amount and the exactness of a pilot's knowledge who carries the Mississippi River in his head. And then, if you will go on until you know every street-crossing, the character, size, and position of the crossing-stones, and the varying depth of mud in each of these numberless places, you will have some idea of what the pilot must know in order to keep a Mississippi steamer out of trouble. Next, if you will take half of the signs in that long street, and *change their places* once a month, and still manage to know their new positions accurately on dark nights, and keep up with these repeated changes without making any mistakes, you will understand what is required of a pilot's peerless memory by the fickle Mississippi.

I think a pilot's memory is about the most wonderful thing in the world. To know the Old and New Testaments by heart, and be able to recite them glibly, forward or backward, or begin at random anywhere in the book and recite both ways and never trip or make a mistake, is no extravagant mass of knowledge, and no marvelous facility, compared to a pilot's massed knowledge of the Mississippi and his marvelous facility in the handling of it. I make this comparison deliberately, and believe I am not expanding the truth when I do it. Many will think my figure too strong, but pilots will not.

And how easily and comfortably the pilot's memory does its work; how placidly effortless is its way; how *unconsciously* it lays up its vast stores, hour by hour, day by day, and never loses or mislays a single valuable package of them all! Take an instance. Let a leadsman cry, "Half twain! half twain! half twain! half twain! half twain!" until it becomes as monotonous as the ticking of a clock; let conversation be going on all the time, and the pilot be doing his share of the talking, and no longer consciously listening to the leadsman; and in the midst of this endless string of half twains let a single "quarter twain!" be interjected, without emphasis, and then the half-twain cry go on again, just as before: two or three weeks later that pilot can describe with precision the boat's position in the river when that quarter twain was uttered, and give you such a lot of head-marks, stern-marks, and side-marks to guide you, that you ought to be able to take the boat there and put her in that same spot again yourself! The

cry of "quarter twain" did not really take his mind from his talk, but his trained faculties instantly photographed the bearings, noted the change of depth, and laid up the important details for future reference without requiring any assistance from *him* in the matter. If you were walking and talking with a friend, and another friend at your side kept up a monotonous repetition of the vowel sound A, for a couple of blocks, and then in the midst interjected an R, thus, A, A, A, A, A, R, A, A, A, etc., and gave the R no emphasis, you would not be able to state, two or three weeks afterward, that the R had been put in, nor be able to tell what objects you were passing at the moment it was done. But you could if your memory had been patiently and laboriously trained to do that sort of thing mechanically.

Give a man a tolerably fair memory to start with, and piloting will develop it into a very colossus of capability. But *only in the matters it is daily drilled in.* A time would come when the man's faculties could not help noticing landmarks and soundings, and his memory could not help holding on to them with the grip of a vise; but if you asked that same man at noon what he had had for breakfast, it would be ten chances to one that he could not tell you. Astonishing things can be done with the human memory if you will devote it faithfully to one particular line of business.

At the time that wages soared so high on the Missouri River, my chief, Mr. Bixby, went up there and learned more than a thousand miles of that stream with an ease and rapidity that were astonishing. When he had seen each division *once* in the daytime and *once* at night, his education was so nearly complete that he took out a "daylight" license; a few trips later he took out a full license, and went to piloting day and night—and he ranked A1, too.

Mr. Bixby placed me as steersman for a while under a pilot whose feats of memory were a constant marvel to me. However, his memory was born in him, I think, not built. For instance, somebody would mention a name. Instantly Mr. Brown would break in:

"Oh, I knew *him.* Sallow-faced, red-headed fellow, with a little scar on the side of his throat, like a splinter under the flesh. He was only in the Southern trade six months. That was thirteen years ago. I made a trip with him. There was five feet in the upper river then; the *Henry Blake* grounded at the foot of Tower Island drawing four and a half; the *George Elliott* unshipped her rudder on the wreck of the *Sunflower*—"

"Why, the *Sunflower* didn't sink until—"

"I know when she sunk; it was three years before that, on the 2d of December; Asa Hardy was captain of her, and his brother John was first clerk; and it was his first trip in her, too; Tom Jones told me these things a week afterward in New Orleans; he was first mate of the *Sunflower*. Captain Hardy stuck a nail in his foot the 6th of July of the next year, and died of the lockjaw on the 15th. His brother John died two years after—3d of March—erysipelas. I never saw either of the Hardys—they were Alleghany River men—but people who knew them told me all these things. And they said Captain Hardy wore yarn socks winter and summer just the same, and his first wife's name was Jane Shook—she was from New England—and his second one died in a lunatic asylum. It was in the blood. She was from Lexington, Kentucky. Name was Horton before she was married."

And so on, by the hour, the man's tongue would go. He could *not* forget anything. It was simply impossible. The most trivial details remained as distinct and luminous in his head, after they had lain there for years, as the most memorable events. His was not simply a pilot's memory; its grasp was universal. If he were talking about a trifling letter he had received seven years before, he was pretty sure to deliver you the entire screed from memory. And then, without observing that he was departing from the true line of his talk, he was more than likely to hurl in a long-drawn parenthetical biography of the writer of that letter; and you were lucky indeed if he did not take up that writer's relatives, one by one, and give you their biographies, too.

Such a memory as that is a great misfortune.

To it, all occurrences are of the same size. Its possessor cannot distinguish an interesting circumstance from an uninteresting one. As a talker, he is bound to clog his narrative with tiresome details and make himself an insufferable bore. Moreover, he cannot stick to his subject. He picks up every little grain of memory he discerns in his way, and so is led aside. Mr. Brown would start out with the honest intention of telling you a vastly funny anecdote about a dog. He would be "so full of laugh" that he could hardly begin; then his memory would start with the dog's breed and personal appearance; drift into a history of his owner; of his owner's family, with descriptions of weddings and burials that had occurred in it, together with recitals of congratulatory verses and obituary poetry provoked by the same; then his memory would recollect that one of these events occurred during the celebrated "hard winter" of such-and-such a year, and a minute description of that winter would follow, along with the names of people who were frozen to death, and statistics showing the high figures which pork and hay went up to. Pork and hay would suggest corn and fodder; corn and fodder would suggest cows and horses; cows and horses would suggest the circus and certain celebrated bare-back riders; the transition from the circus to the menagerie was easy and natural; from the elephant to equatorial Africa was but a step; then of course the heathen savages would suggest religion; and at the end of three or four hours' tedious jaw, the watch would change, and Brown would go out of the pilot-house muttering extracts from sermons he had heard years before about the efficacy of prayer as a means of grace. And the original first mention would be all you had learned about that dog, after all this waiting and hungering.

A pilot must have a memory; but there are two higher qualities which he must also have. He must have good and quick judgment and decision, and a cool, calm courage that no peril can shake. Give a man the merest trifle of pluck to start with, and by the time he has become a pilot he cannot be unmanned by any danger a steamboat can get into; but one cannot quite say the same for judgment. Judgment is a matter of brains, and a man must *start* with a good stock of that article or he will never succeed as a pilot.

The growth of courage in the pilot-house is steady all the time, but it does not reach a high and satisfactory condition until some time after the young pilot has been "standing his own watch" alone and under the staggering weight of all the responsibilities connected with the position. When the apprentice has become pretty thoroughly acquainted with the river, he goes clattering along so fearlessly with his steamboat, night or day, that he presently begins to imagine that it is *his* courage that animates him; but the first time the pilot steps out and leaves him to his own devices he finds out it was the other man's. He discovers that the article has been left out of his own cargo altogether. The whole river is bristling with exigencies in a moment; he is not prepared for them; he does not know how to meet them; all his knowledge forsakes him; and within fifteen minutes he is as white as a sheet and scared almost to death. Therefore pilots wisely train these cubs by various strategic tricks to look danger in the face a little more calmly. A favorite way of theirs is to play a friendly swindle upon the candidate.

Mr. Bixby served me in this fashion once, and for years afterward I used to blush, even in my sleep, when I thought of it. I had become a good steersman; so good, indeed, that I had all the work to do on our watch, night and day. Mr. Bixby seldom made a suggestion to me; all he ever did was to take the wheel on particularly bad nights or in particularly bad crossings, land the boat when she needed to be landed, play gentleman of leisure nine-tenths of the watch, and collect the wages. The lower river was about bank-full, and if anybody had questioned my ability to run any crossing between Cairo and New Orleans without help or instruction, I should have felt irreparably hurt. The idea of being afraid of any crossing in the lot, in the *daytime*, was a thing too preposterous for contemplation. Well, one matchless

summer's day I was bowling down the bend above Island 66, brimful of self-conceit and carrying my nose as high as a giraffe's, when Mr. Bixby said:

"I am going below awhile. I suppose you know the next crossing?"

This was almost an affront. It was about the plainest and simplest crossing in the whole river. One couldn't come to any harm, whether he ran it right or not; and as for depth, there never had been any bottom there. I knew all this, perfectly well.

"Know how to run it? Why, I can run it with my eyes shut."

"How much water is there in it?"

cane-deck; next the chief mate appeared; then a clerk. Every moment or two a straggler was added to my audience; and before I got to the head of the island I had fifteen or twenty people assembled down there under my nose. I began to wonder what the trouble was. As I started across, the captain glanced aloft at me and said, with a sham uneasiness in his voice:

"Where is Mr. Bixby?"

"Gone below, sir."

But that did the business for me. My imagination began to construct dangers out of nothing, and they multiplied faster than I could keep the run of them. All at once I imagined I saw shoal water ahead! The wave of coward agony

THE MISSISSIPPI AT LOW WATER

"Well, that is an odd question. I couldn't get bottom there with a church steeple."

"You think so, do you?"

The very tone of the question shook my confidence. That was what Mr. Bixby was expecting. He left, without saying anything more. I began to imagine all sorts of things. Mr. Bixby, unknown to me, of course, sent somebody down to the forecastle with some mysterious instructions to the leadsmen, another messenger was sent to whisper among the officers, and then Mr. Bixby went into hiding behind a smoke-stack where he could observe results. Presently the captain stepped out on the hurri-

that surged through me then came near dislocating every joint in me. All my confidence in that crossing vanished. I seized the bell-rope; dropped it, ashamed; seized it again; dropped it once more; clutched it tremblingly once again, and pulled it so feebly that I could hardly hear the stroke myself. Captain and mate sang out instantly, and both together:

"Starboard lead there! and quick about it!"

This was another shock. I began to climb the wheel like a squirrel; but I would hardly get the boat started to port before I would see new dangers on that side, and away I would spin to the other; only to find perils accumulating to

starboard, and be crazy to get to port again. Then came the leadsman's sepulchral cry:

"D-e-e-p four!"

Deep four in a bottomless crossing! The terror of it took my breath away.

"M-a-r-k three! M-a-r-k three! Quarter-less-three! Half twain!"

This was frightful! I seized the bell-ropes and stopped the engines.

"Quarter twain! Quarter twain! *Mark* twain!"

I was helpless. I did not know what in the world to do. I was quaking from head to foot, and I could have hung my hat on my eyes, they stuck out so far.

"Quarter-*less*-twain! Nine-and-a-*half!*"

how I was ass enough to heave the lead at the head of 66."

"Well, no, you won't, maybe. In fact I hope you won't; for I want you to learn something by that experience. Didn't you *know* there was no bottom in that crossing?"

"Yes, sir, I did."

"Very well, then. You shouldn't have allowed me or anybody else to shake your confidence in that knowledge. Try to remember that. And another thing: when you get into a dangerous place, don't turn coward. That isn't going to help matters any."

It was a good enough lesson, but pretty hardly learned. Yet about the hardest part of it was

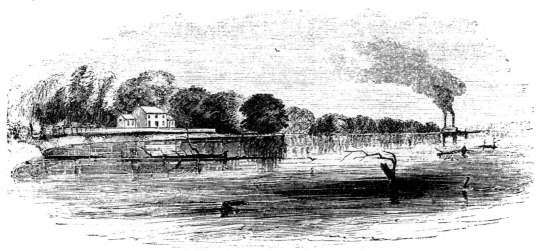

THE SAME SCENE AT HIGH WATER

We were *drawing* nine! My hands were in a nerveless flutter. I could not ring a bell intelligibly with them. I flew to the speaking-tube and shouted to the engineer:

"Oh, Ben, if you love me, *back* her! Quick, Ben! Oh, back the immortal *soul* out of her!"

I heard the door close gently. I looked around, and there stood Mr. Bixby, smiling a bland, sweet smile. Then the audience on the hurricane-deck sent up a thundergust of humiliating laughter. I saw it all, now, and I felt meaner than the meanest man in human history. I laid in the lead, set the boat in her marks, came ahead on the engines, and said:

"It was a fine trick to play on an orphan, *wasn't* it? I suppose I'll never hear the last of

that for months I so often had to hear a phrase which I had conceived a particular distaste for. It was, "Oh, Ben, if you love me, back her!"

IN my preceding chapters I have tried, by going into the minutiae of the science of piloting, to carry the reader step by step to a comprehension of what the science consists of; and at the same time I have tried to show him that it is a very curious and wonderful science, too, and very worthy of his attention. If I have seemed to love my subject, it is no surprising thing, for I loved the profession far better than any I have followed since, and I took a measureless pride in it. The reason is plain: a pilot, in those

days, was the only unfettered and entirely independent human being that lived in the earth. Kings are but the hampered servants of parliament and the people; parliaments sit in chains forged by their constituency; the editor of a newspaper cannot be independent, but must work with one hand tied behind him by party and patrons, and be content to utter only half or two-thirds of his mind; no clergyman is a free man and may speak the whole truth, regardless of his parish's opinions; writers of all kinds are manacled servants of the public. We write frankly and fearlessly, but then we "modify" before we print. In truth, every man and woman and child has a master, and worries and frets in servitude; but, in the day I write of, the Mississippi pilot had *none*. The captain could stand upon the hurricane-deck, in the pomp of a very brief authority, and give him five or six orders while the vessel backed into the stream, and then that skipper's reign was over. The moment that the boat was under way in the river, she was under the sole and unquestioned control of the pilot. He could do with her exactly as he pleased, run her when and whither he chose, and tie her up to the bank whenever his judgment said that that course was best. His movements were entirely free; he consulted no one, he received commands from nobody, he promptly resented even the merest suggestions. Indeed, the law of the United States forbade him to listen to commands or suggestions, rightly considering that the pilot necessarily knew better how to handle the boat than anybody could tell him. So here was the novelty of a king without a keeper, an absolute monarch who was absolute in sober truth and not by a fiction of words. I have seen a boy of eighteen taking a great steamer serenely into what seemed almost certain destruction, and the aged captain standing mutely by, filled with apprehension but powerless to interfere. His interference, in that particular instance, might have been an excellent thing, but to permit it would have been to establish a most pernicious precedent. It will easily be guessed, considering the pilot's boundless authority, that he was a great personage in the old steamboating days. He was treated with marked courtesy by the captain and with marked deference by all the officers and servants; and this deferential spirit was quickly communicated to the passengers, too. I think pilots were about the only people I ever knew who failed to show, in some degree, embarrassment in the presence of traveling foreign princes. But then, people in one's own grade of life are not usually embarrassing objects.

By long habit, pilots came to put all their wishes in the form of commands. It "gravels" me, to this day, to put my will in the weak shape of a request, instead of launching it in the crisp language of an order.

In those old days, to load a steamboat at St. Louis, take her to New Orleans and back, and discharge cargo, consumed about twenty-five days, on an average. Seven or eight of these days the boat spent at the wharves of St. Louis and New Orleans, and every soul on board was hard at work, except the two pilots; *they* did nothing but play gentleman up-town, and receive the same wages for it as if they had been on duty. The moment the boat touched the wharf at either city they were ashore; and they were not likely to be seen again till the last bell was ringing and everything in readiness for another voyage.

When a captain got hold of a pilot of particularly high reputation, he took pains to keep him. When wages were four hundred dollars a month on the Upper Mississippi, I have known a captain to keep such a pilot in idleness, under full pay, three months at a time, while the river was frozen up. And one must remember that in those cheap times four hundred dollars was a salary of almost inconceivable splendor. Few men on shore got such pay as that, and when they did they were mightily looked up to. When pilots from either end of the river wandered into our small Missouri village, they were sought by the best and the fairest, and treated with exalted respect. Lying in port under wages was a thing which many pilots greatly enjoyed and appreciated; especially if they belonged in the Missouri River in the heyday of that trade (Kansas times), and got nine hundred dollars a trip, which was equivalent to about eighteen hundred dollars a month.

My reference, a moment ago, to the fact that a pilot's peculiar official position placed him out of the reach of criticism or command, brings Stephen W. naturally to my mind. He was a gifted pilot, a good fellow, a tireless talker, and had both wit and humor in him. He had a most irreverent independence, too, and was deliciously easy-going and comfortable in the presence of age, official dignity, and even the most august wealth. He always had work, he never saved a penny, he was a most persuasive borrower, he was in debt to every pilot on the river, and to the majority of the captains. He could throw a sort of splendor around a bit of harum-scarum, devil-may-care piloting, that made it almost fascinating—but not to everybody. He made a trip with good old Captain Y. once, and was "relieved" from duty when the boat got to New Orleans. Somebody expressed surprise at the discharge. Captain Y. shuddered at the mere mention of Stephen. Then his poor, thin old voice piped out something like this:

"Why, bless me! I wouldn't have such a wild creature on my boat for the world—not for the whole world! He swears, he sings, he whistles, he yells—I never saw such an Injun to yell. All times of the night—it never made any difference to him. He would just yell that way, not for anything in particular, but merely on account of a kind of devilish comfort he got out of it. I never could get into a sound sleep but he would fetch me out of bed, all in a cold sweat, with one of those dreadful war-whoops. A queer being—very queer being; no respect for anything or anybody. Sometimes he called me 'Johnny.' And he kept a fiddle and a cat. He played execrably. This seemed to distress the cat, and so the cat would howl. Nobody could sleep where that man—and his family— was. And reckless? There never was anything like it. Now you may believe it or not, but as sure as I am sitting here, he brought my boat a-tilting down through those awful snags at Chicot under a rattling head of steam, and the wind a-blowing like the very nation, at that! My officers will tell you so. They saw it. And, sir, while he was a-tearing right down through those snags, and I a-shaking in my shoes and praying, I wish I may never speak again if he didn't pucker up his mouth and go to *whistling!* Yes, sir; whistling 'Buffalo gals, can't you come out to-night, can't you come out to-night, can't you come out to-night'; and doing it as calmly as if we were attending a funeral and weren't related to the corpse. And when I remonstrated with him about it, he smiled down on me as if I was his child, and told me to run in the house and try to be good, and not be meddling with my superiors!"*

Once a pretty mean captain caught Stephen in New Orleans out of work and as usual out of money. He laid steady siege to Stephen, who was in a very "close place," and finally persuaded him to hire with him at one hundred and twenty-five dollars per month, just half wages, the captain agreeing not to divulge the secret and so bring down the contempt of all the guild upon the poor fellow. But the boat was not more than a day out of New Orleans before Stephen discovered that the captain was boasting of his exploit, and that all the officers had been told. Stephen winced, but said nothing. About the middle of the afternoon the captain stepped out on the hurricane-deck, cast his eye around, and looked a good deal surprised. He glanced inquiringly aloft at Stephen, but Stephen was whistling placidly and attending to business. The captain stood around awhile in evident discomfort, and once or twice seemed about to make a suggestion; but the etiquette of the river taught him to avoid that sort of rashness, and so he managed to hold his peace. He chafed and puzzled a few minutes longer, then retired to his apartments. But soon he was out again, and apparently more perplexed than ever. Presently he ventured to remark, with deference:

"Pretty good stage of the river now, ain't it, sir?"

*Considering a captain's ostentatious but hollow chieftainship, and a pilot's real authority, there was something impudently apt and happy about that way of phrasing it.

"Well, I should say so! Bank-full *is* a pretty liberal stage."

"Seems to be a good deal of current here."

"Good deal don't describe it! It's worse than a mill-race."

"Isn't it easier in toward shore than it is out here in the middle?"

"Yes, I reckon it is; but a body can't be too careful with a steamboat. It's pretty safe out here; can't strike any bottom here, you can depend on that."

The captain departed, looking rueful enough. At this rate, he would probably die of old age before his boat got to St. Louis. Next day he

"Mr. W., don't that chute cut off a good deal of distance?"

"I think it does, but I don't know."

"Don't know! Well, isn't there water enough in it now to go through?"

"I expect there is, but I am not certain."

"Upon my word this is odd! Why, those pilots on that boat yonder are going to try it. Do you mean to say that you don't know as much as they do?"

"*They!* Why, *they* are two-hundred-and-fifty-dollar pilots! But don't you be uneasy; I know as much as any man can afford to know for a hundred and twenty-five!"

The captain surrendered.

Five minutes later Stephen was bowling through the chute and showing the rival boat a two-hundred-and-fifty-dollar pair of heels.

appeared on deck and again found Stephen faithfully standing up the middle of the river, fighting the whole vast force of the Mississippi, and whistling the same placid tune. This thing was becoming serious. In by the shore was a slower boat clipping along in the easy water and gaining steadily; she began to make for an island chute; Stephen stuck to the middle of the river. Speech was *wrung* from the captain. He said:

IT was always the custom for the boats to leave New Orleans between four and five o'clock in the afternoon. From three o'clock onward they would be burning rosin and pitch-pine (the sign of preparation), and so one had the picturesque spectacle of a rank, some two or three miles long, of tall, ascending columns of coal-black smoke; a colonnade which sup-

ported a sable roof of the same smoke blended together and spreading abroad over the city. Every outward-bound boat had its flag flying at the jackstaff, and sometimes a duplicate on the verge-staff astern. Two or three miles of mates were commanding and swearing with more than usual emphasis: countless processions of freight barrels and boxes were spinning athwart the levee and flying aboard the stage-planks; belated passengers were dodging and skipping among these frantic things, hoping to reach the forecastle companionway alive, but having their doubts about it; women with reticules and bandboxes were trying to keep up with husbands freighted with carpet sacks and crying babies, and making a failure of it by losing their heads in the whirl and roar and general distraction; drays and baggage-vans were clattering hither and thither in a wild hurry, every now and then getting blocked and jammed together, and then during ten seconds one could not see them for the profanity, except vaguely and dimly; every windlass connected with every fore-hatch, from one end of that long array of steamboats to the other, was keeping up a deafening whizz and whir, lowering freight into the hold, and the half-naked crews of perspiring negroes that worked them were roaring such songs as "De Las' Sack! De Las' Sack!"—inspired to unimaginable exaltation by the chaos of turmoil and racket that was driving everybody else mad. By this time the hurricane and boiler decks of the steamers would be packed black with passengers. The "last bells" would begin to clang, all down the line, and then the powwow seemed to double; in a moment or two the final warning came—a simultaneous din of Chinese gongs, with the cry, "All dat ain't goin', please to git asho'!"—and behold the powwow quadrupled! People came swarming ashore, overturning excited stragglers that were trying to swarm aboard. One more moment later a long array of stage-planks was being hauled in, each with its customary latest passenger clinging to the end of it with teeth, nails, and everything else, and the customary latest procrastinator making a wild spring shoreward over his head.

Now a number of the boats slide backward into the stream, leaving wide gaps in the serried rank of steamers. Citizens crowd the decks of boats that are not to go, in order to see the sight. Steamer after steamer straightens herself up, gathers all her strength, and presently comes swinging by, under a tremendous head of steam, with flag flying, black smoke rolling, and her entire crew of firemen and deck-hands (usually swarthy negroes) massed together on the forecastle, the best "voice" in the lot towering from the midst (being mounted on the capstan), waving his hat or a flag, and all roaring a mighty chorus, while the parting cannons boom and the multitudinous spectators wave their hats and huzza! Steamer after steamer falls into line, and the stately procession goes winging its flight up the river.

In the old times, whenever two fast boats started out on a race, with a big crowd of people looking on, it was inspiring to hear the crews sing, especially if the time were nightfall, and the forecastle lit up with the red glare of the torch-baskets. Racing was royal fun. The public always had an idea that racing was dangerous; whereas the opposite was the case—that is, after the laws were passed which restricted each boat to just so many pounds of steam to the square inch. No engineer was ever sleepy or careless when his heart was in a race. He was constantly on the alert, trying gauge-cocks and watching things. The dangerous place was on slow, plodding boats, where the engineers drowsed around and allowed chips to get into the "doctor" and shut off the water-supply from the boilers.

In the "flush times" of steamboating, a race between two notoriously fleet steamers was an event of vast importance. The date was set for it several weeks in advance, and from that time forward the whole Mississippi valley was in a state of consuming excitement. Politics and the weather were dropped, and people talked only of the coming race. As the time approached, the two steamers "stripped" and got ready. Every encumbrance that added weight, or exposed a resisting surface to wind or water, was removed, if the boat could possibly do without

it. The "spars," and sometimes even their supporting derricks, were sent ashore, and no means left to set the boat afloat in case she got aground. When the *Eclipse* and the *A. L. Shotwell* ran their great race many years ago, it was said that pains were taken to scrape the gilding off the fanciful device which hung between the *Eclipse's* chimneys, and that for that one trip the captain left off his kid gloves and had his head shaved. But I always doubted these things.

If the boat was known to make her best speed when drawing five and a half feet forward and five feet aft, she carefully loaded to that exact figure—she wouldn't enter a dose of homeopathic pills on her manifest after that. Hardly any passengers were taken, because they not only add weight but they never will "trim boat." They always run to the side when there is anything to see, whereas a conscientious and experienced steamboatman would stick to the center of the boat and part his hair in the middle with a spirit-level.

No way-freights and no way-passengers were allowed, for the racers would stop only at the largest towns, and then it would be only "touch and go." Coal-flats and wood-flats were contracted for beforehand, and these were kept ready to hitch on to the flying steamers at a moment's warning. Double crews were carried, so that all work could be quickly done.

The chosen date being come, and all things in readiness, the two great steamers back into the stream, and lie there jockeying a moment, apparently watching each other's slightest movement, like sentient creatures; flags drooping, the pent steam shrieking through safety-valves, the black smoke rolling and tumbling from the chimneys and darkening all the air. People, people everywhere; the shores, the housetops, the steamboats, the ships, are packed with them, and you know that the borders of the broad Mississippi are going to be fringed with humanity thence northward twelve hundred miles, to welcome these racers. Presently tall columns of steam burst from the 'scape-pipes of both steamers, two guns boom a good-by, two red-shirted heroes mounted on capstans wave their small flags

above the massed crews on the forecastles, two plaintive solos linger on the air a few waiting seconds, two mighty choruses burst forth—and here they come! Brass bands bray "Hail Columbia," huzza after huzza thunders from the shores, and the stately creatures go whistling by like the wind.

Those boats will never halt a moment between New Orleans and St. Louis, except for a second or two at large towns, or to hitch thirty-cord wood-boats alongside. You should be on board when they take a couple of those wood-boats in tow and turn a swarm of men into each; by the time you have wiped your glasses and put them on, you will be wondering what has become of that wood.

Two nicely matched steamers will stay in sight of each other day after day. They might even stay side by side, but for the fact that pilots are not all alike, and the smartest pilots will win the race. If one of the boats has a "lightning" pilot, whose "partner" is a trifle his inferior, you can tell which one is on watch by noting whether that boat has gained ground or lost some during each four-hour stretch. The shrewdest pilot can delay a boat if he has not a fine genius for steering. Steering is a very high art. One must not keep a rudder dragging across a boat's stern if he wants to get up the river fast.

There is a great difference in boats, of course. For a long time I was on a boat that was so slow we used to forget what year it was we left port in. But of course this was at rare intervals. Ferry-boats used to lose valuable trips because their passengers grew old and died, waiting for us to get by. This was at still rarer intervals. I had the documents for these occurrences, but through carelessness they have been mislaid. This boat, the *John J. Roe*, was so slow that when she finally sunk in Madrid Bend it was five years before the owners heard of it. That was always a confusing fact to me, but it is according to the record, anyway. She was dismally slow; still, we often had pretty exciting times racing with islands, and rafts, and such things. One trip, however, we did rather well. We went to St. Louis in sixteen days. But even at this rattling gait I think we changed watches

three times in Fort Adams reach, which is five miles long. A "reach" is a piece of straight river, and of course the current drives through such a place in a pretty lively way.

That trip we went to Grand Gulf, from New Orleans, in four days (three hundred and forty miles); the *Eclipse* and *Shotwell* did it in one. We were nine days out, in the chute of 63 (seven hundred miles); the *Eclipse* and *Shotwell* went there in two days. Something over a generation ago, a boat called the *J. M. White* went from New Orleans to Cairo in three days, six hours, and forty-four minutes. In 1853 the *Eclipse* made the same trip in three days, three hours, and twenty minutes.* In 1870 the *R. E. Lee* did it in three days and *one* hour. This last is called the fastest trip on record. I will try to show that it was not. For this reason: the distance between New Orleans and Cairo, when the *J. M. White* ran it, was about eleven hundred and six miles; consequently her average speed was a trifle over fourteen miles per hour. In the *Eclipse*'s day the distance between the two ports had become reduced to one thousand and eighty miles; consequently her average speed was a shade under fourteen and three-eighths miles per hour. In the *R. E. Lee*'s time the distance had diminished to about one thousand and thirty miles; consequently her average was about fourteen and one-eighth miles per hour. Therefore the *Eclipse*'s was conspicuously the fastest time that has ever been made. . . .

THESE dry details are of importance in one particular. They give me an opportunity of introducing one of the Mississippi's oddest peculiarities—that of shortening its length from time to time. If you will throw a long, pliant apple-paring over your shoulder, it will pretty fairly shape itself into an average section of the Mississippi River; that is, the nine or ten hundred miles stretching from Cairo, Illinois,

*Time disputed. Some authorities add 1 hour and 16 minutes to this.

southward to New Orleans, the same being wonderfully crooked, with a brief straight bit here and there at wide intervals. The two-hundred-mile stretch from Cairo northward to St. Louis is by no means so crooked, that being a rocky country which the river cannot cut much.

The water cuts the alluvial banks of the "lower" river into deep horseshoe curves; so deep, indeed, that in some places if you were to get ashore at one extremity of the horseshoe and walk across the neck, half or three-quarters of a mile, you could sit down and rest a couple of hours while your steamer was coming around the long elbow at a speed of ten miles an hour to take you on board again. When the river is rising fast, some scoundrel whose plantation is back in the country, and therefore of inferior value, has only to watch his chance, cut a little gutter across the narrow neck of land some dark night, and turn the water into it, and in a wonderfully short time a miracle has happened: to wit, the whole Mississippi has taken possession of that little ditch, and placed the countryman's plantation on its bank (quadrupling its value), and that other party's formerly valuable plantation finds itself away out yonder on a big island; the old watercourse around it will soon shoal up, boats cannot approach within ten miles of it, and down goes its value to a fourth of its former worth. Watches are kept on those narrow necks at needful times, and if a man happens to be caught cutting a ditch across them, the chances are all against his ever having another opportunity to cut a ditch.

Pray observe some of the effects of this ditching business. Once there was a neck opposite Port Hudson, Louisiana, which was only half a mile across in its narrowest place. You could walk across there in fifteen minutes; but if you made the journey around the cape on a raft, you traveled thirty-five miles to accomplish the same thing. In 1722 the river darted through that neck, deserted its old bed, and thus shortened itself thirty-five miles. In the same way it shortened itself twenty-five miles at Black Hawk Point in 1699. Below Red River Landing, Raccourci cut-off was made (forty or fifty years

ago, I think). This shortened the river twenty-eight miles. In our day, if you travel by river from the southernmost of these three cut-offs to the northernmost, you go only seventy miles. To do the same thing a hundred and seventy-six years ago, one had to go a hundred and fifty-eight miles—a shortening of eighty-eight miles in that trifling distance. At some forgotten time in the past, cut-offs were made above Vidalia, Louisiana, at Island 92, at Island 84, and at Hale's Point. These shortened the river, in the aggregate, seventy-seven miles.

Since my own day on the Mississippi, cut-offs have been made at Hurricane Island, at Island 100, at Napoleon, Arkansas, at Walnut Bend, and at Council Bend. These shortened the river, in the aggregate, sixty-seven miles. In my own time a cut-off was made at American Bend, which shortened the river ten miles or more.

Therefore the Mississippi between Cairo and New Orleans was twelve hundred and fifteen miles long one hundred and seventy-six years ago. It was eleven hundred and eighty after the cut-off of 1722. It was one thousand and forty after the American Bend cut-off. It has lost sixty-seven miles since. Consequently, its length is only nine hundred and seventy-three miles at present.

Now, if I wanted to be one of those ponderous scientific people, and "let on" to prove what had occurred in the remote past by what had occurred in a given time in the recent past, or what will occur in the far future by what has occurred in late years, what an opportunity is here! Geology never had such a chance, nor such exact data to argue from! Nor "development of species," either! Glacial epochs are great things, but they are vague—vague. Please observe:

In the space of one hundred and seventy-six years the lower Mississippi has shortened itself two hundred and forty-two miles. That is an average of a trifle over one mile and a third per year. Therefore, any calm person, who is not blind or idiotic, can see that in the Old Oölitic Silurian Period, just a million years ago next November, the lower Mississippi River was upward of one million three hundred thousand miles long, and stuck out over the Gulf of Mexico like a fishing-rod. And by the same token any person can see that seven hundred and forty-two years from now the Lower Mississippi will be only a mile and three-quarters long, and Cairo and New Orleans will have joined their streets together, and be plodding comfortably along under a single mayor and a mutual board of aldermen. There is something fascinating about science. One gets such wholesale returns of conjecture out of such a trifling investment of fact.

When the water begins to flow through one of those ditches I have been speaking of, it is time for the people thereabouts to move. The water cleaves the banks away like a knife. By the time the ditch has become twelve or fifteen feet wide, the calamity is as good as accomplished, for no power on earth can stop it now. When the width has reached a hundred yards, the banks begin to peel off in slices half an acre wide. The current flowing around the bend traveled formerly only five miles an hour; now it is tremendously increased by the shortening of the distance. I was on board the first boat that tried to go through the cut-off at American Bend, but we did not get through. It was toward midnight, and a wild night it was—thunder, lightning, and torrents of rain. It was estimated that the current in the cut-off was making about fifteen or twenty miles an hour; twelve or thirteen was the best our boat could do, even in tolerably slack water, therefore perhaps we were foolish to try the cut-off. However, Mr. Brown was ambitious, and he kept on trying. The eddy running up the bank, under the "point," was about as swift as the current out in the middle; so we would go flying up the shore like a lightning express-train, get on a big head of steam, and "stand by for a surge" when we struck the current that was whirling by the point. But all our preparations were useless. The instant the current hit us it spun us around like a top, the water deluged the forecastle, and the boat careened so far over that one could hardly keep his feet. The next instant we were away down the river, clawing

with might and main to keep out of the woods. We tried the experiment four times. I stood on the forecastle companionway to see. It was astonishing to observe how suddenly the boat would spin around and turn tail the moment she emerged from the eddy and the current struck her nose. The sounding concussion and the quivering would have been about the same if she had come full speed against a sand-bank. Under the lightning flashes one could see the plantation cabins and the goodly acres tumble into the river, and the crash they made was not a bad effort at thunder. Once, when we spun around, we only missed a house about twenty feet that had a light burning in the window, and in the same instant that house went overboard. Nobody could stay on our forecastle; the water swept across it in a torrent every time we plunged athwart the current. At the end of our fourth effort we brought up in the woods two miles below the cut-off; all the country there was overflowed, of course. A day or two later the cut-off was three-quarters of a mile wide, and boats passed up through it without much difficulty, and so saved ten miles. . . .

During the two or two and a half years of my apprenticeship I served under many pilots, and had experience of many kinds of steamboatmen and many varieties of steamboats; for it was not always convenient for Mr. Bixby to have me with him, and in such cases he sent me with somebody else. I am to this day profiting somewhat by that experience; for in that brief, sharp schooling, I got personally and familiarly acquainted with about all the different types of human nature that are to be found in fiction, biography, or history. The fact is daily borne in upon me that the average shore-employment requires as much as forty years to equip a man with this sort of an education. When I say I am still profiting by this thing, I do not mean that it has constituted me a judge of men—no, it has not done that, for judges of men are born, not made. My profit is various in kind and degree, but the feature of it which I value most is the zest which that early experience has given to my later reading. When I find a well-drawn character in fiction or biography I generally take a warm personal interest in him, for the reason that I have known him before—met him on the river.

The figure that comes before me oftenest, out of the shadows of that vanished time, is that of Brown, of the steamer *Pennsylvania*—the man referred to in a former chapter, whose memory was so good and tiresome. He was a middle-aged, long, slim, bony, smooth-shaven, horse-faced, ignorant, stingy, malicious, snarling, fault-hunting, mote-magnifying tyrant. I early got the habit of coming on watch with dread at my heart. No matter how good a time I might have been having with the off-watch below, and no matter how high my spirits might be when I started aloft, my soul became lead in my body the moment I approached the pilot-house.

I still remember the first time I ever entered the presence of that man. The boat had backed out from St. Louis and was "straightening down." I ascended to the pilot-house in high feather, and very proud to be semi-officially a member of the executive family of so fast and famous a boat. Brown was at the wheel. I paused in the middle of the room, all fixed to make my bow, but Brown did not look around. I thought he took a furtive glance at me out of the corner of his eye, but as not even this notice was repeated, I judged I had been mistaken. By this time he was picking his way among some dangerous "breaks" abreast the wood-yards; therefore it would not be proper to interrupt him; so I stepped softly to the high bench and took a seat.

There was silence for ten minutes; then my new boss turned and inspected me deliberately and painstakingly from head to heel for about —as it seemed to me—a quarter of an hour. After which he removed his countenance and I saw it no more for some seconds; then it came around once more, and this question greeted me:

"Are you Horace Bigsby's cub?"

"Yes, sir."

After this there was a pause and another inspection. Then:

"What's your name?"

I told him. He repeated it after me. It was probably the only thing he ever forgot; for although I was with him many months he never addressed himself to me in any other way than "Here!" and then his command followed.

"Where was you born?"

"In Florida, Missouri."

A pause. Then:

"Dern sight better stayed there!"

By means of a dozen or so of pretty direct questions, he pumped my family history out of me.

The leads were going now in the first crossing. This interrupted the inquest. When the leads had been laid in he resumed:

"How long you been on the river?"

I told him. After a pause:

"Where'd you get them shoes?"

I gave him the information.

"Hold up your foot!"

I did so. He stepped back, examined the shoe minutely and contemptuously, scratching his head thoughtfully, tilting his high sugar-loaf hat well forward to facilitate the operation, then ejaculated, "Well, I'll be dod derned!" and returned to his wheel.

What occasion there was to be dod derned about it is a thing which is still as much of a mystery to me now as it was then. It must have been all of fifteen minutes—fifteen minutes of dull, homesick silence—before that long horse-face swung round upon me again—and then what a change! It was as red as fire, and every muscle in it was working. Now came this shriek:

"Here! You going to set there all day?"

I lit in the middle of the floor, shot there by the electric suddenness of the surprise. As soon as I could get my voice I said apologetically: "I have had no orders, sir."

"You've had no *orders!* My, what a fine bird we are! We must have *orders!* Our father was a *gentleman*—owned slaves—and *we've* been to *school*. Yes, *we* are a gentleman, *too*, and got to have *orders!* ORDERS, is it? ORDERS is what

you want! Dod dern my skin, *I'll* learn you to swell yourself up and blow around *here* about your dod-derned *orders!* G'way from the wheel!" (I had approached it without knowing it.)

I moved back a step or two and stood as in a dream, all my senses stupefied by this frantic assault.

"What you standing there for? Take that ice-pitcher down to the texas-tender! Come, move along, and don't you be all day about it!"

The moment I got back to the pilot-house Brown said:

"Here! What was you doing down there all this time?"

"I couldn't find the texas-tender; I had to go all the way to the pantry."

"Derned likely story! Fill up the stove."

I proceeded to do so. He watched me like a cat. Presently he shouted:

"Put down that shovel! Derndest numskull I ever saw—ain't even got sense enough to load up a stove."

All through the watch this sort of thing went on. Yes, and the subsequent watches were much like it during a stretch of months. As I have said, I soon got the habit of coming on duty with dread. The moment I was in the presence, even in the darkest night, I could feel those yellow eyes upon me, and knew their owner was watching for a pretext to spit out some venom on me. Preliminarily he would say:

"Here! Take the wheel."

Two minutes later:

"*Where* in the nation you going to? Pull her down! pull her down!"

After another moment:

"Say! You going to hold her all day? Let her go—meet her! meet her!"

Then he would jump from the bench, snatch the wheel from me, and meet her himself, pouring out wrath upon me all the time.

George Ritchie was the other pilot's cub. He was having good times now; for his boss, George Ealer, was as kind-hearted as Brown wasn't. Ritchie had steered for Brown the season before; consequently, he knew exactly how

to entertain himself and plague me, all by the one operation. Whenever I took the wheel for a moment on Ealer's watch, Ritchie would sit back on the bench and play Brown, with continual ejaculations of "Snatch her! snatch her! Derndest mud-cat I ever saw!" "Here! Where are you going *now*? Going to run over that snag?" "Pull her *down*! Don't you hear me? Pull her *down*!" "There she goes! *Just* as I expected! I *told* you not to cramp that reef. G'way from the wheel!"

So I always had a rough time of it, no matter whose watch it was; and sometimes it seemed to me that Ritchie's good-natured badgering was pretty nearly as aggravating as Brown's dead-earnest nagging.

I often wanted to kill Brown, but this would not answer. A cub had to take everything his boss gave, in the way of vigorous comment and criticism; and we all believed that there was a United States law making it a penitentiary offense to strike or threaten a pilot who was on duty. However, I could *imagine* myself killing Brown; there was no law against that; and that was the thing I used always to do the moment I was abed. Instead of going over my river in my mind, as was my duty, I threw business aside for pleasure, and killed Brown. I killed Brown every night for months; not in old, stale, commonplace ways, but in new and picturesque ones—ways that were sometimes surprising for freshness of design and ghastliness of situation and environment.

Brown was *always* watching for a pretext to find fault; and if he could find no plausible pretext, he would invent one. He would scold you for shaving a shore, and for not shaving it; for hugging a bar, and for not hugging it; for "pulling down" when not invited, and for *not* pulling down when not invited; for firing up without orders, and for waiting *for* orders. In a word, it was his invariable rule to find fault with *everything* you did; and another invariable rule of his was to throw all his remarks (to you) into the form of an insult.

One day we were approaching New Madrid, bound down and heavily laden. Brown was at one side of the wheel, steering; I was at the other, standing by to "pull down" or "shove up." He cast a furtive glance at me every now and then. I had long ago learned what that ment; viz., he was trying to invent a trap for me. I wondered what shape it was going to take. By and by he stepped back from the wheel and said in his usual snarly way:

"Here! See if you've got gumption enough to round her to."

This was simply *bound* to be a success; nothing could prevent it; for he had never allowed me to round the boat to before; consequently, no matter how I might do the thing, he could find free fault with it. He stood back there with his greedy eye on me, and the result was what might have been foreseen: I lost my head in a quarter of a minute, and didn't know what I was about; I started too early to bring the boat around, but detected a green gleam of joy in Brown's eye, and corrected my mistake. I started around once more while too high up, but corrected myself again in time. I made other false moves, and still managed to save myself; but at last I grew so confused and anxious that I tumbled into the very worst blunder of all—I got too far *down* before beginning to fetch the boat around. Brown's chance was come.

His face turned red with passion; he made one bound, hurled me across the house with a sweep of his arm, spun the wheel down, and began to pour out a stream of vituperation upon me which lasted till he was out of breath. In the course of this speech he called me all the different kinds of hard names he could think of, and once or twice I thought he was even going to swear—but he had never done that, and he didn't this time. "Dod dern" was the nearest he ventured to the luxury of swearing, for he had been brought up with a wholesome respect for future fire and brimstone.

That was an uncomfortable hour; for there was a big audience on the hurricane-deck. When I went to bed that night, I killed Brown in seventeen different ways—all of them new.

TWO trips later I got into serious trouble.

Brown was steering; I was "pulling down." My younger brother appeared on the hurricane-deck, and shouted to Brown to stop at some landing or other, a mile or so below. Brown gave no intimation that he had heard anything. But that was his way: he never condescended to take notice of an under-clerk. The wind was blowing; Brown was deaf (although he always pretended he wasn't), and I very much doubted if he had heard the order. If I had had two heads, I would have spoken; but as I had only one, it seemed judicious to take care of it; so I kept still.

Presently, sure enough, we went sailing by that plantation. Captain Klinefelter appeared on the deck, and said:

"Let her come around, sir, let her come around. Didn't Henry tell you to land here?"

"*No, sir!*"

"I sent him up to do it."

"He *did* come up; and that's all the good it done, the dod-derned fool. He never said anything."

"Didn't *you* hear him?" asked the captain of me.

Of course I didn't want to be mixed up in this business, but there was no way to avoid it; so I said:

"Yes, sir."

I knew what Brown's next remark would be, before he uttered it. It was:

"Shut your mouth! You never heard anything of the kind."

I closed my mouth, according to instructions. An hour later Henry entered the pilot-house, unaware of what had been going on. He was a thoroughly inoffensive boy, and I was sorry to see him come, for I knew Brown would have no pity on him. Brown began, straightway:

"Here! Why didn't you tell me we'd got to land at that plantation?"

"I did tell you, Mr. Brown."

"It's a lie!"

I said:

"You lie, yourself. He did tell you."

Brown glared at me in unaffected surprise; and for as much as a moment he was entirely speechless; then he shouted to me:

"I'll attend to your case in a half a minute!" then to Henry, "And you leave the pilot-house; out with you!"

It was pilot law, and must be obeyed. The boy started out, and even had his foot on the upper step outside the door, when Brown, with a sudden access of fury, picked up a ten-pound lump of coal and sprang after him; but I was between, with a heavy stool, and I hit Brown a good honest blow which stretched him out.

I had committed the crime of crimes—I had lifted my hand against a pilot on duty! I supposed I was booked for the penitentiary sure, and couldn't be booked any surer if I went on and squared my long account with this person while I had the chance; consequently I stuck to him and pounded him with my fists a considerable time. I do not know how long, the pleasure of it probably made it seem longer than it really was; but in the end he struggled free and jumped up and sprang to the wheel; a very natural solicitude, for, all this time, here was this steamboat tearing down the river at the rate of fifteen miles an hour and nobody at the helm! However, Eagle Bend was two miles wide at this bank-full stage, and correspondingly long and deep: and the boat was steering herself straight down the middle and taking no chances. Still, that was only luck—a body *might* have found her charging into the woods.

Perceiving at a glance that the *Pennsylvania* was in no danger, Brown gathered up the big spy-glass, war-club fashion, and ordered me out of the pilot-house with more than Comanche bluster. But I was not afraid of him now; so, instead of going, I tarried, and criticized his grammar. I reformed his ferocious speeches for him, and put them into good English, calling his attention to the advantage of pure English over the bastard dialect of the Pennsylvania collieries whence he was extracted. He could have done his part to admiration in a cross-fire of mere vituperation, of course; but he was not equipped for this species of controversy; so he presently laid aside his glass and took the wheel, muttering and shaking his head; and I retired to the bench. The racket had brought everybody to the hurricane-deck, and I trembled when I saw the old captain looking up from amid the crowd. I said to myself, "Now I *am* done for!" for although, as a rule, he was so fatherly and indulgent toward the boat's family, and so patient of minor shortcomings, he could be stern enough when the fault was worth it.

I tried to imagine what he *would* do to a cub pilot who had been guilty of such a crime as mine, committed on a boat guard-deep with costly freight and alive with passengers. Our watch was nearly ended. I thought I would go and hide somewhere till I got a chance to slide ashore. So I slipped out of the pilot-house, and down the steps, and around to the texas-door, and was in the act of gliding within, when the captain confronted me! I dropped my head, and he stood over me in silence a moment or two, then said impressively:

"Follow me."

I dropped into his wake; he led the way to his parlor in the forward end of the texas. We were alone, now. He closed the after door; then moved slowly to the forward one and closed that. He sat down; I stood before him. He looked at me some little time, then said:

"So you have been fighting Mr. Brown?"

I answered meekly:

"Yes, sir."

"Do you know that that is a very serious matter?"

"Yes, sir."

"Are you aware that this boat was plowing down the river fully five minutes with no one at the wheel?"

"Yes, sir."

"Did you strike him first?"

"Yes, sir."

"What with?"

"A stool, sir."

"Hard?"

"Middling, sir."

"Did it knock him down?"

"He—he fell, sir."

"Did you follow it up? Did you do anything further?"

"Yes, sir."

"What did you do?"

"Pounded him, sir."

"Pounded him?"

"Yes, sir."

"Did you pound him much? that is, severely?"

"One might call it that, sir, maybe."

"I'm deucèd glad of it! Hark ye, never mention that I said that. You have been guilty of a great crime; and don't you ever be guilty of it again, on this boat. *But*—lay for him ashore! Give him a good sound thrashing, do you hear? I'll pay the expenses. Now go—and mind you, not a word of this to anybody. Clear out with you! You've been guilty of a great crime, you whelp!"

I slid out, happy with the sense of a close shave and a mighty deliverance; and I heard him laughing to himself and slapping his fat thighs after I had closed his door.

When Brown came off watch he went straight to the captain, who was talking with some passengers on the boiler-deck, and demanded that I be put ashore in New Orleans—and added:

"I'll never turn a wheel on this boat again while that cub stays."

The captain said:

"But he needn't come round when you are on watch, Mr. Brown."

"I won't even stay on the same boat with him. *One* of us has got to go ashore."

"Very well," said the captain, "let it be yourself," and resumed his talk with the passengers.

During the brief remainder of the trip I knew how an emancipated slave feels, for I was an emancipated slave myself. While we lay at landings I listened to George Ealer's flute, or to his readings from his two Bibles, that is to say, Goldsmith and Shakespeare, or I played chess with him—and would have beaten him sometimes, only he always took back his last move and ran the game out differently.

WE lay three days in New Orleans, but the captain did not succeed in finding another

pilot, so he proposed that I should stand a daylight watch and leave the night watches to George Ealer. But I was afraid; I had never stood a watch of any sort by myself, and I believed I should be sure to get into trouble in the head of some chute, or ground the boat in a near cut through some bar or other. Brown remained in his place, but he would not travel with me. So the captain gave me an order on the captain of the *A. T. Lacey* for a passage to St. Louis, and said he would find a new pilot there and my steersman's berth could then be resumed. The *Lacey* was to leave a couple of days after the *Pennsylvania*.

The night before the *Pennsylvania* left, Henry and I sat chatting on a freight pile on the levee till midnight. The subject of the chat, mainly, was one which I think we had not exploited before—steamboat disasters. One was then on its way to us, little as we suspected it; the water which was to make the steam which should cause it was washing past some point fifteen hundred miles up the river while we talked—but it would arrive at the right time and the right place. We doubted if persons not clothed with authority were of much use in cases of disaster and attendant panic, still they might be of *some* use; so we decided that if a disaster ever fell within our experience we would at least stick to the boat, and give such minor service as chance might throw in the

way. Henry remembered this, afterward, when the disaster came, and acted accordingly.

The *Lacey* started up the river two days behind the *Pennsylvania*. We touched at Greenville, Mississippi, a couple of days out, and somebody shouted:

"The *Pennsylvania* is blown up at Ship Island, and a hundred and fifty lives lost!"

At Napoleon, Arkansas, the same evening, we got an extra, issued by a Memphis paper, which gave some particulars. It mentioned my brother, and said he was not hurt.

Further up the river we got a later extra. My brother was again mentioned, but this time as being hurt beyond help. We did not get full details of the catastrophe until we reached Memphis. This is the sorrowful story:

It was six o'clock on a hot summer morning. The *Pennsylvania* was creeping along, north of Ship Island, about sixty miles below Memphis, on a half-head of steam, towing a wood-flat which was fast being emptied. George Ealer was in the pilot-house—alone, I think; the second engineer and a striker had the watch in the engine-room; the second mate had the watch on deck; George Black, Mr. Wood, and my brother, clerks, were asleep, as were also Brown and the head engineer, the carpenter, the chief mate, and one striker; Captain Klinefelter was in the barber's chair, and the barber was preparing to shave him. There were

A TIMBER RAFT

a good many cabin passengers aboard, and three or four hundred deck passengers—so it was said at the time—and not very many of them were astir. The wood being nearly all out of the flat now, Ealer rang to "come ahead" full of steam, and the next moment four of the eight boilers exploded with a thunderous crash, and the whole forward third of the boat was hoisted toward the sky! The main part of the mass, with the chimneys, dropped upon the boat again, a mountain of riddled and chaotic rubbish—and then, after a little, fire broke out.

Many people were flung to considerable distances and fell in the river; among these were Mr. Wood and my brother and the carpenter. The carpenter was still stretched upon his mattress when he struck the water seventy-five feet from the boat. Brown, the pilot, and George Black, chief clerk, were never seen or heard of after the explosion. The barber's chair, with Captain Klinefelter in it and unhurt, was left with its back overhanging vacancy—everything forward of it, floor and all, had disappeared; and the stupefied barber, who was also unhurt, stood with one toe projecting over space, still stirring his lather unconsciously and saying not a word.

When George Ealer saw the chimneys plunging aloft in front of him, he knew what the matter was; so he muffled his face in the lapels of his coat, and pressed both hands there tightly to keep this protection in its place so that no steam could get to his nose or mouth. He had ample time to attend to these details while he was going up and returning. He presently landed on top of the unexploded boilers, forty feet below the former pilot-house, accompanied by his wheel and a rain of other stuff, and enveloped in a cloud of scalding steam. All of the many who breathed that steam died; none escaped. But Ealer breathed none of it. He made his way to the free air as quickly as he could; and when the steam cleared away he returned and climbed up on the boilers again, and patiently hunted out each and every one of his chessmen and the several joints of his flute.

By this time the fire was beginning to threaten. Shrieks and groans filled the air. A great many persons had been scalded, a great many crippled; the explosion had driven an iron crowbar through one man's body—I think they said he was a priest. He did not die at once, and his sufferings were very dreadful. A young French naval cadet of fifteen, son of a French admiral, was fearfully scalded, but bore his tortures manfully. Both mates were badly scalded, but they stood to their posts, nevertheless. They drew the wood-boat aft, and they and the captain fought back the frantic herd of frightened immigrants till the wounded could be brought there and placed in safety first.

When Mr. Wood and Henry fell in the water they struck out for shore, which was only a few hundred yards away; but Henry presently said he believed he was not hurt (what an unaccountable error!) and therefore would swim back to the boat and help save the wounded. So they parted and Henry returned.

By this time the fire was making fierce headway, and several persons who were imprisoned under the ruins were begging piteously for help. All efforts to conquer the fire proved fruitless, so the buckets were presently thrown aside and the officers fell to with axes and tried to cut the prisoners out. A striker was one of the captives; he said he was not injured, but could not free himself, and when he saw that the fire was likely to drive away the workers he begged that some one would shoot him, and thus save him from the more dreadful death. The fire did drive the axmen away, and they had to listen, helpless, to this poor fellow's supplications till the flames ended his miseries.

The fire drove all into the wood-flat that could be accommodated there; it was cut adrift then, and it and the burning steamer floated down the river toward Ship Island. They moored the flat at the head of the island, and there, unsheltered from the blazing sun, the half-naked occupants had to remain, without food or stimulants, or help for their hurts, during the rest of the day. A steamer came along, finally, and carried the unfortunates to Memphis, and there the most lavish assistance was at once forthcoming. By this time Henry was

insensible. The physicians examined his injuries and saw that they were fatal, and naturally turned their main attention to patients who could be saved.

Forty of the wounded were placed upon pallets on the floor of a great public hall, and among these was Henry. There the ladies of Memphis came every day, with flowers, fruits, and dainties and delicacies of all kinds, and there they remained and nursed the wounded. All the physicians stood watches there, and all the medical students; and the rest of the town furnished money, or whatever else was wanted. And Memphis knew how to do all these things well; for many a disaster like the *Pennsylvania*'s had happened near her doors; and she was experienced, above all other cities on the river, in the gracious office of the Good Samaritan.

The sight I saw when I entered that large hall was new and strange to me. Two long rows of prostrate forms—more than forty in all—and every face and head a shapeless wad of loose raw cotton. It was a gruesome spectacle. I watched there six days and nights, and a very melancholy experience it was. There was one daily incident which was peculiarly depressing: this was the removal of the doomed to a chamber apart. It was done in order that the *morale* of the other patients might not be injuriously affected by seeing one of their number in the death-agony. The fated one was always carried out with as little stir as possible, and the stretcher was always hidden from sight by a wall of assistants; but no matter: everybody knew what that cluster of bent forms, with its muffled step and its slow movement, meant; and all eyes watched it wistfully, and a shudder went abreast of it like a wave.

I saw many poor fellows removed to the "death-room," and saw them no more afterward. But I saw our chief mate carried thither more than once. His hurts were frightful, especially his scalds. He was clothed in linseed oil and raw cotton to his waist, and resembled nothing human. He was often out of his mind; and then his pains would make him rave and shout and sometimes shriek. Then, after a period of dumb exhaustion, his disordered imagination would suddenly transform the great apartment into a forecastle, and the hurrying throng of nurses into the crew; and he would come to a sitting posture and shout, "Hump yourselves, *hump* yourselves, you petrifactions, snail-bellies, pall-bearers! going to be all *day* getting that hatful of freight out?" and supplement this explosion with a firmament-obliterating irruption of profanity which nothing could stay or stop till his crater was empty. And now and then while these frenzies possessed him, he would tear off handfuls of the cotton and expose his cooked flesh to view. It was horrible. It was bad for the others, of course—this noise and these exhibitions; so the doctors tried to give him morphine to quiet him. But, in his mind or out of it, he would not take it. He said his wife had been killed by that treacherous drug, and he would die before he would take it. He suspected that the doctors were concealing it in his ordinary medicines and in his water—so he ceased from putting either to his lips. Once, when he had been without water during two sweltering days, he took the dipper in his hand, and the sight of the limpid fluid, and the misery of his thirst, tempted him almost beyond his strength; but he mastered himself and threw it away, and after that he allowed no more to be brought near him. Three times I saw him carried to the death-room, insensible and supposed to be dying; but each time he revived, cursed his attendants, and demanded to be taken back. He lived to be mate of a steamboat again.

But he was the only one who went to the death-room and returned alive. Dr. Peyton, a principal physician, and rich in all the attributes that go to constitute high and flawless character, did all that educated judgment and trained skill could do for Henry; but, as the newspapers had said in the beginning, his hurts were past help. On the evening of the sixth day his wandering mind busied itself with matters far away, and his nerveless fingers "picked at his coverlet." His hour had struck; we bore him to the death-room, poor boy.

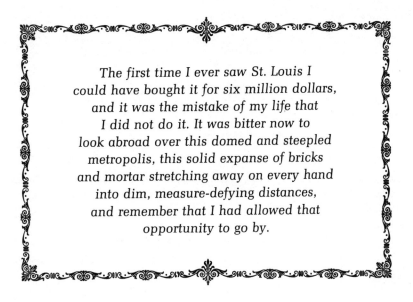

The first time I ever saw St. Louis I
could have bought it for six million dollars,
and it was the mistake of my life that
I did not do it. It was bitter now to
look abroad over this domed and steepled
metropolis, this solid expanse of bricks
and mortar stretching away on every hand
into dim, measure-defying distances,
and remember that I had allowed that
opportunity to go by.

PART THREE

IN due course I got my license. I was a pilot now, full-fledged. I dropped into casual employments no misfortunes resulting, intermittent work gave place to steady and protracted engagements. Time drifted smoothly and prosperously on, and I supposed—and hoped—that I was going to follow the river the rest of my days, and die at the wheel when my mission was ended. But by and by the war came, commerce was suspended, my occupation was gone.

I had to seek another livelihood. So I became a silver-miner in Nevada; next, a newspaper reporter; next, a gold-miner in California; next, a reporter in San Francisco; next, a special correspondent in the Sandwich Islands; next, a roving correspondent in Europe and the East; next, an instructional torch-bearer on the lecture platform; and, finally, I became a scribbler of books, and an immovable fixture among the other rocks of New England.

In so few words have I disposed of the twenty-one slow-drifting years that have come and gone since I last looked from the windows of a pilot-house. . . .

After twenty-one years' absence I felt a very strong desire to see the river again, and the steamboats, and such of the boys as might be left; so I resolved to go out there. I enlisted a poet for company, and a stenographer to "take him down," and started westward about the middle of April.

As I proposed to make notes, with a view to printing, I took some thought as to methods of procedure. I reflected that if I were recognized, on the river, I should not be as free to go and come, talk, inquire, and spy around, as I should be if unknown; I remembered that it was the custom of steamboatmen in the old times to load up the confiding stranger with the most picturesque and admirable lies, and put the sophisticated friend off with dull and ineffectual facts: so I concluded that, from a business point of view, it would be an advantage to disguise our party with fictitious names. The idea was certainly good, but it bred infinite bother; for although Smith, Jones, and Johnson are easy names to remember when there is no occasion to remember them, it is next to impossible to recollect them when they are

wanted. How do criminals manage to keep a brand-new *alias* in mind? This is a great mystery. I was innocent; and yet was seldom able to lay my hand on my new name when it was needed; and it seemed to me that if I had had a crime on my conscience to further confuse me, I could never have kept the name by me at all.

We left per Pennsylvania Railroad, at 8 A.M. April 18. . . .

We reached St. Louis at ten o'clock at night. At the counter of the hotel I tendered a hurriedly invented fictitious name, with a miserable attempt at careless ease. The clerk paused, and inspected me in the compassionate way in which one inspects a respectable person who is found in doubtful circumstances; then he said:

"It's all right; I know what sort of a room you want. Used to clerk at the St. James, in New York."

An unpromising beginning for a fraudulent career! We started to the supper-room, and met two other men whom I had known elsewhere. How odd and unfair it is: wicked impostors go around lecturing under my *nom de guerre*, and nobody suspects them; but when an honest man attempts an imposture, he is exposed at once.

One thing seemed plain: we must start down the river the next day, if people who could not be deceived were going to crop up at this rate: an unpalatable disappointment, for we had hoped to have a week in St. Louis. The Southern was a good hotel, and we could have had a comfortable time there. It is large and well conducted, and its decorations do not make one cry, as do those of the vast Palmer House, in Chicago. True, the billiard-tables were of the Old Silurian Period, and the cues and balls of the Post-Pliocene; but there was refreshment in this, not discomfort; for there are rest and healing in the contemplation of antiquities.

The most notable absence observable in the billiard-room was the absence of the riverman. If he was there, he had taken in his sign; he was in disguise. I saw there none of the swell airs and graces, and ostentatious displays of money, and pompous squanderings of

it, which used to distinguish the steamboat crowd from the dry-land crowd in the bygone days, in the thronged billiard-rooms of St. Louis. In those times the principal saloons were always populous with river-men; given fifty players present, thirty or thirty-five were likely to be from the river. But I suspected that the ranks were thin now, and the steamboatmen no longer an aristocracy. Why, in my time they used to call the "barkeep" Bill, or Joe, or Tom, and slap him on the shoulder; I watched for that. But none of these people did it. Manifestly, a glory that once was had dissolved and vanished away in these twenty-one years. . . .

Next morning we drove around town in the rain. The city seemed but little changed. It *was* greatly changed, but it did not seem so; because in St. Louis, as in London and Pittsburg, you can't persuade a new thing to look new; the coal-smoke turns it into an antiquity the moment you take your hand off it. The place had just about doubled its size since I was a resident of it, and was now become a city of four hundred thousand inhabitants; still, in the solid business parts, it looked about as it had looked formerly. Yet I am sure there is not as much smoke in St. Louis now as there used to be. The smoke used to bank itself in a dense billowy black canopy over the town, and hide the sky from view. This shelter is very much thinner now; still, there is a sufficiency of smoke there, I think. I heard no complaint.

However, on the outskirts changes were apparent enough; notably in dwelling-house architecture. The fine new homes are noble and beautiful and modern. They stand by themselves, too, with green lawns around them; whereas the dwellings of a former day are packed together in blocks, and are all of one pattern, with windows all alike, set in an arched framework of twisted stone; a sort of house which was handsome enough when it was rarer.

There was another change—the Forest Park. This was new to me. It is beautiful and very extensive, and has the excellent merit of having been made mainly by nature. There are other parks, and fine ones, notably Tower Grove and the Botanical Gardens; for St. Louis interested herself in such improvements at an earlier day than did the most of our cities.

The first time I ever saw St. Louis I could have bought it for six million dollars, and it was the mistake of my life that I did not do it. It was bitter now to look abroad over this domed and steepled metropolis, this solid expanse of bricks and mortar stretching away on every hand into dim, measure-defying distances, and remember that I had allowed that opportunity to go by. Why I should have allowed it to go by seems, of course, foolish and inexplicable to-day, at a first glance; yet there were reasons at the time to justify this course.

A Scotchman, Hon. Charles Augustus Murray, writing some forty-five or fifty years ago, said: "The streets are narrow, ill-paved, and ill-lighted." Those streets are narrow still, of course; many of them are ill-paved yet; but the reproach of ill-lighting cannot be repeated now. The "Catholic New Church" was the only notable building then, and Mr. Murray was confidently called upon to admire it, with its "species of Grecian portico, surmounted by a kind of steeple, much too diminutive in its proportions, and surmounted by sundry ornaments" which the unimaginative Scotchman found himself "quite unable to describe"; and therefore was grateful when a German tourist helped him out with the exclamation: "By —, they look exactly like bed-posts!" St. Louis is well equipped with stately and noble public buildings now, and the little church, which the people used to be so proud of, lost its importance a long time ago. Still, this would not surprise Mr. Murray if he could come back; for he prophesied the coming greatness of St. Louis with strong confidence.

The further we drove in our inspection tour, the more sensibly I realized how the city had grown since I had seen it last; changes in detail became steadily more apparent and frequent than at first, too: changes uniformly evidencing progress, energy, prosperity.

But the change of changes was on the "levee." This time, a departure from the rule. Half a dozen sound-asleep steamboats where I used to see a solid mile of wide-awake ones! This was melancholy, this was woeful. The absence of the pervading and jocund steamboatman from the billiard-saloon was explained. He was absent because he is no more. His occupation is gone, his power has passed away, he is absorbed into the common herd; he grinds at the mill, a shorn Samson and inconspicuous. Half a dozen lifeless steamboats, a mile of empty wharves, a negro, fatigued with whisky, stretched asleep in a wide and soundless vacancy, where the serried hosts of commerce used to contend! Here was desolation indeed. . . .

MY idea was to tarry awhile in every town between St. Louis and New Orleans. To do this, it would be necessary to go from place to place by the short packet lines. It was an easy plan to make, and would have been an easy one to follow, twenty years ago—but not now. There are wide intervals between boats, these days.

I wanted to begin with the interesting old French settlements of St. Genevieve and Kaskaskia, sixty miles below St. Louis. There was only one boat advertised for that section—a Grand Tower packet. Still, one boat was enough; so we went down to look at her. She was a venerable rack-heap, and a fraud to boot; for she was playing herself for personal property, whereas the good honest dirt was so thickly caked all over her that she was righteously taxable as real estate. There are places in New England where her hurricane-deck would be worth a hundred and fifty dollars an acre. The soil on her forecastle was quite good—the new crop of wheat was already springing from the cracks in protected places. The companionway was of a dry sandy character, and would have been well suited for grapes, with a southern exposure and a little subsoiling. The soil of the boiler-deck was thin and rocky, but good enough for grazing purposes. A colored boy was on watch here—nobody else visible. We gathered from him that this calm craft would go as advertised, "if she got her trip"; if she didn't get it, she would wait for it.

"Has she got any of her trip?"

"Bless you, no boss! She ain't unloadened, yit. She only come in dis mawnin'."

He was uncertain as to when she might get her trip, but thought it might be to-morrow or maybe next day. This would not answer at all; so we had to give up the novelty of sailing down the river on a farm. We had one more arrow in our quiver: a Vicksburg packet, the *Gold Dust*, was to leave at 5 P.M. We took passage in her for Memphis, and gave up the idea of stopping off here and there, as being impracticable. She was neat, clean, and comfortable. We camped on the boiler-deck, and bought some cheap literature to kill time with. The vendor was a venerable Irishman with a benevolent face and a tongue that worked easily in the socket, and from him we learned that he had lived in St. Louis thirty-four years and had never been across the river during that period. Then he wandered into a very flowing lecture, filled with classic names and allusions, which was quite wonderful for fluency until the fact became rather apparent that this was not the first time, nor perhaps the fiftieth, that the speech had been delivered. He was a good deal of a character, and much better company than the sappy literature he was selling. A random remark, connecting Irishmen and beer, brought this nugget of information out of him:

"They don't drink it, sir. They *can't* drink it, sir. Give an Irishman lager for a month, and he's a dead man. An Irishman is lined with copper, and the beer corrodes it. But whisky polishes the copper and is the saving of him, sir." . . .

Presently I ascended to the hurricane-deck and cast a longing glance toward the pilot-house.

After a close study of the face of the pilot on watch, I was satisfied that I had never seen him before, so I went up there. The pilot inspected me; I reinspected the pilot. These customary preliminaries over, I sat down on the high bench, and he faced about and went on with his work. Every detail of the pilot-house was familiar to me, with one exception—a large-mouthed tube under the breast-board. I puzzled over that thing a considerable time; then gave up and asked what it was for.

"To hear the engine-bells through."

It was another good contrivance which ought to have been invented half a century sooner. So I was thinking when the pilot asked:

"Do you know what this rope is for?"

I managed to get around this question without committing myself.

"Is this the first time you were ever in a pilot-house?"

I crept under that one.

"Where are you from?"

"New England."

"First time you have ever been West?"

I climbed over this one.

"If you take an interest in such things, I can tell you what all these things are for."

I said I should like it.

"This," putting his hand on a backing-bell rope, "is to sound the fire-alarm; this," putting his hand on a go-ahead bell, "is to call the texas-tender; this one," indicating the whistle-lever, "is to call the captain"—and so he went on, touching one object after another and reeling off his tranquil spool of lies.

I had never felt so like a passenger before. I thanked him, with emotion, for each new fact, and wrote it down in my note-book. The pilot warmed to his opportunity, and proceeded to load me up in the good old-fashioned way. At times I was afraid he was going to rupture his invention; but it always stood the strain, and he pulled through all right. He drifted, by easy stages, into revealments of the river's marvelous eccentricities of one sort and another, and backed them up with some pretty gigantic illustrations. For instance:

"Do you see that little boulder sticking out of the water yonder? Well, when I first came on the river, that was a solid ridge of rock, over sixty feet high and two miles long. All washed away but that." [This with a sigh.]

I had a mighty impulse to destroy him, but it seemed to me that killing, in any ordinary way, would be too good for him.

Once, when an odd-looking craft, with a vast coal-scuttle slanting aloft on the end of a beam, was steaming by in the distance, he indifferently drew attention to it, as one might to an object grown wearisome through familiarity, and observed that it was an "alligator-boat."

"An alligator-boat? What's it for?"

"To dredge out alligators with."

"Are they so thick as to be troublesome?"

"Well, not now, because the government keeps them down. But they used to be. Not everywhere; but in favorite places, here and there, where the river is wide and shoal—like Plum Point, and Stack Island, and so on—places they call alligator-beds."

"Did they actually impede navigation?"

"Years ago, yes, in very low water; there was hardly a trip, then that we didn't get aground on alligators."

It seemed to me that I should certainly have to get out my tomahawk. However, I restrained myself and said:

"It must have been dreadful."

"Yes, it was one of the main difficulties about piloting. It was so hard to tell anything about the water; the d—d things shift around so—never lie still five minutes at a time. You can tell a wind-reef, straight off, by the look of it; you can tell a break; you can tell a sand-reef—that's all easy; but an alligator-reef doesn't show up, worth anything. Nine times in ten you can't tell where the water is; and when you *do* see where it is, like as not it ain't there when *you* get there, the devils have swapped around so, meantime. Of course there were some few pilots that could judge of alligator-water nearly as well as they could of any other kind, but they had to have natural talent for it; it wasn't a thing a body could *learn*, you had to be born with it. Let me see: There was Ben Thornburg, and Beck Jolly, and Squire Bell, and Horace Bixby, and Major Downing, and John Stevenson, and Billy Gordon, and Jim Brady, and George Ealer, and Billy Young-blood—all A 1 alligator-pilots. They could tell alligator-water as far as another Christian could tell whisky. Read it? Ah, *couldn't* they, though! I only wish I had as many dollars as

they could read alligator-water a mile and a half off. Yes, and it paid them to do it, too. A good alligator-pilot could always get fifteen hundred dollars a month. Nights, other people had to lay up for alligators, but those fellows never laid up for alligators; they never laid up for anything but fog. They could *smell* the best alligator-water—so it was said. I don't know whether it was so or not, and I think a body's got his hands full enough if he sticks to just what he knows himself, without going around backing up other people's say-so's, though there's a plenty that ain't backward about doing it, as long as they can roust out something wonderful to tell. Which is not the style of Robert Styles, by as much as three fathom—maybe quarter-*less*."

[My! Was this Rob Styles? This mustached and stately figure? A slim enough cub, in my time. How he has improved in comeliness in five-and-twenty years—and in the noble art of inflating his facts.] After these musings, I said aloud:

"I should think that dredging out the alligators wouldn't have done much good, because they could come back again right away."

"If you had had as much experience of alligators as I have, you wouldn't talk like that. You dredge an alligator once and he's *convinced*. It's the last you hear of *him*. He wouldn't come back for pie. If there's one thing that an alligator is more down on than another, it's being dredged. Besides, they were not simply shoved out of the way; the most of the scoopful were scooped aboard; they emptied them into the hold; and when they had got a trip, they took them to Orleans to the government works."

"What for?"

"Why, to make soldier-shoes out of their hides. All the government shoes are made of alligator-hide. It makes the best shoes in the world. They last five years, and they won't absorb water. The alligator fishery is a government monopoly. All the alligators are government property—just like the live-oaks. You cut down a live-oak, and government fines you fifty dollars; you kill an alligator, and up you go for misprision of treason—lucky duck if they don't hang you, too. And they will, if you're a Democrat. The buzzard is the sacred bird of the South, and you can't touch him; the alligator is the sacred bird of the government, and you've got to let him alone."

"Do you ever get aground on the alligators now?"

"Oh, no! it hasn't happened for years."

"Well, then, why do they still keep the alligator-boats in service?"

"Just for police duty—nothing more. They merely go up and down now and then. The present generation of alligators know them as easy as a burglar knows a roundsman; when they see one coming, they break camp and go for the woods."

After rounding out and finishing up and polishing off the alligator business, he dropped easily and comfortably into the historical vein, and told of some tremendous feats of half a dozen old-time steamboats of his acquaintance, dwelling at special length upon a certain extraordinary performance of his chief favorite among this distinguished fleet—and then adding:

"That boat was the *Cyclone*—last trip she ever made—she sunk, that very trip; captain was Tom Ballou, the most immortal liar that ever I struck. He couldn't ever seem to tell the truth, in *any* kind of weather. Why, he would make you fairly shudder. He *was* the most scandalous liar! I left him, finally; I couldn't stand it. The proverb says, 'like master, like man'; and if you stay with that kind of a man, you'll come under suspicion by and by, just as sure as you live. He paid first-class wages; but said I, 'What's wages when your reputation's in danger?' So I let the wages go, and froze to my reputation. And I've never regretted it. Reputation's worth everything, ain't it? That's the way I look at it. He had more selfish organs than any seven men in the world —all packed in the stern-sheets of his skull, of course, where they belonged. They weighed down the back of his head so that it made his nose tilt up in the air. People thought it was vanity, but it wasn't, it was malice. If you only saw his foot, you'd take him to be nineteen feet high, but he wasn't; it was because his foot was out of drawing. He was intended to be nineteen feet high, no doubt, if his foot was made first, but he didn't get there; he was only five feet ten. That's what he was, and that's what he is. You take the lies out of him, and he'll shrink to the size of your hat; you take the malice out of him, and he'll disappear. That *Cyclone* was a rattler to go, and the sweetest thing to steer that ever walked the waters. Set her amidships, in a big river, and just let her go; it was all you had to do. She would hold herself on a star all night, if you let her alone. You couldn't ever feel her rudder. It wasn't any more labor to steer her than it is to count the Republican vote in a South Carolina election. One morning, just at daybreak, the last trip she ever made, they took her rudder aboard to mend it; I didn't know anything about it; I backed her out from the wood-yard and went a-weaving down the river all serene. When I had gone about twenty-three miles, and made four horribly crooked crossings—"

"Without any rudder?"

"Yes—old Captain Tom appeared on the roof and began to find fault with me for running such a dark night—"

"Such a *dark* night? Why, you said—"

"Never mind what I said—'twas as dark as Egypt *now*, though pretty soon the moon began to rise, and—"

"You mean the *sun*—because you started out just at break of—look here! Was this *before* you quitted the captain on account of his lying, or—"

"It was before—oh, a long time before. And as I was saying, he—"

"But was this the trip she sunk, or was—"

"Oh, no! months afterward. And so the old man, he—"

"Then she made *two* last trips, because you said—"

He stepped back from the wheel, swabbing away his perspiration, and said:

"Here!" (calling me by name) "*you* take her and lie awhile—you're handier at it than I am: Trying to play yourself for a stranger and an

innocent! Why, I knew you before you had spoken seven words; and I made up my mind to find out what was your little game. It was to *draw me out*. Well, I let you, didn't I? Now take the wheel and finish the watch; and next time play fair, and you won't have to work your passage."

Thus ended the fictitious-name business. And not six hours out from St. Louis! but I had gained a privilege, anyway, for I had been itching to get my hands on the wheel, from the beginning. I seemed to have forgotten the river, but I hadn't forgotten how to steer a steamboat, nor how to enjoy it, either. . . .

ALL day we swung along down the river, and had the stream almost wholly to ourselves. Formerly, at such a stage of the water, we should have passed acres of lumber-rafts and dozens of big coal-barges; also occasional little trading-scows, peddling along from farm to farm, with the peddler's family on board; possibly a random scow, bearing a humble Hamlet & Co. on an itinerant dramatic trip. But these were all absent. Far along in the day we saw one steamboat; just one, and no more. She was lying at rest in the shade, within the wooded mouth of the Obion River. The spy-glass revealed the fact that she was named for me—or he was named for me, whichever you prefer. As this was the first time I had ever encountered this species of honor, it seems excusable to mention it, and at the same time call the attention of the authorities to the tardiness of my recognition of it.

Noted a big change in the river at Island 21. It was a very large island, and used to lie out toward midstream; but it is joined fast to the main shore now, and has retired from business as an island.

As we approached famous and formidable Plum Point darkness fell, but that was nothing to shudder about—in these modern times. For now the national government has turned the Mississippi into a sort of two-thousand-mile torchlight procession. In the head of every crossing, and in the foot of every crossing, the government has set up a clear-burning lamp. You are never entirely in the dark, now; there is always a beacon in sight, either before you, or behind you, or abreast. One might almost say that lamps have been squandered there. Dozens of crossings are lighted which were not shoal when they were created, and have never been shoal since; crossings so plain, too, and also so straight, that a stream-boat can take herself through them without any help, after she has been through once. Lamps in such places are of course not wasted; it is much more convenient and comfortable for a pilot to hold on them than on a spread of formless blackness that won't stay still; and money is saved to the boat, at the same time, for she can of course make more miles with her rudder amidships than she can with it squared across her stern and holding her back.

But this thing has knocked the romance out of piloting, to a large extent. It and some other things together have knocked all the romance out of it. For instance, the peril from snags is not now what it once was. The government's snag-boats go patrolling up and down, in these matter-of-fact days, pulling the river's teeth; they have rooted out all the old clusters which made many localities so formidable; and they allow no new ones to collect. Formerly, if your boat got away from you, on a black night, and broke for the woods, it was an anxious time with you; so was it, also, when you were groping your way through solidified darkness in a narrow chute, but all that is changed now— you flash out your electric light, transform night into day in the twinkling of an eye, and your perils and anxieties are at an end. Horace Bixby and George Ritchie have charted the crossings and laid out the courses by compass; they have invented a lamp to go with the chart, and have patented the whole. With these helps, one may run in the fog now, with considerable security, and with a confidence unknown in the old days.

With these abundant beacons, and the banishment of snags, plenty of daylight in a box and ready to be turned on whenever needed,

and a chart compass to fight the fog with, piloting, at a good stage of water, is now nearly as safe and simple as driving stage, and is hardly more than three times as romantic.

And now, in these new days of infinite change, the Anchor Line have raised the captain above the pilot by giving him the bigger wages of the two. This was going far, but they have not stopped there. They have decreed that the pilot shall remain at his post, and stand his watch clear through, whether the boat be under way or tied up to the shore. We, that were once the aristocrats of the river, can't go to bed now, as we used to do, and sleep while a hundred tons of freight are lugged aboard; no, we must sit in the pilot-house; and keep awake, too. Verily we are being treated like a parcel of mates and engineers. The government has taken away the romance of our calling; the Company has taken away its state and dignity.

Plum Point looked as it had always looked by night, with the exception that now there were beacons to mark the crossings, and also a lot of other lights on the point and along its shore; these latter glinting from the fleet of the United States River Commission, and from a village which the officials have built on the land for offices and for the employees of the service. The military engineers of the Commission have taken upon their shoulders the job of making the Mississippi over again—a job transcended in size by only the original job of creating it. They are building wing-dams here and there to deflect the current; and dikes to confine it in narrower bounds; and other dikes to make it stay there; and for unnumbered miles along the Mississippi they are felling the timber-front for fifty yards back, with the purpose of shaving the bank down to low-water mark with the slant of a house-roof, and ballasting it with stones; and in many places they have protected the wasting shores with rows of piles. One who knows the Mississippi will promptly aver—not aloud but to himself—that ten thousand River Commissions, with the mines of the world at their back, cannot tame that lawless stream, cannot curb it or confine it, cannot say to it, "Go here," or "Go there," and make it obey; cannot save a shore which it has sentenced; cannot bar its path with an obstruction which it will not tear down, dance over, and laugh at. But a discreet man will not put these things into spoken words; for the West Point engineers have not their superiors anywhere; they know all that can be known of their abstruse science; and so, since they conceive that they can fetter and handcuff that river and boss him, it is but wisdom for the unscientific man to keep still, lie low, and wait till they do it. Captain Eads, with his jetties, has done a work at the mouth of the Mississippi which seemed clearly impossible; so we do not feel full confidence now to prophesy against like impossibilities. Otherwise one would pipe out and say the Commission might as well bully the comets in their courses and undertake to make them behave, as try to bully the Mississippi into right and reasonable conduct.

I consulted Uncle Mumford concerning this and cognate matters; and I give here the result, stenographically reported, and therefore to be relied on as being full and correct; except that I have here and there left out remarks which were addressed to the men, such as "*Where in blazes are you going with that barrel now?*" and which seemed to me to break the flow of the written statement, without compensating by adding to its information or its clearness. Not that I have ventured to strike out all such interjections; I have removed only those which were obviously irrelevant; wherever one occurred which I felt any question about, I have judged it safest to let it remain.

UNCLE MUMFORD'S IMPRESSIONS

Uncle Mumford said:

"As long as I have been mate of a steamboat —thirty years—I have watched this river and studied it. Maybe I could have learned more about it at West Point, but if I believe it I wish I may be—*WHAT are you sucking your fingers there for?—Collar that kag of nails!* Four years at West Point, and plenty of books and schooling, will learn a man a good deal, I reckon, but

it won't learn him the river. You turn one of those little European rivers over to this Commission, with its hard bottom and clear water, and it would just be a holiday job for them to wall it, and pile it, and dike it, and tame it down, and boss it around, and make it go wherever they wanted it to, and stay where they put it, and do just as they said, every time. But this ain't that kind of a river. They have started in here with big confidence, and the best intentions in the world; but they are going to get left. What does Ecclesiastes vii 13 say? Says enough to knock *their* little game galley-west, don't it? Now you look at their methods once. There at Devil's Island, in the Upper River, they wanted the water to go one way, the water wanted to go another. So they put up a stone wall. But what does the river care for a stone wall? When it got ready, it just bulged through it. Maybe they can build another that will stay; that is, up there—but not down here they can't. Down here in the Lower River, they drive some pegs to turn the water away from the shore and stop it from slicing off the bank; very well, don't it go straight over and cut somebody else's bank? Certainly. Are they going to peg *all* the banks? Why, they could buy ground and build a new Mississippi cheaper. They are pegging Bulletin Tow-head now. It won't do any good. If the river has got a mortgage on that island, it will foreclose, sure; pegs or no pegs. Away down yonder, they have driven two rows of piles straight through the middle of a dry bar half a mile long, which is forty foot out of the water when the river is low. What do you reckon that is for? If I know, I wish I may land inHUMP *yourself, you son of an undertaker!—out with that coal-oil, now, lively,* LIVELY! And just look at what they are trying to do down there at Milliken's Bend. There's been a cut-off in that section, and Vicksburg is left out in the cold. It's a country town now. The river strikes in below it; and a

boat can't go up to the town except in high water. Well, they are going to build wing-dams in the bend opposite the foot of 103, and throw the water over and cut off the foot of the island and plow down into an old ditch where the river used to be in ancient times; and they think they can persuade the water around that way, and get it to strike in above Vicksburg, as it used to do, and fetch the town back into the world again. That is, they are going to take this whole Mississippi, and twist it around and make it run several miles *up-stream*. Well, you've got to admire men that deal in ideas of that size and can tote them around without crutches; but you haven't got to believe they can *do* such miracles, have you? And yet you ain't absolutely obliged to believe they can't. I reckon the safe way, where a man can afford it, is to *copper the operation*, and at the same time buy enough property in Vicksburg to square you up in case they win. Government is doing a deal for the Mississippi, now—spending loads of money on her. When there used to be four thousand steamboats and ten thousand acres of coal-barges, and rafts, and trading-scows, there wasn't a lantern from St. Paul to New Orleans, and the snags were thicker than bristles on a hog's back; and now, when there's three dozen steamboats and nary barge or raft, government has snatched out all the snags, and lit up the shores like Broadway, and a boat's as safe on the river as she'd be in heaven. And I reckon that by the time there ain't any boats left at all, the Commission will have the old thing all reorganized, and dredged out, and fenced in, and tidied up, to a degree that will make navigation just simply perfect, and absolutely safe and profitable; and all the days will be Sundays, and all the mates will be Sunday-school suWHAT - *in - the - nation - you - fooling - around - there - for, you sons of un-righteousness, heirs of perdition! Going to be a* YEAR *getting that hogshead ashore?. . . .*

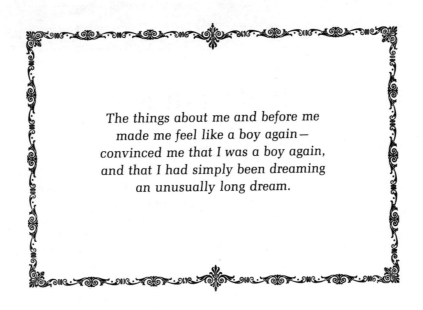

The things about me and before me
made me feel like a boy again —
convinced me that I was a boy again,
and that I had simply been dreaming
an unusually long dream.

PART FOUR

IT was a big river, below Memphis; banks brimming full, everywhere, and very frequently more than full, the waters pouring out over the land, flooding the woods and fields for miles into the interior; and in places to a depth of fifteen feet; signs all about of men's hard work gone to ruin, and all to be done over again, with straitened means and a weakened courage. A melancholy picture, and a continuous one; hundreds of miles of it. Sometimes the beacon lights stood in water three feet deep, in the edge of dense forests which extended for miles without farm, wood-yard, clearing, or break of any kind; which meant that the keeper of the light must come in a skiff a great distance to discharge his trust—and often in desperate weather. Yet I was told that the work is faithfully performed, in all weathers; and not always by men—sometimes by women, if the man is sick or absent. The government furnishes oil, and pays ten or fifteen dollars a month for the lighting and tending. A government boat distributes oil and pays wages once a month.

The Ship Island region was as woodsy and tenantless as ever. The island has ceased to be an island; has joined itself compactly to the main shore, and wagons travel now where the steamboats used to navigate. No signs left of the wreck of the *Pennsylvania*. Some farmer will turn up her bones with his plow one day, no doubt, and be surprised.

We were getting down now into the migrating Negro region. These poor people could never travel when they were slaves; so they make up for the privation now. They stay on a plantation till the desire to travel seizes them; then they pack up, hail a steamboat, and clear out. Not for any particular place; no, nearly any place will answer; they only want to be moving. The amount of money on hand will answer the rest of the conundrum for them. If it will take them fifty miles, very well; let it be fifty. If not, a shorter flight will do.

During a couple of days we frequently answered these hails. Sometimes there was a group of high-water-stained, tumbledown cabins, populous with colored folk, and no whites visible; with grassless patches of dry ground here and there; a few felled trees, with skeleton cattle, mules, and horses, eating the leaves and gnawing the bark—no other food for them in the flood-wasted land. Sometimes there was a single lonely landing-cabin; near it the colored family that had hailed us; little and big, old and young, roosting on the scant pile of household goods; these consisting of a rusty gun, some bedticks, chests, tinware, stools, a crippled looking-glass, a venerable arm-chair, and six or eight base-born and spiritless yellow curs, attached to the family by strings. They must have their dogs; can't go without their dogs. Yet the dogs are never willing; they always object; so, one after another, in ridiculous procession, they are dragged aboard; all four feet braced and sliding along the stage, head likely to be pulled off; but the tugger marching determinedly forward, bending to his work, with the rope over his shoulder for better purchase. Sometimes a child is forgotten and left on the bank; but never a dog.

The usual river gossip going on in the pilot-house. Island No. 63—an island with a lovely "chute," or passage, behind it in the former times. They said Jesse Jamieson, in the *Skylark*, had a visiting pilot with him one trip—a poor old broken-down, superannuated fellow—left him at the wheel, at the foot of 63, to run off the watch. The ancient mariner went up through the chute, and down the river outside; and up the chute and down the river again; and yet again and again; and handed the boat over to the relieving pilot, at the end of three hours of honest endeavor, at the same old foot of the island where he had originally taken the wheel! A darky on shore who had observed the boat go by, about thirteen times, said, "'clar to gracious, I wouldn't be s'prised if dey's a whole line o' dem *Skylarks!*"

Anecdote illustrative of influence of reputation in the changing of opinion. The *Eclipse* was renowned for her swiftness. One day she passed along; an old darky on shore, absorbed in his own matters, did not notice what steamer it was. Presently some one asked:

"Any boat gone up?"

"Yes, sah."

"Was she going fast?"

"Oh, so-so—loafin' along."

"Now, do you know what boat that was?"

"No, sah."

"Why, uncle, that was the *Eclipse*."

"No! Is dat so? Well, I bet it was—cause she jes' went by here a-*sparklin'!*"

Piece of history illustrative of the violent style of some of the people down along here. During the early weeks of high water, A's fence-rails washed down on B's ground, and B's rails washed up in the eddy and landed on A's ground. A said, "Let the thing remain so; I will use your rails, and you use mine." But B objected—wouldn't have it so. One day, A came down on B's grounds to get his rails. B said, "I'll kill you!" and proceeded for him with his revolver. A said, "I'm not armed." So B, who wished to do only what was right, threw down his revolver; then pulled a knife, and cut A's throat all around, but gave his principal attention to the front, and so failed to sever the jugular. Struggling around, A managed to get his hands on the discarded revolver, and shot B dead with it—and recovered from his own injuries.

Further gossip; after which, everybody went below to get afternoon coffee and left me at the wheel, alone. Something presently reminded me of our last hour in St. Louis, part of which I spent on this boat's hurricane-deck, aft. I was joined there by a stranger, who dropped into conversation with me—a brisk young fellow, who said he was born in a town in the interior of Wisconsin, and had never seen a steamboat until a week before. Also said that on the way down from La Crosse he had inspected and examined his boat so diligently and with such passionate interest that he had mastered the whole thing from stem to rudder-blade. Asked me where I was from. I answered, "New England." "Oh, a Yank!" said he; and went chatting straight along, without waiting for assent or denial. He immediately proposed to take me all over the boat and tell me the names of her different parts, and teach me their uses. Before I could enter protest or excuse, he was already rattling glibly away at his benevolent work; and when I perceived that he was misnaming the things, and inhospitably amusing himself

at the expense of an innocent stranger from a far country, I held my peace and let him have his way. He gave me a world of misinformation; and the further he went, the wider his imagination expanded, and the more he enjoyed his cruel work of deceit. Sometimes, after palming off a particularly fantastic and outrageous lie upon me, he was so "full of laugh" that he had to step aside for a minute, upon one pretext or another, to keep me from suspecting. I stayed faithfully by him until his comedy was finished. Then he remarked that he had undertaken to "learn" me all about a steamboat, and had done it: but that if he had overlooked anything, just ask him and he would supply the lack. "Anything about this boat that you don't know the name of or the purpose of, you come to me and I'll tell you." I said I would, and took my departure, disappeared, and approached him from another quarter, whence he could not see me. There he sat, all alone, doubling himself up and writhing this way and that, in the throes of unappeasable laughter. He must have made himself sick; for he was not publicly visible afterward for several days. Meantime, the episode dropped out of my mind.

The thing that reminded me of it now, when I was alone at the wheel, was the spectacle of this young fellow standing in the pilot-house door, with the knob in his hand, silently and severely inspecting me. I don't know when I have seen anybody look so injured as he did. He did not say anything—simply stood there and looked; reproachfully looked and pondered. Finally he shut the door and started away: halted on the texas a minute; came slowly back and stood in the door again, with that grieved look on his face, gazed upon me awhile in meek rebuke, then said:

"You let me learn you all about a steamboat, *didn't* you?"

"Yes," I confessed.

"Yes, you did—*didn't* you?"

"Yes."

"You are the feller that—that—"

Language failed. Pause—impotent struggle for further words—then he gave it up, choked out a deep, strong oath, and departed for good.

Afterward I saw him several times below during the trip; but he was cold—would not look at me. Idiot! if he had not been in such a sweat to play his witless, practical joke upon me, in the beginning, I would have persuaded his thoughts into some other direction, and saved him from committing that wanton and silly impoliteness.

I had myself called with the four-o'clock watch, mornings, for one cannot see too many summer sunrises on the Mississippi. They are enchanting. First, there is the eloquence of silence; for a deep hush broods everywhere. Next, there is the haunting sense of loneliness, isolation, remoteness from the worry and bustle of the world. The dawn creeps in stealthily; the solid walls of black forest soften to gray, and vast stretches of the river open up and reveal themselves; the water is glass-smooth, gives off spectral little wreaths of white mist, there is not the faintest breath of wind, nor stir of leaf; the tranquillity is profound and infinitely satisfying. Then a bird pipes up, another follows, and soon the pipings develop into a jubilant riot of music. You see none of the birds; you simply move through an atmosphere of song which seems to sing itself. When the light has become a little stronger, you have one of the fairest and softest pictures imaginable. You have the intense green of the massed and crowded foliage near by; you see it paling shade by shade in front of you; upon the next projecting cape, a mile off or more, the tint has lightened to the tender young green of spring; the cape beyond that one has almost lost color, and the furthest one, miles away under the horizon, sleeps upon the water a mere dim vapor, and hardly separable from the sky above it and about it. And all this stretch of river is a mirror, and you have the shadowy reflections of the leafage and the curving shores and the receding capes pictured in it. Well, that is all beautiful; soft and rich and beautiful; and when the sun gets well up, and distributes a pink flush here and a powder of gold yonder and a purple haze where it will yield the best effect, you grant that you have seen something that is worth remembering. . . .

WE used to plow past the lofty hill-city, Vicksburg, down-stream; but we cannot do that now. A cut-off has made a country town of it, like Osceola, St. Genevieve, and several others. There is currentless water—also a big island—in front of Vicksburg now. You come down the river the other side of the island, then turn and come up to the town, that is, in high water: in low water you can't come up, but must land some distance below it.

Signs and scars still remain, as reminders of Vicksburg's tremendous war experiences; earthworks, trees crippled by the cannon-balls, cave refuges in the clay precipices, etc. The caves did good service during the six weeks' bombardment of the city—May 18 to July 4, 1863. They were used by the non-combatants—mainly by the women and children; not to live in constantly, but to fly to for safety on occasion. They were mere holes, tunnels driven into the perpendicular clay-bank, then branched Y-shape, within the hill. Life in Vicksburg during the six weeks was perhaps—but wait; here are some materials out of which to reproduce it:

Population, twenty-seven thousand soldiers and three thousand non-combatants; the city utterly cut off from the world—walled solidly in, the frontage by gunboats, the rear by soldiers and batteries; hence, no buying and selling with the outside; no passing to and fro; no god-speeding a parting guest, no welcoming a coming one; no printed acres of world-wide news to be read at breakfast, mornings—a tedious dull absence of such matter, instead; hence, also, no running to see steamboats smoking into view in the distance up or down, and plowing toward the town—for none came, the river lay vacant and undisturbed; no rush and turmoil around the railway-station, no struggling over bewildered swarms of passengers by noisy mobs of hackmen—all quiet there; flour two hundred dollars a barrel, sugar thirty, corn ten dollars a bushel, bacon five dollars a pound, rum a hundred dollars a gallon, other things in proportion; consequently, no roar and racket of drays and carriages tearing along the streets; nothing for them to do, among that handful of noncombatants of exhausted means;

at three o'clock in the morning, silence—silence so dead that the measured tramp of a sentinel can be heard a seemingly impossible distance; out of hearing of this lonely sound, perhaps the stillness is absolute: all in a moment come ground-shaking thunder-crashes of artillery, the sky is cobwebbed with the crisscrossing red lines streaming from soaring bombshells, and a rain of iron fragments descends upon the city, descends upon the empty streets—streets which are not empty a moment later, but mottled with dim figures of frantic women and children scurrying from home and bed toward the cave dungeons—encouraged by the humorous grim soldiery, who shout "Rats, to your holes!" and laugh.

The cannon-thunder rages, shells scream and crash overhead, the iron rain pours down, one hour, two hours, three, possibly six, then stops; silence follows, but the streets are still empty; the silence continues; by and by a head projects from a cave here and there and yonder, and reconnoitres cautiously; the silence still continuing, bodies follow heads, and jaded, half-smothered creatures group themselves about, stretch their cramped limbs, draw in deep draughts of the grateful fresh air, gossip with the neighbors from the next cave; maybe straggle off home presently, or take a lounge through the town, if the stillness continues; and will scurry to the holes again, by and by, when the war-tempest breaks forth once more.

There being but three thousand of these cave-dwellers—merely the population of a village—would they not come to know each other, after a week or two, and familiarly; insomuch that the fortunate or unfortunate experiences of one would be of interest to all?

Those are the materials furnished by history. From them might not almost anybody reproduce for himself the life of that time in Vicksburg? Could you, who did not experience it, come nearer to reproducing it to the imagination of another non-participant than could a Vicksburger who *did* experience it? It seems impossible; and yet there are reasons why it might not really be. When one makes his first voyage in a ship, it is an experience which

multitudinously bristles with striking novelties; novelties which are in such sharp contrast with all this person's former experiences that they take a seemingly deathless grip upon his imagination and memory. By tongue or pen he can make a landsman live that strange and stirring voyage over with him; make him see it all and feel it all. But if he wait? If he makes ten voyages in succession—what then? Why, the thing has lost color, snap, surprise; and has become commonplace. The man would have nothing to tell that would quicken a landsman's pulse.

The war history of Vicksburg has more about it to interest the general reader than that of any other of the river towns. It is full of variety, full of incident, full of the picturesque. Vicksburg held out longer than any other important river town, and saw warfare in all its phases, both land and water—the siege, the mine, the assault, the repulse, the bombardment, sickness, captivity, famine.

The most beautiful of all the national cemeteries is here. Over the great gateway is this inscription:

"HERE REST IN PEACE 16,600 WHO DIED FOR
THEIR COUNTRY IN THE YEARS
1861 TO 1865"

The grounds are nobly situated; being very high and commanding a wide prospect of land and river. They are tastefully laid out in broad terraces, with winding roads and paths; and there is profuse adornment in the way of semi-tropical shrubs and flowers; and in one part is a piece of native wild-wood, left just as it grew, and, therefore, perfect in its charm. Everything about this cemetery suggests the hand of the national government. The government's work is always conspicuous for excellence, solidity, thoroughness, neatness. The government does its work well in the first place, and then takes care of it.

By winding roads—which were often cut to so great a depth between perpendicular walls that they were mere roofless tunnels—we drove out a mile or two and visited the monument which stands upon the scene of the surrender of Vicksburg to General Grant by General Pemberton. Its metal will preserve it from the hackings and chippings which so defaced its predecessor, which was of marble; but the brick foundations are crumbling, and it will tumble down by and by. It overlooks a picturesque region of wooded hills and ravines; and is not unpicturesque itself, being well smothered in flowering weeds. The battered remnant of the marble monument has been removed to the National Cemetery.

On the road, a quarter of a mile townward, an aged colored man showed us, with pride, an unexploded bombshell which had lain in his yard since the day it fell there during the siege.

"I was a-stannin' heah, an' de dog was a-stannin' heah; de dog he went for the shell, gwine to pick a fuss wid it; but I didn't; I says, 'Jes' make youseff at home heah; lay still whah you is, or bust up de place, jes' as you's a mind to, but *I's* got business out in de woods, I has!' "

Vicksburg is a town of substantial business streets and pleasant residences; it commands the commerce of the Yazoo and Sunflower rivers; is pushing railways in several directions, through rich agricultural regions, and has a promising future of prosperity and importance.

Apparently, nearly all the river towns, big and little, have made up their minds that they must look mainly to railroads for wealth and upbuilding, henceforth. They are acting upon this idea. The signs are that the next twenty years will bring about some noteworthy changes in the valley, in the direction of increased population and wealth, and in the intellectual advancement and the liberalizing of opinion which go naturally with these. And yet, if one may judge by the past, the river towns will manage to find and use a chance, here and there, to cripple and retard their progress. They kept themselves back in the days of steamboating supremacy, by a system of wharfage dues so stupidly graded as to prohibit what may be called small *retail* traffic in freights and passengers. Boats were charged such heavy wharfage that they could not afford to land for one or two passengers or a light lot of freight. Instead of encouraging the bringing of trade to

their doors, the towns diligently and effectively discouraged it. They could have had many boats and low rates; but their policy rendered few boats and high rates compulsory. It was a policy which extended—and extends—from New Orleans to St. Paul.

THE approaches to New Orleans were familiar; general aspects were unchanged. When one goes flying through London along a railway propped in the air on tall arches, he may inspect miles of upper bedrooms through the open windows, but the lower half of the houses is under his level and out of sight. Similarly, in high-river stage, in the New Orleans region, the water is up to the top of the inclosing levee-rim, the flat country behind it lies low—representing the bottom of a dish—and as the boat swims along, high on the flood, one looks down upon the houses and into the upper windows. There is nothing but that frail breastwork of earth between the people and destruction.

The old brick salt-warehouses clustered at the upper end of the city looked as they had always looked: warehouses which had had a kind of Aladdin's lamp experience, however, since I had seen them; for when the war broke out the proprietor went to bed one night leaving them packed with thousands of sacks of vulgar salt, worth a couple of dollars a sack, and got up in the morning and found his mountain of salt turned into a mountain of gold, so to speak, so suddenly and to so dizzy a height had the war news sent up the price of the article.

The vast reach of plank wharves remained unchanged, and there were as many ships as ever: but the long array of steamboats had vanished; not altogether, of course, but not much of it was left.

The city itself had not changed—to the eye. It had greatly increased in spread and population, but the look of the town was not altered. The dust, waste-paper-littered, was still deep in the streets; the deep troughlike gutters along the curbstones were still half full of reposeful water with a dusty surface; the sidewalks were still—in the sugar and bacon region—encumbered by casks and barrels and hogsheads; the great blocks of austerely plain commercial houses were as dusty-looking as ever.

Canal Street was finer and more attractive and stirring than formerly, with its drifting crowds of people, its several processions of hurrying street-cars, and—toward evening—its broad second-story verandas crowded with gentlemen and ladies clothed according to the latest mode.

Not that there is any "architecture" in Canal Street: to speak in broad, general terms, there is no architecture in New Orleans, except in the cemeteries. It seems a strange thing to say of a wealthy, far-seeing, and energetic city of a quarter of a million inhabitants, but it is true. There is a huge granite United States custom-house—costly enough, genuine enough, but as to decoration it is inferior to a gasometer. It looks like a state prison. But it was built before the war. Architecture in America may be said to have been born since the war. New Orleans, I believe, has had the good luck—and in a sense the bad luck—to have had no great fire in late years. It must be so. If the opposite had been the case, I think one would be able to tell the "burnt district" by the radical improvement in its architecture over the old forms. One can do this in Boston and Chicago. The "burnt district" of Boston was commonplace before the fire; but now there is no commercial district in any city in the world that can surpass it—or perhaps even rival it—in beauty, elegance, and tastefulness.

However, New Orleans has begun—just this moment, as one may say. When completed, the new Cotton Exchange will be a stately and beautiful building: massive, substantial, full of architectural graces; no shams or false pretenses or ugliness about it anywhere. To the city it will be worth many times its cost, for it will breed its species. What has been lacking hitherto was a model to build toward, something to educate eye and taste: a *suggester*, so to speak.

The city is well outfitted with progressive men—thinking, sagacious, long-headed men.

The contrast between the spirit of the city and the city's architecture is like the contrast between waking and sleep. Apparently there is a "boom" in everything but that one dead feature. The water in the gutters used to be stagnant and slimy, and a potent disease-breeder; but the gutters are flushed now two or three times a day by powerful machinery; in many of the gutters the water never stands still, but has a steady current. Other sanitary improvements have been made; and with such effect that New Orleans claims to be (during the long intervals between the occasional yellow-fever assaults) one of the healthiest cities in the Union. There's plenty of ice now for everybody, manufactured in the town. It is a driving place commercially, and has a great river, ocean, and railway business. At the date of our visit it was the best-lighted city in the Union, electrically speaking. The New Orleans electric lights were more numerous than those of New York, and very much better. One had this modified noonday not only in Canal and some neighboring chief streets, but all along a stretch of five miles of river-frontage. There are good clubs in the city now—several of them but recently organized—and inviting modern-style pleasure resorts at West End and Spanish Fort. The telephone is everywhere. One of the most notable advances is in journalism. The newspapers, as I remember them, were not a striking feature. Now they are. Money is spent upon them with a free hand. They get the news, let it cost what it may. The editorial work is not hack-grinding, but literature. As an example of New Orleans journalistic achievement, it may be mentioned that the *Times-Democrat* of August 26, 1882, contained a report of the year's business of the towns of the Mississippi valley, from New Orleans all the way to St. Paul—two thousand miles. That issue of the paper consisted of *forty* pages; seven columns to the page; two hundred and eighty columns in all; fifteen hundred words to the column; an aggregate of four hundred and twenty thousand words. . . .

I have been speaking of public architecture only. The domestic article in New Orleans is reproachless, notwithstanding it remains as it always was. All the dwellings are of wood—in the American part of the town, I mean—and all have a comfortable look. Those in the wealthy quarter are spacious; painted snow-white usually, and generally have wide verandas, or double verandas, supported by ornamental columns. These mansions stand in the center of large grounds, and rise, garlanded with roses, out of the midst of swelling masses of shining green foliage and many-colored blossoms. No houses could well be in better harmony with their surroundings, or more pleasing to the eye, or more homelike and comfortable-looking.

One even becomes reconciled to the cistern presently; this is a mighty cask, painted green, and sometimes a couple of stories high, which is propped against the house-corner on stilts. There is a mansion-and-brewery suggestion about the combination which seems very incongruous at first. But the people cannot have wells, and so they take rain-water. Neither can they conveniently have cellars or graves, the town being built upon "made" ground; so they do without both, and few of the living complain, and none of the others.

WE took passage in one of the fast boats of the St. Louis and St. Paul Packet Company, and started up the river.

When I, as a boy, first saw the mouth of the Missouri River, it was twenty-two or twenty-three miles above St. Louis, according to the estimate of pilots; the wear and tear of the banks has moved it down eight miles since then; and the pilots say that within five years the river will cut through and move the mouth down five miles more, which will bring it within ten miles of St. Louis.

About nightfall we passed the large and flourishing town of Alton, Illinois, and before daylight next morning the town of Louisiana, Missouri, a sleepy village in my day, but a brisk railway-center now; however, all the towns out there are railway-centers now. I could not clearly recognize the place. This seemed odd

to me, for when I retired from the rebel army in '61 I retired upon Louisiana in good order; at least in good enough order for a person who had not yet learned how to retreat according to the rules of war, and had to trust to native genius. It seemed to me that for a first attempt at a retreat it was not badly done. I had done no advancing in all that campaign that was at all equal to it.

There was a railway bridge across the river here well sprinkled with glowing lights, and a very beautiful sight it was.

At seven in the morning we reached Hannibal, Missouri, where my boyhood was spent. I had had a glimpse of it fifteen years ago, and another glimpse six years earlier, but both were so brief that they hardly counted. The only notion of the town that remained in my mind was the memory of it as I had known it when I first quitted it twenty-nine years ago. That picture of it was still as clear and vivid to me as a photograph. I stepped ashore with the feeling of one who returns out of a dead-and-gone generation. I had a sort of realizing sense of what the Bastille prisoners must have felt when they used to come out and look upon Paris after years of captivity, and note how curiously the familiar and the strange were mixed together before them. I saw the new houses—saw them plainly enough—but they did not affect the older picture in my mind, for through their solid bricks and mortar I saw the vanished houses, which had formerly stood there, with perfect distinctness.

It was Sunday morning, and everybody was abed yet. So I passed through the vacant streets, still seeing the town as it was, and not as it is,

and recognizing and metaphorically shaking hands with a hundred familiar objects which no longer exist; and finally climbed Holiday's Hill to get a comprehensive view. The whole town lay spread out below me then, and I could mark and fix every locality, every detail. Naturally, I was a good deal moved. I said, "Many of the people I once knew in this tranquil refuge of my childhood are now in heaven; some, I trust, are in the other place."

The things about me and before me made me feel like a boy again—convinced me that I was a boy again, and that I had simply been dreaming an unusually long dream; but my reflections spoiled all that; for they forced me to say, "I see fifty old houses down yonder, into each of which I could enter and find either a man or a woman who was a baby or unborn when I noticed those houses last, or a grandmother who was a plump young bride at that time."

From this vantage-ground the extensive view up and down the river, and wide over the wooded expanses of Illinois, is very beautiful —one of the most beautiful on the Mississippi, I think; which is a hazardous remark to make, for the eight hundred miles of river between St. Louis and St. Paul afford an unbroken succession of lovely pictures. It may be that my affection for the one in question biases my judgment in its favor; I cannot say as to that. No matter, it was satisfyingly beautiful to me, and it had this advantage over all the other friends whom I was about to greet again: it had suffered no change; it was as young and fresh and comely and gracious as ever it had been; whereas, the faces of the others would be old, and scarred with the campaigns of life, and

THE EADS BRIDGE AT ST. LOUIS, COMPLETED IN 1874

marked with their griefs and defeats, and would give me no upliftings of spirit.

An old gentleman, out on an early morning walk, came along, and we discussed the weather, and then drifted into other matters. I could not remember his face. He said he had been living here twenty-eight years. So he had come after my time, and I had never seen him before. I asked him various questions; first about a mate of mine in Sunday-school—what became of him?

"He graduated with honor in an Eastern college, wandered off into the world somewhere, succeeded at nothing, passed out of knowledge and memory years ago, and is supposed to have gone to the dogs."

"He was bright, and promised well when he was a boy."

"Yes, but the thing that happened is what became of it all."

I asked after another lad, altogether the brightest in our village school when I was a boy.

"He, too, was graduated with honors, from an Eastern college; but life whipped him in every battle, straight along, and he died in one of the territories, years ago, a defeated man."

I asked after another of the bright boys.

"He is a success, always has been, always will be, I think."

I inquired after a young fellow who came to the town to study for one of the professions when I was a boy.

"He went at something else before he got through—went from medicine to law, or from law to medicine—then to some other new thing; went away for a year, came back with a young wife; fell to drinking, then to gambling behind the door; finally took his wife and two children to her father's, and went off to Mexico; went from bad to worse, and finally died there, without a cent to buy a shroud, and without a friend to attend the funeral."

"Pity, for he was the best-natured and most cheery and hopeful young fellow that ever was."

I named another boy.

"Oh, he is all right. Lives here yet; has a wife and children, and is prospering."

Same verdict concerning other boys.

I named three school-girls.

"The first two live here, are married and have children; the other is long ago dead—never married."

I named, with emotion, one of my early sweethearts.

"She is all right. Been married three times; buried two husbands, divorced from the third, and I hear she is getting ready to marry an old fellow out in Colorado somewhere. She's got children scattered around here and there, most everywheres."

The answer to several other inquiries was brief and simple:

"Killed in the war."

I named another boy.

"Well now, his case *is* curious! There wasn't a human being in this town but knew that that boy was a perfect chucklehead; perfect dummy; just a stupid ass, as you may say. Everybody knew it, and everybody said it. Well, if that very boy isn't the first lawyer in the state of Missouri to-day, I'm a Democrat!"

"Is that so?"

"It's actually so. I'm telling you the truth."

"How do you account for it?"

"Account for it? There ain't any accounting for it, except that if you send a d—d fool to St. Louis, and you don't tell them he's a d—d fool, *they'll* never find it out. There's one thing sure—if I had a d—d fool I should know what to do with him: ship him to St. Louis—it's the noblest market in the world for that kind of property. Well, when you come to look at it all around, and chew at it and think it over, *don't* it just bang anything you ever heard of?"

"Well, yes; it does seem to. But don't you think maybe it was the Hannibal people who were mistaken about the boy, and not the St. Louis people?"

"Oh, nonsense! The people here have known him from the very cradle—they knew him a hundred times better than the St. Louis idiots *could* have known him. No; if you have got any d—d fools that you want to realize on, take my advice—send them to St. Louis."

I mentioned a great number of people whom

I had formerly known. Some were dead, some were gone away, some had prospered, some had come to naught; but as regarded a dozen or so of the lot, the answer was comforting:

"Prosperous—live here yet—town littered with their children."

I asked about Miss —.

"Died in the insane asylum three or four years ago—never was out of it from the time she went in; and was always suffering too; never got a shred of her mind back."

If he spoke the truth, here was a heavy tragedy, indeed. Thirty-six years in a madhouse, that some young fools might have some fun! I was a small boy at the time; and I saw those giddy young ladies come tiptoeing into the room where Miss — sat reading at midnight by a lamp. The girl at the head of the file wore a shroud and a doughface; she crept behind the victim, touched her on the shoulder, and she looked up and screamed, and then fell into convulsions. She did not recover from the fright, but went mad. In these days it seems incredible that people believed in ghosts so short a time ago. But they did.

After asking after such other folk as I could call to mind, I finally inquired about *myself*.

"Oh, he succeeded well enough—another case of d—d fool. If they'd sent him to St. Louis, he'd have succeeded sooner."

It was with much satisfaction that I recognized the wisdom of having told this candid gentleman, in the beginning, that my name was Smith.

BEING left to myself, up there, I went on picking out old houses in the distant town, and calling back their former inmates out of the moldy past. Among them I presently recognized the house of the father of Lem Hackett (fictitious name). It carried me back more than a generation in a moment, and landed me in the midst of a time when the happenings of life were not the natural and logical results of great general laws, but of special orders, and were freighted with very precise and distinct purposes—partly punitive in intent, partly admonitory; and usually local in application.

When I was a small boy, Lem Hackett was drowned—on a Sunday. He fell out of an empty flatboat, where he was playing. Being loaded with sin, he went to the bottom like an anvil. He was the only boy in the village who slept that night. We others all lay awake, repenting. We had not needed the information, delivered from the pulpit that evening, that Lem's was a case of special judgment—we knew that, already. There was a ferocious thunder-storm that night, and it raged continuously until near dawn. The wind blew, the windows rattled, the rain swept along the roof in pelting sheets, and at the briefest of intervals the inky blackness of the night vanished, the houses over the way glared out white and blinding for a quivering instant, then the solid darkness shut down again and a splitting peal of thunder followed which seemed to rend everything in the neighborhood to shreds and splinters. I sat up in bed quaking and shuddering, waiting for the destruction of the world, and expecting it. To me there was nothing strange or incongruous in Heaven's making such an uproar about Lem Hackett. Apparently it was the right and proper thing to do. Not a doubt entered my mind that all the angels were grouped together, discussing this boy's case and observing the awful bombardment of our beggarly little village with satisfaction and approval. There was one thing which disturbed me in the most serious way: that was the thought that this centering of the celestial interest on our village could not fail to attract the attention of the observers to people among us who might otherwise have escaped notice for years. I felt that I was not only one of those people, but the very one most likely to be discovered. That discovery could have but one result: I should be in the fire with Lem before the chill of the river had been fairly warmed out of him. I knew that this would be only just and fair. I was increasing the chances against myself all the time, by feeling a secret bitterness against Lem for having attracted this fatal attention to me, but I could not help it—this sinful thought persisted in infesting my breast in spite of me. Every time the lightning glared I caught my breath, and judged I was gone. In my terror and misery I meanly began to suggest other boys, and mention acts of theirs which were wickeder than mine, and peculiarly needed punishment—and I tried to pretend to myself that I was simply doing this in a casual way, and without intent to divert the heavenly attention to them for the purpose of getting rid of it myself. With deep sagacity I put these mentions into the form of sorrowing recollections and left-handed sham-supplications that the sins of those boys might be allowed to pass unnoticed—"Possibly they may repent.". "It is true that Jim Smith broke a window and lied about it—but maybe he did not mean any harm. And although Tom Holmes says more bad words than any other boy in the village, he probably intends to repent—though he has never said he would. And while it is a fact that John Jones did fish a little on Sunday, once, he didn't really catch anything but only just one small useless mudcat; and maybe that wouldn't have been so awful if he had thrown it back—as he says he did, but he didn't. Pity but they would repent of these dreadful things—and maybe they will yet."

But while I was shamefully trying to draw attention to these poor chaps—who were doubtless directing the celestial attention to me at the same moment, though I never once suspected that—I had heedlessly left my candle burning. It was not a time to neglect even trifling precautions. There was no occasion to add anything to the facilities for attracting notice to me—so I put the light out.

It was a long night to me, and perhaps the most distressful one I ever spent. I endured agonies of remorse for sins which I knew I had committed, and for others which I was not certain about, yet was sure that they had been set down against me in a book by an angel who was wiser than I and did not trust such important matters to memory. It struck me, by and by, that I had been making a most foolish and calamitous mistake, in one respect; doubtless I had not only made my own destruction sure by directing attention to those other boys, but had already accomplished theirs! Doubtless the lightning had stretched them all dead in their beds by this time! The anguish and the fright which this thought gave me made my previous sufferings seem trifling by comparison.

Things had become truly serious. I resolved to turn over a new leaf instantly; I also resolved to connect myself with the church next day, if I survived to see its sun appear. I resolved to cease from sin in all its forms, and to lead a high and blameless life forever after. I would be punctual at church and Sunday-school; visit the sick; carry baskets of victuals to the poor (simply to fulfil the regulation conditions, although I knew we had none among us so poor but they would smash the basket over my head for my pains); I would instruct other boys in right ways, and take the resulting trouncings meekly; I would subsist entirely on tracts; I would invade the rum shop and warn the drunkard—and finally, if I escaped the fate of those who early become too good to live, I would go for a missionary.

The storm subsided toward daybreak, and I dozed gradually to sleep with a sense of obligation to Lem Hackett for going to eternal suffering in that abrupt way, and thus preventing a far more dreadful disaster—my own loss.

But when I rose refreshed, by and by, and found that those other boys were still alive, I had a dim sense that perhaps the whole thing was a false alarm; that the entire turmoil had been on Lem's account and nobody's else. The world looked so bright and safe that there did not seem to be any real occasion to turn over a new leaf. I was a little subdued during that day, and perhaps the next; after that, my purpose of reforming slowly dropped out of my mind, and I had a peaceful, comfortable time again, until the next storm.

That storm came about three weeks later; and it was the most unaccountable one, to me, that I had ever experienced; for on the afternoon of that day, "Dutchy" was drowned. Dutchy belonged to our Sunday-school. He was a German lad who did not know enough to come in out of the rain; but he was exasperatingly good, and had a prodigious memory.

One Sunday he made himself the envy of all the youth and the talk of the admiring village, by reciting three thousand verses of Scripture without missing a word: then he went off the very next day and got drowned.

Circumstances gave to his death a peculiar impressiveness. We were all bathing in a muddy creek which had a deep hole in it, and in this hole the coopers had sunk a pile of green hickory hoop-poles to soak, some twelve feet under water. We were diving and "seeing who could stay under longest." We managed to remain down by holding on to the hoop-poles. Dutchy made such a poor success of it that he was hailed with laughter and derision every time his head appeared above water. At last he seemed hurt with the taunts, and begged us to stand still on the bank and be fair with him and give him an honest count—"be friendly and kind just this once, and not miscount for the sake of having the fun of laughing at him." Treacherous winks were exchanged, and all said, "All right, Dutchy—go ahead, we'll play fair."

Dutchy plunged in, but the boys, instead of beginning to count, followed the lead of one of their number and scampered to a range of blackberry bushes close by and hid behind it. They imagined Dutchy's humiliation, when he should rise after a superhuman effort and find the place silent and vacant, nobody there to applaud. They were "so full of laugh" with the idea that they were continually exploding into muffled cackles. Time swept on, and presently one who was peeping through the briers said, with surprise:

"Why, he hasn't come up yet!"

The laughing stopped.

"Boys, it's a splendid dive," said one.

"Never mind that," said another, "the joke on him is all the better for it."

There was a remark or two more, and then a pause. Talking ceased, and all began to peer through the vines. Before long, the boys' faces began to look uneasy, then anxious, then terrified. Still there was no movement of the placid water. Hearts began to beat fast, and faces to turn pale. We all glided out silently, and stood on the bank, our horrified eyes wandering back and forth from each other's countenances to the water.

"Somebody must go down and see!"

Yes, that was plain; but nobody wanted that grisly task.

"Draw straws!"

So we did—with hands which shook so that we hardly knew what we were about. The lot fell to me, and I went down. The water was so muddy I could not see anything, but I felt around among the hoop-poles, and presently grasped a limp wrist which gave me no response—and if it had I should not have known it, I let it go with such a frightened suddenness.

The boy had been caught among the hoop-poles and entangled there, helplessly. I fled to the surface and told the awful news. Some of us knew that if the boy were dragged out at once he might possibly be resuscitated, but we never thought of that. We did not think of anything; we did not know what to do, so we did nothing—except that the smaller lads cried piteously, and we all struggled frantically into our clothes, putting on anybody's that came handy, and getting them wrong side out and upside down, as a rule. Then we scurried away and gave the alarm, but none of us went back to see the end of the tragedy. We had a more important thing to attend to: we all flew home, and lost not a moment in getting ready to lead a better life.

The night presently closed down. Then came on that tremendous and utterly unaccountable storm. I was perfectly dazed; I could not understand it. It seemed to me that there must be some mistake. The elements were turned loose, and they rattled and banged and blazed away in the most blind and frantic manner. All heart and hope went out of me, and the dismal thought kept floating through my brain, "If a boy who knows three thousand verses by heart is not satisfactory, what chance is there for anybody else?"

Of course I never questioned for a moment that the storm was on Dutchy's account, or that he or any other inconsequential animal was worthy of such a majestic demonstration

from on high; the lesson of it was the only thing that troubled me; for it convinced me that if Dutchy, with all his perfections, was not a delight, it would be vain for me to turn over a new leaf, for I must infallibly fall hopelessly short of that boy, no matter how hard I might try. Nevertheless I did turn it over—a highly educated fear compelled me to do that —but succeeding days of cheerfulness and sunshine came bothering around, and within a month I had so drifted backward that again I was as lost and comfortable as ever.

Breakfast-time approached while I mused these musings and called these ancient happenings back to mind; so I got me back into the present and went down the hill.

On my way through town to the hotel, I saw the house which was my home when I was a boy. At present rates, the people who now occupy it are of no more value than I am; but in my time they would have been worth not less than five hundred dollars apiece. They are colored folk.

After breakfast I went out alone again, intending to hunt up some of the Sunday-schools and see how this generation of pupils might compare with their progenitors who had sat with me in those places and had probably taken me as a model—though I do not remember as to that now. By the public square there had been in my day a shabby little brick church called the "Old Ship of Zion," which I had attended as a Sunday-school scholar; and I found the locality easily enough, but not the old church; it was gone, and a trig and rather hilarious new edifice was in its place. The pupils were better dressed and better looking than were those of my time; consequently they did not resemble their ancestors; and consequently there was nothing familiar to me in their faces. Still, I contemplated them with a deep interest and a yearning wistfulness, and if I had been a girl I would have cried; for they were the offspring, and represented, and occupied the places, of boys and girls some of whom I had loved to love, and some of whom I had loved to hate, but all of whom were dear to me for the one reason or the other, so many

years gone by—and, Lord, where be they now!

I was mightily stirred, and would have been grateful to be allowed to remain unmolested and look my fill; but a bald-summited superintendent who had been a towheaded Sunday-school mate of mine of that spot in the early ages, recognized me, and I talked a flutter of wild nonsense to those children to hide the thoughts which were in me, and which could not have been spoken without a betrayal of feeling that would have been recognized as out of character with me.

Making speeches without preparation is no gift of mine; and I was resolved to shirk any new opportunity, but in the next and larger Sunday-school I found myself in the rear of the assemblage; so I was very willing to go on the platform a moment for the sake of getting a good look at the scholars. On the spur of the moment I could not recall any of the old idiotic talks which visitors used to insult me with when I was a pupil there; and I was sorry for this, since it would have given me time and excuse to dawdle there and take a long and satisfying look at what I feel at liberty to say was an array of fresh young comeliness not matchable in another Sunday-school of the same size. As I talked merely to get a chance to inspect, and as I strung out the random rubbish solely to prolong the inspection, I judged it but decent to confess these low motives, and I did so.

If the Model Boy was in either of these Sunday-schools, I did not see him. The Model Boy of my time—we never had but the one—was perfect: perfect in manners, perfect in dress, perfect in conduct, perfect in filial piety, perfect in exterior godliness; but at bottom he was a prig; and as for the contents of his skull, they could have changed place with the contents of a pie, and nobody would have been the worse off for it but the pie. This fellow's reproachlessness was a standing reproach to every lad in the village. He was the admiration of all the mothers, and the detestation of all their sons. I was told what became of him, but as it was a disappointment to me, I will not enter into details. He succeeded in life.

(Previous page) Samuel Clemens in the pilothouse of the steamer Calamity Jane 1883.

In a splendid excess of imagination, William Henry Powell depicted De Soto's discovery of the Mississippi with more style than accuracy.

On January 8, 1815, American troops successfully defended New Orleans against a British assault—two weeks after the War of 1812 had ended. Some of the carnage and most of the smoke of that battle are suggested by this lithograph of 1827.

Fort Snelling, Minnesota, founded in 1819 at the confluence of the Mississippi and Minnesota rivers as a buffer against Indian attacks.

With the ceremony appropriate to the acquisition of an inland empire, the American flag is raised at New Orleans on December 20, 1803.

It was such a busy river, this American Mississippi—crawling with barges and keelboats and ambitious little steamers. Everything seemed possible, even probable, and little towns like Cairo, Illinois, dreamed huge dreams in the 1830s.

Lusty, boozy, and incredibly hard-working, the flatboatmen of the Mississippi lived with death every day—and with life. In probably his most famous painting, George Caleb Bingham captured the whole-souled vigor of these vanished beings in "The Jolly Flatboatmen in Port," a work completed in 1857, long after steam had supplanted muscle on the great river.

Towns become cities: By the 1840s a generation of enterprise in the Mississippi Valley had transformed New Orleans from a charming Creole town into one of the largest shipping ports in the world.

St. Louis, seen here at about the same time as the lithograph of New Orleans at the top of the page, could not boast a forest of masts, but there was no mistaking her role as one of the major inland ports of the river.

*Unlike New Orleans and St. Louis, St. Paul, Minnesota, very near the
head of navigation on the Mississippi, had not quite made the transition
from town to city when this view was painted by S. Holmes Andrews in 1855.
Yet the enterprise was there, and the dreams; St. Paul would have its day.*

(Previous two pages) Perhaps no painting has better captured the power and presence of steam on the Mississippi than this view of the New Orleans sugar levee by Henri Sebron, done in 1853.

The ritual of "wooding up" on the Mississippi was a procedure in which not only a boat's deck hands but her able-bodied deck passengers were expected to participate.

156

Steamboat racing was incredibly dangerous for all concerned and the bane of boat owners. It was also a matter of some excitement and enormously popular. One of the most famous of the races was that between the Natchez *and the* Robert E. Lee *in 1870, documented here in a modern painting by Dean Cornwell.*

The Mississippi had not seen human conflict since the War of 1812, but in 1862 it came again, this time with all the flash and horror of industrial warfare, as the American North and the American South struggled to define what America was supposed to mean. Late in April 1862, the ships and gunboats of the North met those of the South to see which would possess New Orleans. The South lost New Orleans, and the Mississippi soon after became a Northern river.

The Key to a Continent

WITH ALL THE CENTURIES of human history behind the Mississippi, the river itself had not yet been a battleground. That privilege did not come to it until the Civil War split this "more perfect union" into antagonistic halves, each of which struggled to enforce its version of the American dream on the other. And since this was the heartland river of America, the Mississippi experienced modern warfare.

When the war began, the Mississippi was a Confederate stream, for the Confederacy effectively controlled its banks from Columbus, Kentucky, all the way down to New Orleans. The snouts of artillery spouted from embankments and fortifications at Columbus, Island No. 10, in the middle of the river itself, and from Fort Pillow, Fort Randolph, Memphis, Vicksburg, and New Orleans. And on the Ohio tributaries of the Cumberland and Tennessee rivers, forts Donelson and Henry guarded entrance into the interior valley. Like a kind of Maginot Line, the waters ringed the American South.

The Civil War was the first major conflict of the Age of Steam, the first industrial war, the first to be fought with machines as well as men. The machines that the Union forces brought to bear on the Confederate defenses of the river valley were ironclad gunboats, a small fleet of unlikely-looking craft that sat low in the water, sheathed with armor plate and bristling with guns. Most of them were designed and constructed by a riverman of much experience, James Eads, a former peddler and steamboat clerk who had realized a fortune by putting together the first fleet of salvage boats in the river's history. Eads had long been an advocate of iron-clad gunboats, and when the Navy Department asked for bids to build seven such boats for the defense of the western rivers, he put in a bid and won the contract. On October 12, 1861, the first of the vessels, the *St. Louis*, slid off the ways at Eads's Union Iron Works in Carondolet, a suburb of St. Louis, and a little over one hundred days after he had taken the contract, the last boat was completed.

Brigadier General Ulysses S. Grant put the gunboats to good use almost immediately. In February 1862 they steamed up the Tennessee River under the command of Flag Officer Andrew H. Foote, bound for the Confederate stronghold of Fort Henry, while Grant and seventeen thousand men followed in various river craft. From behind a cover of smoke, the gunboats poured round after round into the fort, a bombardment one Confederate officer said "exceeded in terror anything that the imagination had pictured of shot and shell, plowing roads through the earthworks and sandbags, dismantling guns . . . setting on fire and bringing down buildings within the fortification, and cutting in two, as with a scythe, large trees in the neighborhood." Fort Henry fell on February 6, and one week later the gunboats repeated their deadly performance in front of Fort Donelson, while Grant and his soldiers attacked it from the rear. The second fort surrendered on February 16, and the first crack in the Confederate river defenses had been forced by Eads's cumbersome, lethal machines.

More was to come. On February 22 the gunboats bombarded Columbus, Kentucky, so fiercely that her commander, General Leonidas Polk, surrendered himself

The machines of war: ramming, blasting, and steaming, Federal and Confederate gunboats meet in the Battle of Memphis, June 6, 1862.

*Called the "key to the Mississippi," the Confederate stronghold on Island No. 10
surrendered to Union forces on April 7, 1862.*

and the twenty thousand troops of his command. On April 4, the gunboat *Carondolet* successfully ran the gauntlet of Confederate guns at Island No. 10, a journey through "checkers of darkness and flame," as a reporter on board described it; two nights later, the gunboat *Pittsburgh* duplicated the feat, while Union soldiers dug their way through a swamp and presented themselves to the astonished Confederates. Island No. 10 was surrounded on two sides, cut off from aid, and helpless to resist the fire of the two gunboats. It surrendered with seven thousand men on April 7, the same day Grant defeated southern forces at Shiloh Church near Pittsburg Landing, Tennessee.

THE SECOND JAW of Union power on the Mississippi clamped down at New Orleans when seagoing fighting ships and gunboats under the command of Flag Officer David G. Farragut passed the Confederate batteries of Chalmette (where Andrew Jackson had annihilated a British army thirty-seven years before) and

accepted the surrender of the city on May 1. But Farragut could not bring his deep-draft vessels up the river; the gunboats and soldiers of Grant would have to do the rest. They did. In an engagement on May 10, eight Confederate rams and the seven Union ironclads battered each other in the river opposite Fort Pillow; at day's end, two of the ironclads and two of the rams were sunk.

It was a Confederate victory, technically, but the remaining six ironclads would not be driven off, bombarding the fort continuously while the army's land forces came down from Shiloh to drive off the Confederate Army at Corinth. Shelled in front and threatened from the rear, Fort Pillow was abandoned, the Confederate boats retreating to Memphis. There was no escape. Irresistibly, the federal ironclads followed after, and on the morning of June 6, while the citizens of Memphis stood on the bluffs and watched, the ironclads—joined now by several federal ramboats—systematically destroyed the river navy of the Confederates. In twenty minutes it was done, and Memphis fell to the Union.

Only Vicksburg was left now, but it was no easy task

Guerrilla-like, Confederate sharpshooters attack a Union mortar boat.

to subdue it. If the Mississippi was the key to the continent, then Vicksburg was the key to the Mississippi, and no one knew this better than the Confederates, who set up their defenses with a last-stand desperation, while generals Grant and William Tecumseh Sherman laid attack plans and rested and resupplied their forces. The first attempt to assault the Confederate entrenchments in the bluffland of Vicksburg was made by Sherman on December 26 and 27, 1862; the attack was repulsed by the well-dug-in Confederates at tremendous cost to the Union forces, as noted by Horace Greeley, editor of the *New York Tribune* and an observer: What, he said, "could valor avail against rifle pits filled with sharp-shooters whose every bullet drew blood? Against gunners who poured grape and canister into our dauntless heroes, who could not advance and were stung by the consciousness that they were dying in vain? This attempt on Vicksburg cost us no less than 2,000 men."

Since attack from the north appeared impossible, Grant ultimately determined to float his army at night through the great bend of the Mississippi that passed beneath the city; once below the city, he would send Sherman east to capture Jackson, cutting off Vicksburg's only railroad communication, and he himself would turn to the river town for a major assault from a more advantageous position.

One of Grant's staff officers, William E. Strong, described that historic April night passage of the Union fleet (including Eads's surviving ironclads): "As the fleet approached the city and passed it, fire was opened from batteries which had hitherto been unable to bring their guns to bear. Field batteries were hurried into position on the main streets near the river and on the sloping hillside, until it seemed as though every square foot of soil possessed a gun. Heavy bodies of infantry along the levee and wharf kept up a deadly fire upon the boats as long as these were within range. Houses and barns on the shores were set on fire, and the bright glare, added to the incessant flashing of the guns, made the night as light as day. The men at the batteries and in the streets of Vicksburg could be distinctly seen from the vessels of the fleet when they were opposite the Vicksburg Courthouse, and

On April 24, 1862, Union forces ran a gauntlet near Carondelet below New Orleans.

Union officers ran their own kind of gauntlet of jeering, defiant citizens when they landed to demand the surrender of New Orleans on April 25, 1862.

Troops and citizens alike dug in for the duration of the forty-seven-day siege of Vicksburg in 1863; shown here are the caves of the Union's Illinois contingent.

Casualties of war: 1,547 Union soldiers died when the Sultana's *boiler exploded shortly after this photograph was taken.*

it was here that each vessel was exposed to the heaviest and most destructive fire. A storm of solid shot and shell, of almost every variety and size, poured upon the fleet, crashing through hull and pilothouse, shivering the machinery, cutting ropes and chimney guys and bursting in the cabins. . . . The fleet was under fire for two and a half hours. But at length the last boat was out of range; the blazing bonfires burned low, flickered, and went out. The heavy guns ceased firing, and silence once more reigned over the beleaguered city."

The conquest went more or less according to plan.

Jackson fell to Sherman on May 14, 1863, and on May 15 and 16 Grant defeated Vicksburg's defenders at Champion's Hill and Black River Bridge, driving them back into the city. Unable to achieve any more decisive a victory, Grant settled down and laid siege to the city, a siege which lasted forty-seven days.

It was a hell the city remembers to this day. "On June twenty-eighth," a Confederate soldier related after the war, "orders were issued to select the finest and fattest mules and slaughter them. Mule-flesh is coarse-grained and darker than beef, but really delicious, sweet and juicy. Besides this meat, traps were set for rats, which were consumed in such numbers that ere the termination of the siege they actually became a scarcity. I once made a hearty breakfast on fried rats and found the flesh very good." Day after day, Union shells rained on the town, while the people took to living in their basements and digging caves and dugouts for protection. "One evening," a woman resident of the city wrote, "I heard the most heart-rending screams and moans. I was told that a mother had taken a child into a cave about a hundred yards from us and laid it on its bed. A mortar shell entered the earth about it, crushing in the upper part of the little sleeping head."

On July 4, 1863, Vicksburg surrendered. The Union now held the Mississippi from source to mouth, and would hold it unchallenged until the end of the war on April 18, 1865. But there was damage done, not only to the hearts and minds of the river's people but to the river itself. War had ended romance.

THE RIVER III

St. Louis in 1872: steamboats still line the city's levee, but the nearly complete Eads railroad bridge (far right) spells an end to the glory days of steam on the Mississippi.

The Conquest of Steel

IN 1856 there occurred one of those minor events that stand in history as a metaphor. On a spring day that year, the steamboat *Effie Alton* pushed off from her wharf in Davenport, Iowa, and headed upriver. Crossing under the railroad bridge at Rock Island, completed just a few weeks before, the boat's captain miscalculated both his distances and the bridge's effect on the river currents. The *Effie Alton* slammed into one of the bridge piers, burst into flame, and soon burned to the waterline. The boat's owners promptly sued the proprietor of the bridge, the Rock Island Railroad, claiming that the bridge constituted an unlawful and unnatural obstruction to navigation.

The Rock Island line was a mighty fine line and could afford the best of legal help. The lawyer that it hired was one Abraham Lincoln of Springfield, Illinois. Lincoln, probably as good a country lawyer as any other in the nation, studied the bridge and the river personally, taking his own measurements and calculations, and weighing them against the plaintiff's charge that the bridge had been constructed at a point that was dangerous even without obstruction, and that the piers of the bridge had been built not only too close together but at such an angle as seriously to affect the river's natural currents. Lincoln's argument, presented at trial, was that the piers had actually improved the river's currents, that the *Effie Alton* had lost power and therefore steerage way, in no way the fault of the bridge, and that her pilot had not exercised reasonable caution in his approach. The result was a hung jury, and the bridge remained.

Even though it resulted in no decision, that otherwise insignificant event in Abraham Lincoln's life featured the lines of a major contest drawn hard and true, a contest between two forms of the same technology for dominance in the Mississippi Valley: the steamboats of the river and the railroads of the land. The railroads were the future and the steamboats were the past, and the past has never yet won out against the pressures of the future; the phenomenon is called Progress.

In the years before the Civil War, the railroads, like the pioneer wagons before them, had crossed the Appalachian plateau into the Ohio and Mississippi valleys. Beginning in 1852, when the Pennsylvania Railroad had been stretched from Philadelphia to Pittsburgh on the Ohio River, one railroad after another laid its tracks down until by the middle of the 1850s, like the latticework crust on a pie, there were railroad connections between all the major cities in the upper valley, from Cairo in the south to Galena in the north; from Rock Island, Burlington, Alton, and East St. Louis on the west to Chicago, Cleveland, Cincinnati, and Pittsburgh on the east—and from these points even farther east, all the way across the mountains to the harbors of Philadelphia, New York, and Boston. The Civil War, whose men and supplies had been moved brilliantly by the railroads, only accelerated the process, and the years following the war saw a veritable rash of railroad construction. Soon agitation began to develop for a railroad bridge across the Mississippi at one of its widest points: St. Louis. Impossible, most people said.

Passengers arriving at the levee for the New Orleans Exposition of 1885 (Harper's Weekly, January 10, 1885).

Harbinger of a new era, Minnesota's first steam locomotive, the **William Crooks,**
shows its mettle at St. Paul, 1862.

ENTER ONCE AGAIN James Eads, whose ironclad gunboats had driven the Confederates from the Mississippi. He was not impressed with the word *impossible.*
There were those who had told him that profitable salvage on the Mississippi was impossible, even those who
had said that ironclad gunboats were impossible. He had
given them the lie, and he would do it again. "Must we
admit," he once asked loftily, "that because a thing never
has been done, it never can be?" Intrigued with this new
challenge, he drew up plans for an arch bridge with
spans of five hundred feet in length; its piers would be
sunk to bedrock in the middle of the turbulent river,
and its spans would be of steel. He organized a bridge
company and raised funds, and in July 1867 construction
was started on the first bridge foundation on the west
bank of the river.

The work went slowly, painfully. At one point his
doctors forced Eads to take a leave of absence for rest. He
went off to Europe, where he spent most of his time talking to bridge builders and looking at bridges. By the
time of his return, his bridge had become an object of
derision, as illustrated by an item from the St. Louis
Missouri Republican: "A gentleman crossing the river
by ferry pointed out to a stranger the site of the prospec-
tive bridge. 'How much will it cost to build the bridge?'
the stranger asked.

" 'Seven million dollars,' the other exaggerated.

" 'How long will it take to build it?'

" 'Seven million years.' "

It took seven years and nine million dollars, but on
July 4, 1874 — after engineering difficulties, construction
deaths, floods, financial panics, and corporate antagonisms had all been overcome, the St. Louis bridge opened
to wagon and railroad traffic. It was one of the engineering marvels of the day and proved that the river could
be bridged almost anywhere. In the years that followed,
one bridge after another came into existence with dull
regularity, until by 1887 fifteen bridges crossed the
upper Mississippi alone. And over the bridges came the
railroads, inexorably sucking the lifeblood of the river-

Technology in progress: the first link of the Eads Bridge nears completion in 1872.

boat trade. In 1871, for example, the tonnage moved by rail at East St. Louis was twice that of the tonnage moved on the river at St. Louis. Ten years later, seven times as much tonnage was transported by rail as by river at the same point.

The riverboats did not give up the ghost immediately, however. The years immediately following the Civil War were a period of stupendous economic growth, the first flush of unrestrained industrialism. There was commerce enough for all, for a time, and the steamboats of the interior rivers enjoyed a reprieve from the inevitable. It was the passenger trade that improved most dramatically, for this was the era of the river packets, vessels so ambitious in size, luxuriance, and speed that the great boats of the 1840s and '50s paled by comparison. Consider the *Ruth,* for example: Launched in 1865, she rose four decks high and could comfortably carry 1,600 passengers. Her dining and drawing room was 268 feet long, and her staterooms, one report said, were nothing more or less than "two long rows of cosy white cottages with marble steps and rosewood doors." There were rooms for servants, a saloon, a nursery, a

Technology complete and lasting: the Eads Bridge today, still in use.
In the far background is another engineering marvel—the Gateway Arch.

The saloon of the Grand Republic (*nee* Great Republic), *one of the largest and inarguably most elegant of the great river packets.*

Holding on in spite of time, circumstance, and inevitability, the steamer Natchez *takes on a load at New Orleans, ca. 1885.*

laundry, and a barber shop on board. And she was fast: four and one-half days between St. Louis and New Orleans. She burned in 1869.

Or consider the *Great Republic,* launched from Pittsburgh in 1867, the largest ship then on the river system: "Legends quickly grew around her," historian Walter Havighurst has written. "She was given calendar dimensions—365 feet long, for the days in the years, 52 feet wide for the weeks, 12 feet deep for the months, 7 decks high for the days in the week; and it was said she cost $365,000—a thousand dollars a foot. What her admirers did not know was that she dragged a $100,000 mortgage up and down the river and burned $5,000 worth of fuel on every trip." Her owners went bankrupt, and the boat was sold for $48,000, enlarged, and put back into service. She burned in 1877.

Finally, consider the greatest steamboat in the history of the breed—the *J. M. White,* launched in 1878: She cost $300,000 to build and featured a five-tone whistle, a roof bell that weighed 2,880 pounds, smokestacks eighty

feet high decorated with flaring, seven-foot leaves, a pilot wheel eleven feet in diameter (it took two pilots to handle it), chinaware engraved with her own picture, silver engraved with her silhouette, and linen monogrammed with her initials. The most impressive of the more than four thousand wedding-cakes-on-water that had plied the river, she inspired a newspaper reporter to outright doggerel: "Alladin built a palace,/ He built it in a night;/ And Captain Tobin bought it/ And named it *J. M. White.*" She burned in 1886.

LIKE THE LAST BLOOM of the riverboat trade itself, the packets *Ruth, Great Republic,* and *J. M. White* had enjoyed one final flash of glory before burning out their lives. The furiously active decade of the 1870s came to an end, and in 1880 the riverboat trade entered a long period of decline, lamented by William Faulkner sixty years later: "There were railroads in the wilderness now. People who used to go overland by carriage

A hostage to memory: the wreck of the steamer Mississippi, *1888.*

And here, finally, was the new age of steam, given definition by the great bridge at St. Louis and by the several that followed it.

or on horseback to the river landings for the Memphis and New Orleans steamboats could take the train from almost anywhere now. And presently Pullmans too, all the way from Chicago and the Northern cities and the Northern money, the Yankee dollars arriving."

The figures simply would not be denied; they marched down the columns like a dirge: in 1880 the volume handled at St. Louis on riverboats to and from the upper Mississippi, for example, was 1,314,379 tons; in 1885 it dropped by almost half, to 775,517 tons; in 1895, to 501,152 tons; in 1900, to 347,000 tons; in 1905, to 70,776 tons; and in 1910, to only 43,090 tons—a little over 3 percent of the original volume.

River towns from St. Paul to New Orleans could have come up with similarly depressing figures, but nothing more evocatively symbolized the end of an era than the fate of the small towns scattered along the river,

towns whose whole existence had been based on and justified by the river trade, whose citizens, like those of Mark Twain's Hannibal, could be raised to a feverish excitement whenever the cry of "Steamboat a-comin'!" echoed up from their levees. Marie Meyer gave them an elegy in 1926: "Along the western banks of the Mississippi are little towns that have been made and broken by the river. Many are quaint, old-fashioned villages hugging the banks of the river and sheltered by high bluffs from the cold winds that often sweep across the outlying prairies. . . . Facing the river, they seem to belong to it, having no desire to climb the bluffs and live on the prairie beyond. Uneven sidewalks of flagstones, abandoned sawmills, warehouses gauntly fronting the river now overgrown with weeds and willows— all are mute evidence of a past that was part of the great river."

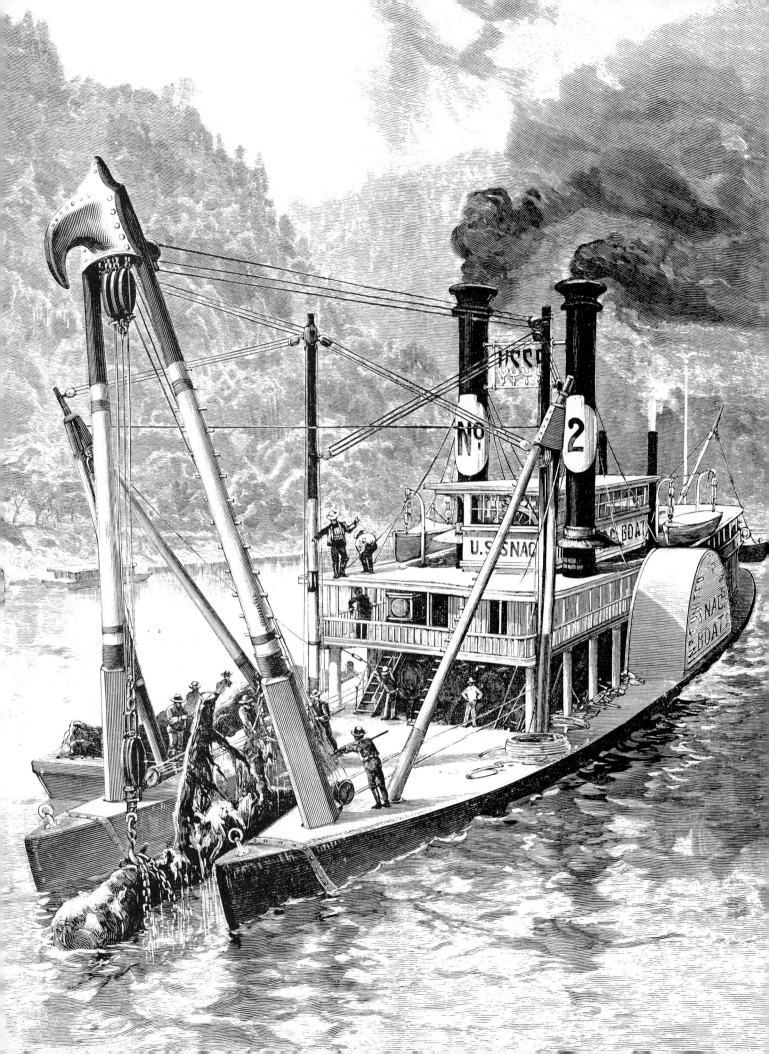

The River Reborn

MISSISSIPPI IMPROVEMENT is a mighty topic, down yonder," Mark Twain wrote in 1882. "Every man on the river banks, south of Cairo, talks about it every day, during such moments as he is able to spare from talking about the war; and each of the several chief theories has its host of zealous partisans. . . . All were agreed on one point, however: if Congress would make a sufficient appropriation, a colossal benefit would result."

Someone had been doing something along those lines even as Twain wrote. In 1877, James Eads (perhaps in unconscious atonement for what he had done to the river trade with his railroad bridge at St. Louis) had dredged through the sandbar that lay outside South Pass in the delta country of the Mississippi's mouth, lowering the channel's depth from eight feet to twenty-two. No longer would ships have to wait outside the bar for high water before crossing and moving on to New Orleans. Even the government had not been idle. The River Commission's snag boats carried on a regular campaign to keep the river free of bottom-ripping debris and, begining in 1874, had erected a string of nearly 1,100 beacon lights from Pittsburgh on the Ohio to New Orleans (". . . piloting, at a good stage of water," Twain wrote somewhat derisively in *Life on the Mississippi*, "is nearly as safe and simple as driving a stage").

Still, these modifications were not nearly enough, and the river's commercial life continued its fearful decline, boat after boat disappearing from service, company after company of freight lines going into receivership, river town after river town taking on a spectral aspect. Little was done to halt the deterioration even while everyone agreed that to ignore the potential of the greatest waterway network in the western hemisphere defied both logic and common sense.

That logic and common sense were documented by a clipping Mark Twain snipped out of the *Cincinnati Commercial*: "The towboat *Jos. B. Williams* is on her way to New Orleans with a tow of thirty-two barges, containing six hundred thousand bushels (seventy-six pounds to the bushel) of coal exclusive of her own fuel, being the largest tow ever taken to New Orleans or anywhere else in the world. Her freight bill, at 3 cents a bushel, amounts to $18,000. It would take eighteen hundred cars, of three hundred and thirty-three bushels to the car, to transport this amount of coal. At $10 per ton, or $100 per car, which would be a fair price for the distance by rail, the freight bill would amount to $180,000, or $162,000 more by rail than by river. The tow will be taken from Pittsburgh to New Orleans in fourteen to fifteen days. It would take one hundred trains of eighteen cars to the train to transport this one tow of six hundred thousand bushels of coal, and even if it made the usual speed of fast freight lines, it would take one whole summer to put it through by rail."

As the century turned, the need for major improvements in shipping on the Mississippi river system became apparent even to railroad men. Speaking on the subject before Congress in 1907, railroad magnate James J. Hill pointed out that "in view of the inability of the railroads to move the heavier classes of freight there has been no subject before Congress for twenty years

River improvement, 1889 style: a U.S. snag boat hauls up a chunk of detritus to help clear a river channel.

Some of the desperation and danger of the Mississippi's constant rampages
were suggested by this night scene of rescue during the great floods of 1882.

which interests so many people, and will prove so great a benefit to the entire basin of the Mississippi and Missouri rivers, as a deep channel or canal from St. Louis to the Gulf of Mexico." The following year President Theodore Roosevelt appointed an Inland Waterways Commission to look into ways and means, but for the next decade the commission did little more than issue annual reports on what might be done, could be done, or should be done.

As usual in the affairs of men, it took a large-scale crisis to bring action. This came after the United States' entry into World War I, when it was discovered that the railroads alone could not handle the volume of traffic that full mobilization required. The government, in the form of the War Department, got to work, reviving forgotten stern-wheelers and ancient barges, hiring pilots to steer whatever would float, merging local carriers into a unified transportation network called the Federal Barge Lines. The rivers moved the goods throughout the war and continued to move them after the war. (In fact, it was not until 1953 that the Federal Barge Lines was reorganized and turned back to the private sector of business.) Powerful new diesel and gasoline-powered tugboats and towboats slid down the ways of shipyards that had once built the river packets of the Age of Steam, and steel-hulled barges were constructed at a pace that a factory might turn out bottle-caps. By the end of the 1920s, the resurgence of river trade—specializing now in such bulk cargoes as coal, oil, iron and steel, sulfur, and limestone—had swelled to a business whose total value of tonnage handled every year had reached $20 million.

HAVING REVITALIZED the river's commercial life, the government finally turned to those improvements rivermen had been demanding for more than forty years. In 1922, Congress appropriated $42 million for navigational and flood-control works, and the following year upped the ante to $56 million. Under the direction of the U.S. Army Corps of Engineers, the work began. Dredges began gouging into the river bottom to create a permanent shipping channel, nine feet deep and 200 feet wide, from New Orleans to Minneapolis–St. Paul on the Mississippi and from Pittsburgh to Cairo on the Ohio. A system of forty-six locks and dams on the Ohio between Pittsburgh and Cairo was finished in 1929, converting that great river into an enormous, watery stairstep. Ten years later, a system of twenty-six locks and dams had been constructed on the Mississippi itself between Minneapolis–St. Paul and St. Louis (a final one, St. Anthony's Falls Upper Lock and Dam, was added to the system in 1963). A bewildering variety of flood-control and abatement projects was begun and completed, from holding basins to reconstructed levees, from spillways to breakwaters and seawalls.

Year after year appropriations mounted and projects proliferated, as the inland waterway developments of the Corps of Engineers swelled that organization to one of the largest bureaucratic institutions in the world. Applying its considerable energies to the river, the corps since 1936 has spent $1.8 billion on flood-control projects alone on the lower Mississippi from Cape Girardeau southward to the Gulf of Mexico. Called the Mississippi River and Tributaries Project, this effort includes a mighty complex of dams, reservoirs, auxiliary channels, and pumping plants along the Mississippi and its tributaries; 1,332 miles of levees and flood walls (with more than two hundred additional miles in the planning stage); 135 miles of dikes to control the direction and speed of the river, a system expected to reach 296 miles by completion; and four major floodways designed to divert river water during times of flood: the Birds Point–New Madrid Floodway, completed in 1933 and used once; the Bonnet Carre Spillway, completed in 1937, used that year and again in 1945, 1950, and 1972; the West Atchafalaya Floodway, completed in 1938 and never used; and the Moganza Floodway, completed in 1953 and also never used.

Flood control remains the corps' chief interest, although it has initiated harbor improvements, hydropower establishments, navigation facilities, recreational areas, and water supply and quality systems. Along the lower river alone, the corps directs a work and research force of more than four thousand people from its district office in Vicksburg. By its own calculations, its various flood-control projects since 1928 have prevented a total of $12,140,830,000 in damage on the Ohio and the upper and lower Mississippi rivers.

WHILE THE CORPS OF ENGINEERS kept itself busy with these sundry improvements, commerce on the river system entered a period of steady, then spectacular growth. It was almost exclusively barge commerce, the hauling of bulk cargoes, and if it lacked something in romance, it lacked nothing at all in the way of financial excitement.

After the hiatus of the Great Depression, which affected river commerce as much as any other sector of the national economy, the river trade was given an immense boost forward by the onslaught of World War II. (It is perhaps ironic that as the Civil War marked the beginning of the river's commercial decline, so two twentieth-century wars have given it new life.) By the early 1950s, there were more than seven hundred individual transportation lines in operation on the Mississippi and its tributaries, with more than a thousand tugs or towboats and ten thousand steel barges. In 1960 the Corps of Engineers, seeking authorization money for one more of its drawing-board projects, reminded Congress of the "dramatic growth of industry in the river valleys which has brought about rapid increase in the use of the inland waterways. . . . In twenty more years, the demands of industry will double the freight load now carried on the rivers."

Ten years later the prediction was well on the way toward fulfillment. In 1971 the main channels and all

*The railroad ferry of the Missouri & Illinois (the "Mike & Ike" line) lands
a cargo of freight cars near Ste. Genevieve, Missouri.*

tributaries of the Mississippi, Missouri, Illinois, and
Ohio rivers carried a total of 303,246,248 tons of cargo
whose individual components provided an encyclopedia
to the rich and varied industries of the entire Mississippi
Valley: 10,802,402 tons of corn, 8,275,435 tons of soybeans (the new money crop), 96,748,822 tons of coal and
lignite, 26,232,090 tons of crude petroleum, 35,668,353
tons of sand, gravel, and crushed rock, 2,422,874 tons of
liquid sulfur, 2,352,282 tons of grain mill products,
10,959,268 tons of basic chemicals, 24,849,875 tons of
gasoline, 8,763,542 tons of residual fuel oil, and 2,479,-
576 tons of iron and steel plates, as well as no less than
106 additional items, ranging from 3,687,247 tons of

"unmanufactured marine shells" (one wonders what a
manufactured marine shell might be) to 1,711 tons of
"rubber and miscellaneous plastics products."

A healthy share of this unimaginably wealthy cornucopia finds its way down the Mississippi River to New
Orleans, which is enjoying a flush of prosperity not even
the most glorious years of the antebellum period could
match. Its port is the second largest in the United States
now (New York–New Jersey being the first), and it
handles some 20 million tons of freight a year, valued
at nearly $3 billion. Grain is the principal export cargo,
of which the port moves 500 million bushels a year from
an immense public grain elevator with a capacity of one

million bushels. One hundred and fifty barge lines serve the port of New Orleans, as well as one hundred steamship lines and eight trunkline railroads. Its 48,086 feet of wharf frontage provides berths for 135 ships. In any given year, as many as 4,800 ships will be serviced there. If these wharves are no longer crowded with a wilderness of masts and steamboat stacks or lined with a mile of flatboats and keelboats, you will hear few laments in the modern city of New Orleans.

WHAT, THEN, OF THE MACHINES that make this riverport abundance possible—the twentieth-century equivalents of the steamboats whose churning wakes were once penciled on the great river? First, it is necessary to remember that while they are called tugboats and towboats, they do not tug, neither do they tow; they push. In the early days the barges were in fact towed, dragged along behind like the tail on a kite, but they had a tendency to drift and lash about uncomfortably in unseasonable weather. Eventually someone came up with the idea of binding several barges together with steel cables, locking a snub-nosed boat to the rear of them, and chugging off down the river like a composite ship. Today, many of these barge-ships stretch more than twelve hundred feet in length, longer than an ocean-going liner, comprised of as many as forty individual barges, enough to cover an area five acres in size. The average steel barge costs $85,000 to build, weighs 350 tons, and can carry up to 1,500 tons in cargo, but some specialized barges, like those used to carry grain or oil, can have a capacity of 3,000 tons.

The sheer bulk of what is called bulk cargo on the Mississippi these days is shown by these grain barges at Lock & Dam No. 21, Quincy, Illinois.

The new machine of Mississippi commerce: a towboat pushes a line of barges upriver from Memphis.

These are not barges; they are floating warehouses, and the boats that thrust twenty or thirty or forty of them at a time through the still-powerful currents of the river are great beasts that bear no more resemblance to the erstwhile steamboats than they do to the tugboats with which they are sometimes confused. Their massive diesel engines will deliver, on the average, up to 8,500 horsepower, although two now on the river—the *America* and the *United States* (fittingly enough owned by the Federal Barge Lines)—have the capacity for 16,500 horsepower, the equivalent, say, of the engine power of one hundred Chevrolet Vegas. The only similarity the modern towboat does bear to its ancestors is its size: from the below-water engine deck it will rise six levels high through a main deck, a boiler deck (a term left over from earlier days), a texas deck, a pilothouse, and a radar platform. There is no spoked wheel in the pilothouse now, but a system of levers, two for steering and two for controlling the engines; the pilot sits in a padded swivel chair with everything he needs to have his hands or eyes upon within easy reach—a whistle pull overhead, levers to control the searchlight, radio phone, intercom, swing meter, radar screen, RPM indicator, fathometer.

These are twentieth-century machines, and the men who operate them are technicians, not romantics. Yet there is something that gets into some of them, some hint of strut and hyperbole that is not dissimilar to the cockwalk air of confidence and color that marked the steamboat pilot. Writing in *Look Down That Winding River,* Ben Lucien Burman told of one such pilot, a technician much given to intricate country phrases and pungent imagery and anecdote. As he steered twenty-five barges through the river night, the pilot explained why it was that an approaching boat both blew its whistle and flashed a light to indicate its presence. "That's something else new on the river—the whistle-light," he said. "Riverman that invented it said some captains might be deaf and some captains might be blind, but the whistle-light'd take care of 'em, because he didn't know any captain who was both deaf and blind."

He was no Mark Twain, this twentieth-century technician, but he was in there trying.

Following its traditional role, New Orleans remains one of the largest seaports in the world.

THE
RIVER IV

Dam, lock, bridge, barges, towboat, and grain elevator—all the accoutrements of the Mississippi's twentieth-century industrial life are shown in this view near Alton, Illinois.

Fathoms of the Future

THE MISSISSIPPI TODAY does not lend itself to easy definition, for it is as vulnerable as any other geographic phenomenon to the consistent inconsistencies of human use and interpretation. Its meaning, if not lost entirely, is at least confused by all the caterwauling bustle of this end of the twentieth century. Men see this river as they want to see it: For some it is the great road of commerce, the artery of progress and enterprise, the heartline for an industrial civilization. For others it is a river of memory, rich with the ghosts of a time called history, a simpler, more understandable, more human time. For yet others it is a recreational resource, an escape hatch from the pressures of a more complicated world, a place for lazing in the sun, boating, water-skiing, fishing, and hunting. And for those who would preserve what has so far been left untouched, it is an abundant natural force whose existence can serve to remind us from time to time that we are, after all, natural creatures living in a natural world, no matter what we have tried to do to that world with plastic and concrete. The river is each of these things—and all of them.

It is a river of commerce, for the region through which it flows is one of stupendous proportions and variety, with a population of nearly sixty-six million people and an industrial and agricultural output that can be counted in the billions of dollars. The valley of the Mississippi today would be big enough and rich enough and varied enough to stand as a nation on its own if it chose to do so. A largely rural land still, it is a region of farms and plantations. From the dairy farms of Minnesota, with their old-world barns and silos, to the little empires of wheat and corn in Iowa, from the truck farms of Missouri to the sweeping sugar cane plantations and fields of soybeans in Louisiana and Mississippi, it is an open land, a land that still reflects the energies and ambitions of those pioneers who crossed into the trans-Appalachian West nearly two hundred years ago driven, as Francis Parkman put it, "by an insane desire to better their condition in life."

Scattered like islands in a sea are the cities of this land; and if the character of the valley is shaped by its farms, the vigor of the land is best defined by its cities, which busily embrace the best and some of the worst expressions of the twentieth century. In the Twin Cities of Minneapolis and St. Paul, for example, high-rise towers are climbing into the sky with startling rapidity, particularly in Minneapolis, where the city plans a complex network of street overpasses as well, linking the major downtown buildings and giving the shopper the opportunity to walk two or three miles without once having to stand on a street corner waiting for a traffic light. There is nothing particularly attractive about the new buildings; like most high rises, they look like ice-cube trays turned on end. But the speed at which they are being built suggests something of the energy that invests the city.

In Dubuque, Iowa, urban renewal money and local enterprise have created a truly beautiful shopping mall in the center of the downtown district, and it is the pride of the region. Contrarily, a few score miles down the river, the metropolitan complex of Bettendorf and

Some of the harsher elements of progress are suggested in this scene of a power plant near Genoa, Wisconsin, one of many strung along the modern Mississippi.

*The new St. Louis: high-rises and a sports complex dwarf two of the city's
more venerable buildings—the Old Cathedral (bottom) and City Hall (right).*

The new New Orleans: little of the city's past is visible in this aerial scene, but some of its future is—the "Super Dome" in the center is an artist's rendering.

Davenport on the Iowa bank, and Moline, East Moline, and Rock Island in Illinois, present to the traveler a definitive picture of the industrial revolution, a panorama of smokestacks, factories, grain elevators, and railroad cars. This is commerce pared to the essentials, and its edges are raw and vital.

In St. Louis, the river's central city, the high rises are going up, too, though not so many and not quite so high as those in Minneapolis, but it is the sprawling new sports complex near the river's edge that symbolizes most tellingly the city's vigorous acceptance of the demands of the twentieth century—that, and the graceful, shining curve of the 630-foot Gateway Arch, one of the engineering marvels of the century.

Cairo, Illinois, at the junction of the Mississippi and Ohio rivers, finds little to celebrate in the twentieth century. Trade has passed the city by, and its past is more pleasant to contemplate than its future.

In Memphis, the high rises loom on the bluffs above the river, not many, but a hint of more to come, while the city plans a complete overhaul of its dilapidated Beale Street section, where W. C. Handy composed his immortal songs and the "Memphis sound" was born.

Natchez, bustles energetically, invigorated by the local discovery of oil and natural gas supplies, but it builds more often out than up.

Baton Rouge, has a skyline utterly dwarfed by the stacks and tubes and towers of the huge petrochemical manufacturing complex that lies north of the city and gives it life. And finally, after 130 miles of smokestacks south of Baton Rouge, there is New Orleans itself, old town and new town, with its own sports center and its huge, rich, and extremely active port.

The cities of the valley are no better and no worse than those of any other part of the United States. They have their racial problems to stand in contrast to their art museums and community theaters; their traffic congestion, to their freeway complexes; their inadequate housing, to their high-rise development; their inner-city decay, to their industrial progress—just like other cities all over the country. Yet if we are to think of the Mississippi as the road of commerce, then they are the stations that govern its traffic, monuments to what the river has given the valley's latest civilization.

What that civilization has done to the river in return is another matter.

The river has its wild beauty, always; but what of the works of man?
This dam is at Little Falls, Minnesota. It is one of many.

THERE IS NO QUESTION but that man has learned through the centuries to use the Mississippi to his advantage and to his pleasure, but there is a real question as to whether he has learned to respect it. Like all major rivers, the Mississippi has functioned as a kind of *cloaca maxima* for most of the time that civilized man has clustered on its banks, dumping his garbage, his sewage, his industrial and agricultural effluents into the convenience of its currents. But it was a big and a powerful river, and it could handle the load.

No longer. Man has grown too many on this river, too many and too competent at producing waste. Technology has its by-products, and one of these, environmental damage, is no stranger to the Mississippi. There have been indications that pollutants dumped into the river far upstream may be having an effect on the Gulf of Mexico itself, and the river waters around such points as the petrochemical complex at Baton Rouge have at times been so polluted as to be downright lethal. Even today, when pollution-control devices have been installed to clean the waste from such plants, every day some 4,800 pounds of lead and 80 pounds of arsenic disappear into the Mississippi between Baton Rouge

and New Orleans, according to the Environmental Protection Agency.

That contamination need not be accepted is illustrated by what the city of St. Louis did to curb its daily discharge of raw sewage. In the 1950s, following the tremendous growth period after the war, St. Louis was dumping 300 million gallons of human waste into the river every day through eighty outfalls—a volume capable of filling 50,000 railroad tank cars a day. By 1958 the problem had become so serious that the U.S. Public Health Service and the Missouri Water Pollution Board were forced to order the city to clean up the river.

St. Louis citizens responded nobly, passing a $95 million bond issue for that purpose in November 1962. Within ten years the city had constructed one of the largest and most effective sewage treatment complexes in the world: two huge primary treatment plants on the shores of the Mississippi and twenty-three miles of large interceptor sewers to catch the flow of raw waste to the river, together with a complicated network of smaller lines and pump stations. Its capacity is 434 million gallons a day, and it services more than one-and-a-half million people. *(Continued on page 209)*

Scattered along the bluffs and little valleys of the river are hints of
a quieter, more gentle age; this one is near Fountain City, Wisconsin.

That the spirit and experiences that moved Mark Twain to remember and memorialize his boyhood may still be present is suggested by these modern followers of the Huckleberry instinct.

If Mark Twain remembered Hannibal, Hannibal remembers him—and has memorialized him in its fashion. At the left is the "Tom and Huck" statue that stands at the foot of Cardiff Hill; below is the Mark Twain home and museum; and at the right, a modern Tom and Becky visit the Mark Twain Cave during the city's annual "Tom Sawyer Days" celebration.

Of all the towns of the lower Mississippi that have institutionalized their past, none has gone at it with more enthusiasm and success than Natchez, Mississippi. The modern town contains more than forty antebellum mansions that have been preserved in a condition approaching that of the plantation days. Each year, some thirty of the homes are opened to the public for the "Natchez Pilgrimage." At the left is the splendid approach to the D'Evereaux mansion. At the right is a detail of one of the columns that graces the front of Stanton Hall.

197

Like a gay, glittering ghost, the sternwheeler
Delta Queen *churns up and down the river
system, re-creating—however briefly, however
imperfectly—the days when hundreds and finally
thousands of the great boats made the river a
highway of commerce and romance. Built in San
Francisco in 1926 and moved to the Mississippi
and Ohio rivers a generation later, she is the
last overnight passenger steamboat to ply these
inland waters.*

If the Delta Queen *denotes some of what is left of romance on the river, it is the snub-nosed, grunting, utilitarian towboats that perpetuate the river's economic life today. They are ugly, powerful, and ubiquitous. At the left, the* Omaha *forces her way through the breaking ice of the upper river. Below, the* Badger *prepares to lock up to a "tow" at Lock & Dam No. 8 near Genoa, Wisconsin.*

For most of the length of the river, barge traffic is a year-round proposition; with snow or without it, the cargo moves.

The barge "tows" of the Mississippi are immense; this one, being shoved through a lock near Quincy, Illinois, is the size of two or three football fields.

Cotton may no longer be king in the American South, but it is at least still a prince—one of the major crops of the lower Mississippi Valley. It is no longer a job for stoop-backed field hands, however, but a thoroughly mechanized and sophisticated industry. Below, a field of defoliated cotton near Parkin, Arkansas, lies ready for the picker; at the left, a load of freshly picked bolls is dumped into a truck for shipment to the gin.

*Oil, land, and water are made to mix, more or less, along much of the
river; this refinery is near Paradise, Louisiana.*

*The Port of New Orleans is
prosperity defined. It is the
second largest port in the United
States (next only to New York–
New Jersey), handling more than
20 million tons of freight every
year, valued at nearly $3 billion.
It has nearly fifty thousand feet
of wharf frontage and loads and
unloads as many as 4,800 ships in
any given year.*

203

Like some kind of immense staple, the glittering Gateway Arch encircles the skyline of modern St. Louis.

St. Paul, Minnesota, has come a long way from the near-village it was in the view on pages 152–153; it now has a "twin" city—Minneapolis—a collection of high-rises giving it a respectable skyline, as well as the "steamer" Jonathan L. Paddleford.

The modern vigor of New Orleans is found in her downtown section, but most of the city's charm is found in her French Quarter, which contains some of the most distinctive and antique architecture in the United States. At the right is a typical street scene in the Quarter, facades of ironwork and brick that have graced a million postcards. Below, St. Charles Cathedral faces Jackson Square at dusk.

Steamboats in the street? Well, sort of. Motorized steamers are only part of the action that takes place in the French Quarter of New Orleans during the annual bachannalia called Mardi Gras.

New Orleans' Old Town has buildings of an age to compare well with the oldest that colonial New England has to offer. One of the oldest of these is Lafitte's blacksmith shop, a structure that looks every hour of its nearly 150 years.

That this expensive system was worthwhile is documented by the difference in river water quality near the city. Before the plants were constructed, anyone strolling idly along the bank could glance down and see raw sewage bobbing along, oil floating on the surface, grease and garbage drifting by, and if he had the nerve to poke his head under the water, sludge on the bottom. He could also smell the effluvium, and perhaps speculate on the possibility of an outbreak of typhoid or salmonella. Now, says district sewer engineer Robert Flick, "Some citizens don't notice any difference in the river. But if you really look, go down to the waterfront, you can see the difference: floating materials, such as grease balls, animal guts, oils, are gone—and the odor with them."

Expensive solutions are rarely popular solutions, and St. Louis is so far alone in the degree to which it has gone to prevent pollution from corrupting the river. But water pollution—man's oldest form of the art—isn't the only example of environmental shortsightedness taking place. More than a thousand miles to the south, in the marshlands of the Louisiana delta, there are plans afoot that some environmental experts say would utterly destroy one of the major estuarine environments in the country. One plan is for the construction of a major shipping channel straight across the marshes; those who advocate digging the channel say it would bring $5 million in new industry to the area and create 200,000 new jobs, but conservationists say, quite simply, that it isn't worth it. Another proposal is for Texas to be allowed to tap into the Mississippi, pump the water 4,000 feet uphill, and deliver it to dry lands in that state a thousand miles to the west; conservationists say this would destroy the marshlands. A third proposal is to drain 113,000 acres of the marshland so as to free the area for agricultural purposes; conservationists maintain that this procedure would bring salt water into the estuarine system and alter its delicate ecological balance. A fourth scheme is to throw a highway across the marsh; again, conservationists say no.

Even the flood-control projects of the Army Corps of Engineers have come under fire from environmentalists, who would agree with the words of Owen P. White written for *Collier's* in 1916: "You are going to build levees, you have been building them, and this is the proposition that you are up against: You wipe out all natural overflow regulation and constrain the entire volume to the river channel and take it as it comes. The maximum volume is greatly increased, the flood heights raised, the velocity accelerated. You have greatly increased the dynamic energy of the stream. You have not only magnified the surplus horsepower but you have also increased the speed of the application, thus multiplying the destructive powers; in other words, you have stimulated the energy, filed the teeth, and ground the claws of your tiger." The Corps of Engineers, conservationists have now been known to mutter, have been at work on this river for nearly fifty years—and it has indeed ground the claws of a tiger, producing annual floods of the dimensions of that of 1973, when seven million acres went under the water, with $161 million in estimated property damage. Is it possible, conservationists ask, that some sort of miscalculation was made—and if so, does it make sense for us to go on using the same measuring devices?

IN THE SUMMER OF 1973, four young men from Canada re-created the 1673 canoe voyage of Marquette and Jolliet down the Wisconsin and Mississippi rivers. At each of their stops along the way, they pleaded with the people who lived there to resist further damage to the great river. It was, in a way, the past reaching out to touch us, to tell us that the river is greater than we are, that it, and not we, ultimately will endure. The message was an appropriate one, for this river has an almost unique kinship with the past. Americans have always had an ungodly fascination for their history, but it would be difficult to find a region more willing to celebrate the trait than the Mississippi Valley. Consider steamboats, for example. It is not possible, one ventures to say, to travel anywhere on the river from Minneapolis–St. Paul to New Orleans without encountering some reminder of the Age of Steam, from the little, steel-filagreed *Jonathan L. Paddleford* in Minneapolis, which makes an hour-long tour of the Mississippi as it winds through the Twin Cities, to the *Becky Thatcher* in St. Louis, a permanently docked old steamboat, which offers an indifferent meal with splendid service at prices that would stop a clock. In Winona, Minnesota, a little lumbering town beneath the bluffs of the river above St. Croix, there is a first-rate steamboat museum housed in

In spite of commerce, of enterprise, of a commercialized past, some of the peace and space and beauty of this river can still be found.

a genuine, landlocked steamboat, the *Julius C. Wilkie,* where a trim and pretty young guide will tell the tourist more than he may have wanted to know about steamboats; and down the river in Vicksburg the old stern-wheeler *Sprague* lies docked beneath the hill, its restaurant waiting for hungry tourists.

The most impressive example of steamboat mania, of course, is the magnificent stern-wheeler *Delta Queen,* which makes the long run between Pittsburgh and New Orleans, giving her passengers the experience of river travel as it was in the grandly vigorous days of the past. Curiously enough, the *Delta Queen* is not native to the Mississippi River. She was built and spent most of her life in California on the Sacramento–San Francisco run and did not see the Mississippi River until the Golden Gate and San Francisco–Oakland Bay bridges helped put an end to significant passenger-boat traffic on San Francisco Bay in the 1930s—just as the railroads and James Eads's bridge at St. Louis once discouraged similar traffic on the Mississippi. A further curiosity has caught the *Delta Queen* in the middle of an uneasy truce between past and present: as an authentic steam craft, she cannot meet the rigid safety standards now demanded by maritime law. Only periodic reprieves by

The past as a living memory: the Delta Queen *slips by the ferry crossing at Grafton, Illinois.*

Congress have kept her in service at all; how long they will continue is open to question. She may be a floating institution, but her days appear to be numbered.

Another kind of memorial can be found in Hannibal, Missouri, and this too finds itself dead up against the sometimes peculiar demands of the twentieth century. On one tiny block the town has preserved Mark Twain's boyhood home, the house where his creation, Tom Sawyer, once endured the gentle civilizing of Aunt Polly and from which he escaped whenever he heard the secret whistle of Huckleberry Finn beneath his bedroom window; the "home" of Becky Thatcher, Tom's unearthly sweetheart; the office where Sam Clemens' father worked before his death; and the "haunted house" that once stood on Cardiff Hill and filled his boyhood days with delicious speculations of spectral horror. A little stone museum next door to the Clemens' home features photographs, clothing, signed copies of Twain's writing, his second typewriter, the original Norman Rockwell illustrations for an edition of *Tom Sawyer*, and other memorabilia from the Twainian past. The site is now a national monument, as it should be.

Yet this country could have done better by its greatest writer, for the memorial is surrounded by tasteless claptrap and gewgaws, wretched excesses of commercialism. Inside the museum a person can buy genuine rubber shrunken heads and other remarkable items; if this is not enough, across the street a little souvenir shop advertises one thousand—count 'em, one thousand—items for under a dollar, not including real plastic Indian moccasins that retail somewhat higher. The haunted house, moved down from Cardiff Hill, has been converted into what someone, somewhere, might believe a haunted house should be. For a suitable fee one can walk through it in a darkness replete with rubber spiders, plastic skeletons, and vague, tinny screams. Nearby, the Mark Twain Dinette serves a thin hamburger and a glass of root beer and something called Mark Twain Fried Chicken; and the Twainland Express, a motorized little train that parks alongside the dinette, provides a tour of historic Hannibal.

It should not be this way, and there are those in Hannibal itself who would like to change the scene. Chief among them is Charles Rendlen, Jr., a fast-talking,

The past as an entrepreneur's delight: a restaurant sign less than 100 feet from Mark Twain's boyhood home.

quick-witted, and utterly enthusiastic lawyer who has a dream of some day clearing out the neon and plastic, of building a new kind of museum—a Twain library—and of refurbishing Hannibal's Main Street so that it reflects the town's past with style and grace. So far his dream is only a dream; in the twentieth century making dreams real costs money.

For all the neon and plastic, a visitor can still stand in one of the little rooms of the house where Mark Twain searched out the "bones" of his art, and feel touched by something out of the past. One can have that same awareness as one drives along the river highways of the South, past antebellum mansions half hidden in trees and sharecroppers' cabins that cannot be much different from the slave quarters of more than a century ago. The Civil War itself has been given a

*At New Iberia, Louisiana—as in so many other places on the lower river—
the plantation South is preserved in the mansion called "Shadows-on-the-Teche".*

River as recreation: water-skiing on Lake Pepin . . .

and day-sailing south of Alton, Illinois.

proper memorial in Vicksburg National Park, and the people of Vicksburg and Natchez have preserved some of the most beautiful of the old colonnaded mansions that exist anywhere in the South.

The past is there in New Orleans, in the French Quarter that surrounds Jackson Square; it is there in St. Louis, beneath the great arch that marks the city's role as the gateway to the west in the nineteenth century and the St. Louis Cathedral that memorializes the city's French beginnings; it is there in Minneapolis–St. Paul, in old Fort Snelling; it is there in Port Gibson, Mississippi, in the woods where Grant skirmished with Confederate defenders of Vicksburg; it is there in Lorman, Mississippi, where a ninety-eight-year-old general store still caters to the people who live and work on the land around it. For two thousand miles, the past and the Mississippi are one in the river of time.

A RIVER OF COMMERCE, a river of memory. . . . Finally, there is the river itself, its own true definition, and one of this country's major recreational resources. Its easy pleasures are accessible and varied. In water no higher than your knees, you can wade across the river at its source in Lake Itasca State Park, Minnesota, or watch the sun rise over its wooded islands from a camp on the bluffs of Wyalusing State Park, Wisconsin; you can rent a boat and row out to fish and explore, or launch your own boat and go water-skiing—particularly at Lake Pepin between Minnesota and Wisconsin, where the sport was invented in 1922; you can sail almost anywhere and swim more often than you might expect in a river too frequently polluted; you can take an excursion boat and skim around Jackson's Island opposite Hannibal, or take another and see the Bayou country of Louisiana; you can hike and picnic and camp and fish from its banks in hundreds of spots scattered along its two-thousand-mile length.

For all its accessibility, there are stretches along this river yet that approach a wilderness state, particularly along its northern and central stems, places of bogs and islands and thick cottonwood stands, where wild ducks gather and great blue herons and egrets ornament the landscape, where some sense of the peace and eternality of this great river can still be found by simply going out after them. In some sections of the river, this wilderness

Steeeeeeeamboat a'goin!—the Mark Twain, *out of New Orleans, takes tourists on a bayou tour.*

sense has been deliberately preserved (although the nation does not have a Mississippi National Park, as it should). One of these regions is the Upper Mississippi River Wildlife and Fish Refuge, a 284-mile stretch of river and islands between Lake Pepin and Rock Island, Illinois. Another is the Horseshoe Lake Wildlife Refuge near Cairo, Illinois, and yet another is the National Audubon Society's Rainey Wildlife Sanctuary in Louisiana's marsh country, part of the river's estuarine delta.

It is this wilderness world that speaks most eloquently of the essence of the river, of its timelessness in an age that rushes in confusion toward a future we cannot know. In the river's woods and sandy banks and islands, its still backwaters and rippling eddies, in the simple unconquerable power of its mile-wide tide, we find something we *can* know and in comprehending that, perhaps we can understand something more of ourselves. It is this world that Mark Twain himself could still love today, in spite of all that man and his works have done to the river in the years since the old pilot last saw it. The Mississippi River, some say, was Twain's god, the same expression of divine purpose that Melville found in Moby Dick. If so, it is good to know that there are places yet where he could sit in the sun on a sandy bank smoking one of his huge cigars, worshiping his god-river, and dreaming back to the days of joy and love where he found the only true measure of himself that he would ever know.

The Mississippi as Mark Twain might remember it, with the marks of man at a minimum and a sternwheeler heading off for God only knows what mystery.

Suggested Reading

ON THE LIFE AND WORK OF MARK TWAIN

Even though he was the acknowledged American writer of his century, Mark Twain did not begin to receive serious critical attention until a generation after his death. After that, the studies and biographies began to proliferate. The following list indicates those titles which the author feels have come closest to touching the sense and feel of the man, the times, and his work.

Mark Twain, A Biography: The Personal and Literary Life of Samuel Langhorne Clemens by Albert Bigelow Paine (New York, 1912).

Mark Twain: An American Prophet by Maxwell Geismar (Boston, 1970).

Mark Twain: A Profile edited by Justin Kaplan (New York, 1967).

Mark Twain at Work by Bernard DeVoto (Cambridge, 1942).

Mark Twain's America by Bernard DeVoto (Boston, 1932).

Mr. Clemens and Mark Twain: A Biography by Justin Kaplan (New York, 1966).

The Ordeal of Mark Twain by Van Wyck Brooks (New York, 1955).

ON THE MISSISSIPPI AND ITS HISTORY

As befits its rank as the central river in American life and history, the Mississippi has inspired a wealth of bibliographic material. As an aid to the general reader however—who may or may not want to know absolutely everything there is to know about the Mississippi—the author offers the following titles, which provide a fairly comprehensive survey of the periods of the river's history.

A Raft Pilot's Log: A History of the Great Rafting Industry on the Upper Mississippi, 1840–1915 by Walter A. Blair (Cleveland, 1930).

Civil War on Western Waters by Fletcher Pratt (New York, 1956).

Explorers of the Mississippi by Timothy Severin (New York, 1968).

Father Mississippi by Lyle Saxon (New York, 1927).

From Canoe to Steel Barge on the Upper Mississippi by Mildred L. Hartsough (St. Paul, 1934).

Man and the River: The Mississippi by Hodding Carter (Chicago, 1970).

The Mighty Mississippi by Bern Keating (Washington, 1971).

The Mississippi Valley Frontier by John Anthony Caruso (Indianapolis, 1966).

River World: Wildlife of the Mississippi by Virginia Louise Eifert (New York, 1959).

Road to the Sea: The Story of James B. Eads by Florence Dorsey (New York, 1947).

Steamboats on the Western Rivers by Louis C. Hunter (Cambridge, 1949).

Voices on the River: The Story of the Mississippi Waterways by Walter Havighurst (New York, 1964).

Acknowledgments

The author and editors wish to express their deep appreciation to the many individuals and organizations whose cooperation made this book possible, with special gratitude to Louise Walker of the St. Louis Art Museum, Bonnie Wilson of the Minnesota Historical Society, and Mary Frances Rhymer of the Chicago Historical Society, as well as to the trustees of those three institutions, without whose assistance no history of the Mississippi River Valley could be adequately illustrated. Special thanks are also due August A. Busch, Jr., of Anheuser-Busch, Inc., and to the directors of the Boatmen's National Bank of St. Louis, who made available paintings from their private collections. Invaluable services were also rendered by Mrs. Philip S. Haring of Knox College, Francis Heldner of the Louisiana State Museum, John L. Lochhead of the Mariners Museum, Paul Gratke of Marquette University, F. M. Cohn of the Missouri Historical Society, Adelaide Hawn and Connie Griffith of Tulane University, and Anne G. McGuffie of the Vicksburg Old Court House Museum. Last but by no means least, extensive information and advice was provided by R. Patrick White of the Great River Road Association and by the state tourism offices of the ten states bordering the Mississippi River.

PICTURE CREDITS

The Bettmann Archive: Pages 43, 80. The Boatmen's National Bank of St. Louis: Pages 156–157. Warren E. Brant: Page 31 (bottom, left). August A. Busch, Jr.: Pages 44, 49, 58. Eric Carle from Shostal: Page 32. Chicago Historical Society: Pages 50–51, 152 (bottom), 160. Convention & Tourist Board of Greater St. Louis: Page 173 (bottom). Culver Pictures, Inc.: Page 60. Kent & Donna Dannen: Pages 30, 31 (top), 183, 194 (bottom, left), 201 (top). Ken Dequaine: Pages 2–3, 27 (bottom), 193. Ken Dequaine from Shostal: Page 28. L. Douthat from Photo Researchers: Page 199 (bottom). Thomas Gilcrease Institute of American History & Art, Tulsa, Oklahoma: Pages 52–53, 65. Grant Heilman: Pages 18, 20, 25, 29, 185, 202. Jefferson National Expansion Memorial, National Park Service: Page 61. Keokuk Public Library, Keokuk, Iowa: Page 79 (top). The Library of Congress: Pages 158–159, 177. Louisiana State Museum, New Orleans: Pages 56, 71. Louisiana State Museum from The Louisiana Historical Society: Page 148. Louisiana Tourist Development Commission, Baton Rouge: Pages 206, 207 (bottom). The Mariners Museum, Newport News, Virginia: Pages 72–73, 75, 79 (bottom), 167, 174, 175. Memorial Library Archives, Marquette University, Milwaukee, Wisconsin: Pages 40, 48. Minnesota Historical Society, St. Paul: Pages 62, 67, 68, 69, 74 (bottom), 149 (bottom), 153, 172. Mississippi Department of Archives and History, Jackson: Page 54. Missouri Department of Commerce, Jefferson City: Page 59. Missouri Historical Society, St. Louis: Pages 1, 173 (top). Missouri Tourism Commission, Jefferson City: Page 195. State Historical Society of Missouri, Columbia: Page 78. J. Mack Moore Photographic Collection, Old Court House Museum, Vicksburg, Mississippi: Page 166. National Collection of Fine Arts, Smithsonian Institution: Page 38. National Geographic Photographer George F. Mobley, courtesy U.S. Capitol Historical Society: Pages 146–147. E. E. Ayer Collection, The Newberry Library, Chicago: Page 57. New Orleans Museum of Art, gift of William E. Groves: Page 39. New Orleans Tourist Commission: Page 184, 191. Harold Owens: Page 145. Joan Parker: Pages 8, 16–17, 26, 27 (top), 31 (bottom, right), 200 (bottom), 205. The Peabody Museum, Harvard University: Page 34. Robert Perron: Page 22. Alan Pitcairn from Grant Heilman: Pages 6–7, 190, 203, 212, 214. Preston Player Collection, Knox College, Galesburg, Illinois: Page 149 (top). The St. Louis Art Museum: Pages 4–5, 35, 74 (top, left & right), 150–151. Paul Slade from Globe Photos: Page 199 (top). J. L. Stage from Photo Researchers: Page 194 (top). Stanford University Libraries: Pages 37, 64, 76, 82, 86, 89, 90, 96, 98, 104, 105, 108, 118, 122, 132, 139, 163–165, 168–169, 170, 176, 178, 180. Tulane University, New Orleans: Pages 152 (top), 154–155. U.S. Navy: Pages 45, 162. Bert Vogel from Shostal: Page 208. T. H. Watkins: Pages 188, 192, 197 (right), 211. State Historical Society of Wisconsin, Madison: Page 42. Jack Zehrt: Pages 182, 186–187, 194 (bottom, right), 196, 198, 200 (top), 207 (top), 210, 213, 215. Jack Zehrt from Freelance Photographers Guild: Pages 201 (bottom), 204.

Index

MISSISSIPPI RIVER REGION
Physical Features

Scale in Miles

0   50   100   150

© Jeppesen & Co., Denver, Colo. Reprinted by permission
of the H. M. Gousha Co., proprietors, San Jose, Calif.

MISSOURI

KENTUCKY

TENNESSEE

★ NASHVILLE

Tennessee R.

Cairo

Cape Girardeau ●

● Memphis

M I S S I S S I P P I

OKLAHOMA

ARKANSAS

Helena ●

Arkansas R.

★ LITTLE ROCK

Greenville ●

MISSISSIPPI

VICKSBURG NAT'L
MIL. PARK
□ Vicksburg

★ JACKSON

ALABAMA

GEORGIA

FLORIDA

Natchez ●

Ouachita R.

Red R.

LOUISIANA

★ BATON ROUGE

New Orleans

CHALMETTE NAT'L
HIST. PA.

TEXAS

GULF OF MEXICO